Everyday & Extraordinary

ALMANAC

OF THE PROVINCE OF

PRINCE EDWARD ISLAND

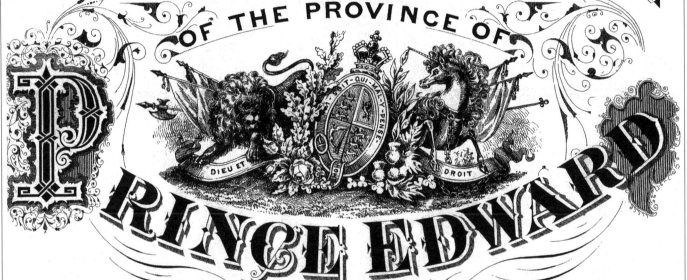

text written by

BOYDE BECK & EDWARD MACDONALD

PUBLISHED WITH THE SPECIAL ASSISTANCE OF
THE McINNIS PUBLISHING TRUST

P.E.I. MUSEUM AND HERITAGE FOUNDATION

— PUBLISHERS —

1999

Design & Layout by Henry Dunsmore
Victoria, Prince Edward Island

Printed by Williams & Crue
Summerside, Prince Edward Island

©1999 by Prince Edward Island Museum and Heritage Foundation
ISBN 0-920434-34-7

Design: Henry Dunsmore
Printing: Williams and Crue (1982) Ltd.

Prince Edward Island Museum and Heritage Foundation
2 Kent Street
Charlottetown, Prince Edward Island
Canada, C1A 1M6

Published with the assistance of the McInnis Publishing Trust

---

Canadian Cataloguing in Publication Data

Beck, E. Boyde (Edwin Boyde), 1960-

    Everyday and extraordinary

    Includes index.
    ISBN 0-920434-34-7

1. Prince Edward Island – History – Miscellanea. I. MacDonald, George Edward, 1957-
       II. Prince Edward Island Museum and Heritage Foundation. III. Title.

FC2601.5 .B42 1999   971.7'003   C99-950172-0
F1047 .B42 1999

INTRODUCTION

This book has its genesis in the *Island History Calendar* published by the P.E.I. Museum and Heritage Foundation between 1992 and 1998.

As Museum staff and volunteer researchers dug up more nuggets of information, the database used for the Calendar grew. Soon it was one of our most-consulted research tools. The phone would ring with a question: "When did ... happen?" "Where did.... take place?" "Who was the one who...?" Many times we simply opened the precious "supercal" file on the computer, told it to look for a certain name or date and were able to reel off an answer on the spot. It made us look very knowledgeable. People were very impressed.

Now our secret is out.

History is in the details. Names, dates, places and events – gather enough data and gradually a story emerges. This book presents the details, organized by year and in nineteen handy categories. The number of stories that emerge – one big one or hundreds of little ones – depend on how you view history and how you read the book. It's designed for use as a reference tool *and* as a rattling good read. We hope you find it performs well on both levels.

LEGEND

The order in the following themes or categories appear is an editorial convenience and does not represent any opinion on their relative importance in Island history. Most are self-explanatory, but two might need a little more definition.

The "Away" category is quintessentially "Prince Edward Island." It features entries about Islanders who left home — or "went away" — and did especially well for themselves. You will note that this category begins to appear more frequently as the "Shipbuilding" category fades in importance.

The "Everyday and Extraordinary," besides being a nifty title, is our "catch-all" category. It features entries that give the flavour of everyday life and unusual happenings that would have raised eyebrows.

Some entries tried to fall between categories. Is a map, for instance, a symbol or a publication? Should an epidemic be classified as a health issue or a disaster? Was Prohibition a political issue, or should it go in the "Law and Order" category? Instead of creating new categories or cross-listing entries, we simply tried to be consistent in where we placed these more troublesome bits of information.

LORNE HOTEL

Landmarks and Symbols

 Transportation and Communications

 Law and Order

 Politics

 Population

 Arts and Letters

 Sports and Leisure

 Land and Sea

 Health and Medicine

 Everyday and Extraordinary

 Education

 Military Events

 Religion

 Natural and Other Disasters

 Commerce

 Science and Technology

 Weather

Away

Shipbuilding

ACKNOWLEDGMENTS

In addition to the many books, articles, community histories and newspapers we plundered for information, we would like to thank the following for their assistance in creating both this volume and the database it is built on.

The staff at UPEI's Robertson Library and the staff at the Public Archives and Records Office. The Publishing Committee of the PEIMHF: Andy Robb (Chair), Sheryl MacKay, Alan Buchanan and Laurie Brinklow. An extra thank you to Laurie Brinklow for her services as proofreader and advice on supervising the publication. Mel Gallant ran his laser-like eye over the text, looking for errors and inconsistencies. Vounteers Joe Malone, Tammy MacAleer, and Len Driscoll helped contribute to and maintain the database over the years.

This book was published with the assistance of the McInnis Publishing Trust.

c9000 BCE

Following the end of the ice age, the first human inhabitants arrive here. Since sea levels are lower than today, what is now known as the Northumberland Strait is above water. Archaeologists call this landmass "Northumbria." Since the "island" is connected to the mainland, migration is simple.

c1000 BCE

Rising sea levels submerge Northumbria, cutting the Island off from the mainland.

c1000

Recent re-interpretations of Icelandic sagas indicate that Viking explorers may have landed and even over-wintered on the Island.

1497

On 24 June, diplomats once argued, John Cabot "discovered" Prince Edward Island and claimed it for England. Later historians carried on the argument but there was always more evidence than proof. Today Cabot's claim is largely discounted.

1534

On 30 June, having sighted land the previous evening, Jacques Cartier "discovers" Prince Edward Island and claims it for France. Compared to what he thinks of Newfoundland — "This is the land God gave Cain" — he's quite impressed with what he sees here. "The fairest land it is possible to see," he notes in his log. "Full of fine meadows and trees."

1535

Using information from Cartier's voyage, Jean Rotz prints the first map of the Gulf of St. Lawrence. We're not on it.

1561

Italian cartographer Girolamo Ruscelli prints a map, *Terra Nueva*, which includes an "Île St. Jean." He places the Island in the northern Gulf of St. Lawrence — hard by Isola de Demoni.

Cabot Building

Designed by William C. Harris, and named for the supposed-discoverer of the Island, the Cabot Building occupied part of Charlottetown's Queen's Square from the 1880s until it was demolished in the 1960s to make way for the Confederation Centre.

1584

French cartographer Jacques de Vaulx publishes the first chart to accurately place Île St. Jean in the Gulf of St. Lawrence.

1653

Île St. Jean is included in a grant to Nicholas Denys. He says he will build a fishing and trading colony here. He doesn't.

1663

Sieur François Doublet convinces the French crown that, since Nicholas Denys has done nothing with Île St. Jean, he should be given a chance. Denys' grant is revoked and given to Doublet, who

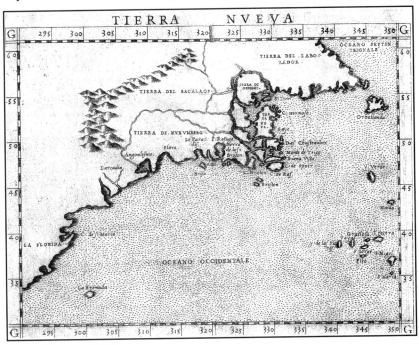

Terra Nueva, 1561

by Girolamo Ruscelli

(James and Barbara Macnutt Collection of Historic Maps), P.E.I. Museum and Heritage Foundation

says he will build a fishing and trading colony here. He doesn't.

1713

The Treaty of Utrecht transfers most of Acadia to British control. Even though France is left with only Île St. Jean and Île Royale (Cape Breton), officials in Paris are optimistic that they can rebuild their fortunes in the Gulf area. They design a huge fortress — Louisbourg — to protect the Gulf of St. Lawrence and the route to Quebec. They doubt that Île Royale can grow sufficient food to supply a large garrison, but aren't worried, since they anticipate a flood of Acadian farmers to move over to Île St. Jean and grow enough for both islands. Unfortunately for this plan, the British, at least at first, treat the Acadians so well they don't want to leave. Île St. Jean remains largely ignored by European colonists.

1720

The Island is granted to another private developer — the Comte de St. Pierre's Compagnie de l'Île Saint Jean. He recruits 300 settlers and sends them out on three ships from the port of Rochefort. Landing on 23 August, they establish the first permanent European settlement on Île St. Jean at Port La Joye.

1721

Île St. Jean's European population is estimated at 300. Unfortunately, nobody ever thinks to count or even estimate the Mi 'kmaq population.

1724

A plague of mice, probably field mice (*Microtus pennsylvannicus*) does great damage to crops. This is the first of a dozen outbreaks that will be recorded over the next 90 years. Biologists are still puzzled over the origins of the outbreaks.

1728

A census tallies the Island's European population at 423. About 70% are permanent settlers — the rest are fishermen, many of whom leave for the winter.

Jacques De Pensens, Commandant of Île St. Jean, reports "a plague of an infinite number of rats" has devastated the crops.

1730

Not satisfied with the slow progress being made, the French crown revokes Comte de St. Pierre's title to Île St. Jean. St. Pierre's losses are not known, but his merchant partners have lost heavily on the failed colony.

1731

The European population has grown to 464.

The French Crown grants the Three Rivers region to Pierre Roma and his Company of the East.

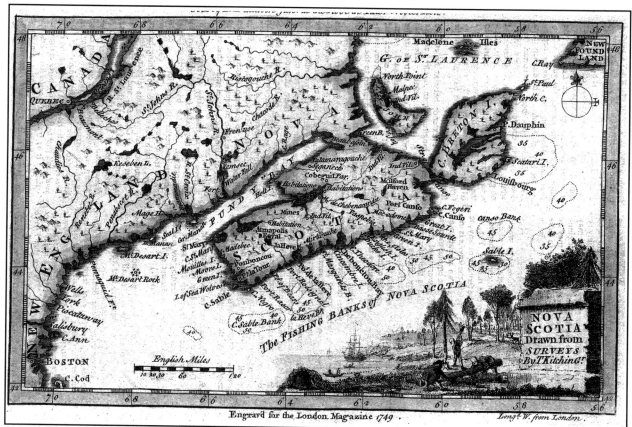

Nova Scotia, 1749

"Drawn from Surveys by T[homas] Kitchen"

(James and Barbara Macnutt Collection of Historic Maps), P.E.I. Museum and Heritage Foundation

He arrives the following year and establishes a fishing and trading settlement at present-day Brudenell Point.

1735

 The European population has grown to 563.

1736

A huge forest fire devastates settlements in northeastern part of the Island. Thousands of acres in what is now known as central Kings County are consumed.

1737

On 10 April, one of the earliest settlers at Port La Joye, Michel Haché-Gallant drowns when he breaks through the rotting spring ice on the North River. He is not rich, but he leaves a rich legacy. He is ancestor of all Hachés and Gallants.

1738

In November the Governor of the colony makes a desperate appeal to Louisbourg for supplies. "An immense quantity of mice ... have entirely and generally devoured wheat and other grains." Settlers face famine if no assistance is forthcoming.

1739

A major forest fire devastates the area around Île St. Jean's major settlement, St. Pierre.

1742

Another major fire, the second in three years, devastates area around St. Pierre. Thirteen people are killed.

1745

On 20 June, New Englanders detached from the siege of the Louisbourg raid and burn Pierre Roma's settlement at Three Rivers (Brudenell Point). It is the last blow for Roma's struggling colony, which is entirely abandoned. The raiders then push on to Port La Joye, destroying it as well. A week later, while pushing up the Northeast (or Hillsborough) River to sack St. Pierre, the British troops are ambushed by François Duport Duvivier's makeshift force of French soldiers and Mi 'kmaq. In the ensuing battle, the British are decimated, losing 28 killed, captured or wounded. St. Pierre is saved, but Duvivier concedes the Island is lost, and removes his tiny force to Quebec.

1746

The British think about deporting the French population from Île St. Jean, but decide against it. In July, Joseph-Michel Legardeur de Croisille et de Montesson and a raiding party of 200 Mi 'kmaq leave Baie Verte for the British-held island. On 21 July they surprise a British provisioning party, killing or capturing about 40.

1748

 With Île St. Jean's return to France, and growing uncertainty over the future of British-controlled Acadia, the Island's population begins to swell. A census puts the total at 735.

The Treaty of Aix-La-Chapelle brings the War of the Austrian Succession to an end. Britain trades Île St. Jean and Île Royale back to France. In return, they get to keep the Indian city of Madras. New

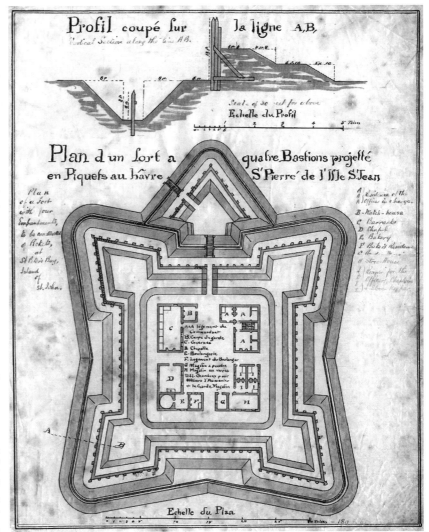

Plans for Fortifications at St. Pierre

(James and Barbara Macnutt Collection of Historic Maps), P.E.I. Museum and Heritage Foundation
Although it looked very good on paper, Colonel Franquet's scheme to fortify the fishing port of St. Pierre was never executed.

England, which spent a good deal of blood and treasure to capture the two islands, is understandably annoyed by this deal.

1749

A plague of mice devour the grain crops in many parts of the Island.

1751

Colonel Franquet, a respected military engineer, is sent from Louisbourg to inspect Île St. Jean. Although the fortifications he designs are never built, his report affords later generations a valuable description of the French colony.

1752

The European population is now 2,223. Another 400 will arrive by 1753.

1754

In Europe, the conflict will begin in 1756, end in 1763 and thus be called "The Seven Years' War." British and French colonists in North America can't wait for the official declaration and begin fighting two years early. The victorious British colonists will dub their version of the conflict: "The French and Indian War."

1755

Infuriated by their refusal to swear an oath of loyalty, and suspicious of their promise of neutrality, British authorities expel the Acadian populations in their territory. Hundreds of dispossessed refugees flood across the Strait to Île St. Jean, swelling the population to an estimated 5,000 and putting a serious strain on the colony's ability to feed itself.

1758

Thomas Pichon publishes an account of the Island. He gathered the material while touring the colony in 1752 with the Governor of Louisbourg, who was probably not aware that his travel companion was an English spy. Pichon's account is received with great inter-

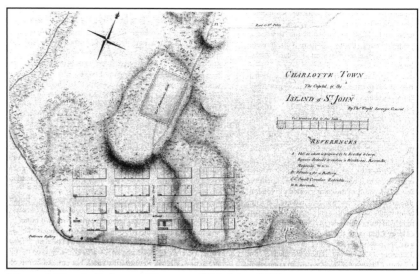

Plan of Charlottetown, Thomas Wright, c1780
Surveyor Thomas Wright based his plan on Captain Charles Morris' design.

est in Britain, where his lavish assessment of the Island's potential turns many greedy heads.

On 27 July, British forces capture Fortress Louisbourg for the second time in 12 years. The subsequent conquest of Île St Jean is a formality. On 17 August Lt. Colonel Andrew Rollo arrives with four ships, 500 troops and orders to deport the entire French and Acadian population. Although many evade capture, by November 3,000 are placed on transports and expelled.

On 12 December the *Violet*, bound for France with 400 deported Island Acadians, is lost in the north Atlantic in a heavy gale. The next day the *Duke William*, with some 300 deportees on board, sinks in the same storm. Of an estimated 3,100 deportees embarked on 11 British transports, close to 1,700 die of disease or drowning before reaching Europe.

1760

On 24 October, according to some traditions, John Webster, Jr. becomes the first "British subject" born on the Island.

1763

The Treaty of Paris brings to a close the Seven Years' War, leaving Britain in possession of Quebec, Île Royale and Île St. Jean.

Île Royale becomes "Cape Breton." Île St. Jean becomes "St. John's Island." For administrative purposes, the two islands are annexed to the existing British colony of Nova Scotia.

Governor Walter Patterson

1764

With treasury seriously strained by the recent war against France, Britain decides to let the private sector settle and develop its new colony of St. John's Island. Major Samuel Holland is despatched to survey the colony and divide it into 20,000-acre estates. These will then be granted to individuals interested in, and capable of developing the properties. The rents thus generated will pay for the colony's civil infrastructure. Britain will get a happy, prosperous colony without having to spend a penny of public money. What could be simpler?

1765

On 6 October, Samuel Holland completes his survey. In dividing the island into three counties, 67 townships, and 14 parishes, he has managed to flatter just about every important British official by naming landmarks after them. A grateful Crown rewards Holland with Lot 28 and a promotion to Surveyor General. Holland never does much to develop his estate but, then again, also pays little attention to collecting rents. He himself settles in Quebec.

Major Robert Rogers fuels interest in St. John's Island. His book, *A Concise Account of North America*, it perhaps a little too concise, for there is little evidence Rogers actually visited the Island before writing about it. Forecasts of the colony's potential suggest it could support 500,000 or more. The "Granary of New France" will swiftly become "The Granary of British America." Interest in getting a piece of the colony grows.

1767

On 23 July, the Board of Trade and Plantations holds a "Great Lottery," to grant 66 of the Island's 67 townships to various individuals with claims on the Crown's largesse. "Thus in a single afternoon," historians will later write, "the entire Island was given away." The lucky winners agree to settle their properties to a certain density within ten years. They promise not to attract settlers from the British Isles, but to recruit "foreign Protestants" only. They also agree to pay an annual "quit rent" to the Crown.

1768

Captain Charles Morris is ordered to lay out "the ground on which the town of Charlotte Town will be built." Inspired by new theories in urban design, Morris creates an elegant street grid with plenty of common areas.

The first British census of St. John's Island puts the population at 271. All but 68 of the residents are Acadians who either escaped deportation or returned when things settled down.

1769

On 10 July, the Lords of Trade and Plantations submit to George III their plan for a seal for the new colony of St. John's Island. It features a large oak tree sheltering three saplings joined at the root. The legend below reads, PARVA SUB INGENTI ("the small under the great"). The seal is adopted four days later.

The Island receives the first (and arguably only) benefit from its system of leasehold tenure. Its 70-odd proprietors lobby forcefully to have the colony detached from the administration of Nova Scotia and set up with a government of its own. On 28 June, St. John's Island is granted separate status on condition that it not become a burden on the British Treasury. Proprietor Walter Patterson, an army Captain from Donegal, is later commissioned as the Island's first governor. He is talented, energetic, and none too honest — but this hardly makes him unique in his generation.

1770

The first legislation ever passed by an Island government is an act to protect the walrus fishery. It doesn't work.

The colony's civil administration slowly takes shape. Governor Patterson arrives and on 19 September swears in John Duport as the colony's first chief justice. Civil service salaries are to come from quit rents paid by Island proprietors on their properties. Most don't pay, and people like Duport soon find themselves in severe circumstances. When his daughter Jane dies a few years later, starvation is listed as the cause.

On 1 June, the *Falmouth*, 53 days out from Greenock, arrives off St. Peter's with 120 settlers. They were sent out by James Montgomery, Lord Advocate of Scotland, to settle his lands on Lot 34. They call their settlement Stanhope.

On 27 September, the brigantine *Annabella*, two months out of Campbellton, Scotland, arrives off Darnley Point bearing 200 settlers.

The British experience their first mouse plague. As with his French predecessors, Governor Patterson reports devastated crops and destitute settlers.

1771

On 27 July, the *Edinburgh* clears Campbellton, Scotland, with about 70 Scots emigrants bound for Col. Robert Stewart's settlement at Malpeque.

1772

On 17 May some 210 Highlanders — the "Glenaladale Settlers" — set sail on the *Alexander* for Tracadie. Their sponsor, Captain John MacDonald, Laird of the Glenaladale MacDonalds, hopes to transplant the best parts of the clan system in the New World while leaving its more unpleasant aspects behind. MacDonald's is the first large-scale emigration of Catholic Highlanders to the Maritimes.

1773

On 7 July, in the absence of any public buildings, the Island's first Assembly meets at the Crossed Keys Tavern in Charlottetown. "Damn queer Parliament," the doorkeeper allegedly remarks. He is censured for his lack of respect.

1774

The Quit Rent Act marks the first attempt to force the Is-

proprietors to pay the annual tax due on their land holdings. It sets the pattern for subsequent attempts — it doesn't work.

Governor Walter Patterson puts the Island's population at very modest 1,215. By the terms of their grants, the Island's proprietors have promised to bring out 6,600 settlers by 1777.

Quaker Robert Clark sends 100 emigrants to his new estate, optimistically named "New London." Clark is hoping to become another William Penn, a fellow Quaker who founded the colony of Pennsylvania. Unlike Penn, Clark sends his settlers out with little preparation for the harsh conditions of the New World.

1775

As rebellion erupts in the American colonies, Governor Patterson leaves for England to try and straighten out the colony's finances. His 12-month leave of absence lasts five years.

Benjamin Chappell emigrates to Robert Clark's settlement at New London. He makes his living as a wheelwright and postmaster and is considered the father of Methodism on the Island. He also keeps a diary that will be considered a treasure trove of insights into pioneer life on Prince Edward Island.

Using information from Samuel Holland's survey, Thomas Jeffreys creates the first map to accurately show the shape of the Island.

Schooner Franklin
Watercolour by Thomas Russell, 1776

When last seen in Island waters, the *Franklin* was headed south with several kidnapped officials and the Colony's Great Seal of office.

 On 17 November two American privateers, the *Lynch* and *Franklin*, appear off Hillsborough Bay. They were commissioned to prey on British shipping, but decide to raid Charlottetown instead. They find little worth liberating in the tiny village, so content themselves with kidnapping two senior civil servants and stealing the colony's official seal of office. Rebel commander George Washington is not impressed with the privateers' actions, and orders the prisoners released. They make their way back to the colony but the great seal, made of silver, is never seen again.

On 5 November the *Elizabeth* runs aground off Malpeque Bay. Among her passengers are Chief Justice Peter Stewart and his family. Also on board is a sawyer named James Curtis. The Stewarts become a dominant force in the colony's politics. Curtis suffers through a bitterly cold — and disillusioning — winter and leaves as soon as he can. He later pens *An Account of a Voyage to the Island of St. John*, based on his experiences. "Many Instances of Severyty in the Climate," he concludes, "convinced me that this Island would not be agreeable to an English constitution."

Another infestation of mice hits the colony.

1776

Patrick M'Robert publishes *A Tour Through Part of the North Provinces of America*. Unlike some of his contemporaries, M'Robert actually visits the places he writes about before writing about them.

1778

On 19 February, the first sentence of death ever pronounced in the colony condemns servant Elizabeth Mukely for stealing £7.7s from her master, Gideon Ticeborn. She is pardoned when no one will consent to act as hangman.

***Charlottetown**, 1778.* From a sketch by Charles Randle

I have no doubt, but some time hence, it will form as fine a city as any in Nova Scotia.
— Patrick M'Robert, 1775

In a few minutes I found Charlottetown to be wicked enough for a larger town. Swearing and Drunkeness abounded.
— Reverend James MacGregor, 1791

1779

Under official pressure, Thomas DesBrisay finally arrives on the Island to take up his duties as lieutenant governor — ten years after his appointment. When the governor's position is downgraded to lieutenant governor in 1784, DesBrisay will lose his job.

1780

There are too many "St. John's" — cities, rivers, etc. — in the Gulf of St Lawrence. So Irish-born Governor Patterson forwards to Britain an act changing the name of St. John's Island to "New Ireland." The act is disallowed because the name is already taken and, besides, the colony should petition for a change, not legislate one. The Island isn't crazy about Britain's suggestions: New Guernsey or New Anglesea.

The Militia Act decrees all males between 16 and 60 should bear arms and attend musters and military exercises. There is allegedly more drinking than drilling at the annual musters.

Theophilus DesBrisay, son of Lt. Governor Thomas DesBrisay, is named the first rector of the Anglican parish of Charlotte. He considers Charlottetown "a wicked place" and moves to Covehead.

On 27 October, Dr. John Clarke (a Harvard man) and Surveyor General Thomas Wright, use a two-foot-long reflecting telescope to observe a solar eclipse. Their observations are forwarded to the American Academy of Art and Sciences.

1781

The Crown has a legal mechanism called "escheat" for repossessing estates of proprietors who can't meet the obligations of the 1767 land grants. On 15 November, Governor Patterson escheats almost half of the estates in the colony for failure to submit quit rents. Since he

Angus MacEachern

Even though the terms of the 1767 land grants specified only "Foreign Protestants" were to settle here, the Island's population was almost 50% Catholic by 1790. Father Angus MacEachern, portrayed here after his elevation to Bishop, was for many years the only Catholic priest in the colony.

and his fellow administrators have not been paid for many years, he offers land in lieu of back wages. At a single stroke, title to over 600,000 acres changes hands. Patterson's personal holdings swell to 170,000 acres. Suddenly-landless proprietors in Britain are soon demanding both the return of their land, and Patterson's dismissal.

1782

The Acadian settlers of Rustico petition Lt. Governor DesBrisay for assistance after a plague of mice destroy their crops. It's the third such outbreak in the last 12 years.

1784

Governor Patterson and other beneficiaries of the 1781 land escheat try to strengthen their hand by granting a quarter of their property for settlement by Loyalists. When the Crown later overturns Patterson's escheat, the Loyalists who settled the "free" land find their deeds are worthless.

On 4 November, a party of American Loyalists arrives at Charlottetown aboard the *Stag*. Thousands are fleeing the newly independent United States, but the difficulty in attracting them to this colony is that it has no Crown Lands to offer.

7

$ John Cambridge arrives in the colony to manage Robert Clark's estate at New London, but soon strikes out on his own. By the time of his death in 1831, he is the Island's leading merchant and biggest landowner. His 102,000-acre estate will include mills, stores, and shipyards, but it is an empire built on credit. Within a decade of his death, his mortgagers, the powerful Cunard family, will have gained the entire estate.

Lt. Governor Edmund Fanning

1785

An act prohibiting all masters of ships or vessels... from transporting any person out of this Island or adjacent territories... without a license is repealed. Passed in 1773, designed to prevent people owing money from absconding without paying their debts, "...the said act has been misconstrued to the prejudice of the settlement of this Island by the enemies thereof, insinuating to people who were coming to settle that after their arrival they would never be able to leave, which malicious reports have served to discourage many useful people from coming to settle in this Island."

1786

Jupiter Wise, a black slave condemned to death for theft and attempted murder, has his sentence reduced to transportation.

Governor Patterson is dismissed and, on 4 November

Col. Edmund Fanning arrives in Charlottetown to assume the government. Claiming he never received his notice of recall, Patterson declines to surrender his office. As a result, the tiny colony spends the winter with two governors.

The Legislature passes *An act for quieting the minds of, and establishing certain privileges to His Majesty's subjects possessing the Popish religion, now residing or who may hereafter reside on this Island.* While guaranteeing that their legal transactions will be backed by law, the Act insists that Roman Catholics first swear a long oath promising allegiance to King George III and his heirs and renouncing any allegiance to the House of Stuart or "other pretenders to the throne." The oath also calls on the taker to reject "as an unchristian and impious position that it is lawful to murder or destroy any person or persons... under the pretence of their being heretics and.... that princes excommunicated by the Church of Rome may be lawfully deposed or murdered by their subjects."

1787

As soon as the ice is out of the harbour, ex-governor Patterson departs for London to try and get his job back. There he fails, and is formally censured for trying to transfer title to an eighth of the colony to his own hands. He dies a pauper in London in 1798.

James Robertson begins the Island's first newspaper, the *Royal Gazette and Weekly Intelligencer of the Island of Saint John.* The reading public is tiny, and Robertson's paper lasts less than a year

Future Island missionary Angus Bernard MacEachern is ordained at the Royal Scots College, Valladolid, Spain.

On 12 May the schooner *St. Patrick*, built at Rustico by John B. Peters, becomes the first vessel ever registered on the Island.

Over 4,500 more will follow over the next 15 decades.

1788

A sturdy boat is constructed to convey the mails across the treacherous ice floes of the Northumberland Strait. The first "iceboat" service is sporadic, but within a generation becomes part of the colony's winter routine.

When Collector of Customs William Townshend seizes a cargo of American goods landed at ex-governor Walter Patterson's property at Rocky Point, Patterson's henchmen seize the seizers, imprisoning them overnight. Townshend comes back next day with the militia, but the merchandise has disappeared.

Attorney General Phillips Callbeck, one of former governor Patterson's highest officials, is elected Speaker by an Assembly opposed to Lt. Governor Fanning. In 1789, when the charges against Patterson and his officials are maintained, Callbeck is stripped of his offices. His career ruined by his allegiance to Patterson, Callbeck dies a year later.

1789

Lt. Governor Fanning sets aside 100 acres of Town Common for the "use and residence" of the Crown's representative. The land will eventually provide the setting for both Fanningbank (Government House) and Victoria Park.

Charles Inglis, first Anglican Bishop of Nova Scotia, begins a nine-day tour of the Island. He finds one Church of England clergyman and no churches (services are held in a local "coffee and ball room"). He is appalled; plans to build a suitable edifice are immediately set afoot.

The Legislature grants dissenting Protestants – Presbyterians, Quakers, etc — the right to build churches, hire clergy and administer sacraments "according to their several opinions." It also excuses them from paying taxes levied to support the Church of England

1790

On 28 August the *Jane* and *Lucy*, both out of Greenock, Scotland, arrive at Charlottetown with 253 Scottish immigrants.

Father Angus MacEachern arrives to minister to the Island's Roman Catholic congregation. He's the first Catholic priest in the colony since Father James MacDonald died in 1785. He's also the only Catholic priest in the colony. Soon his charge will be expanded to include Cape Breton and Nova Scotia's north shore.

The Island's first paper currency, £500 in treasury notes, is issued to combat the colony's shortage of specie. The term of circulation is three years. Despite bearing the warning, "Death to Counterfeiters," the results are disappointing.

1791

The *Royal Gazette* announces that Charlottetown finally has a wharf; erected not with public but private funds. "It is astonishing that in a place where the difficulty of landing is so great, no attempt, worthy of the name, has yet been made to erect a work of so useful and obvious a nature."

On 3 September the *Molly* arrives from Greenock, Scotland with 174 immigrants.

Reverend James MacGregor pays a visit to Charlottetown. He's not impressed. "In a few minutes I found Charlottetown to be wicked enough for a larger town. Swearing and drunkenness abounded."

1792

The colony passes its own criminal code. Included in the list of capital offenses are: high treason, murder and mayhem, assault,

issuing threatening letters, buggery, rape, theft and arson.

Joseph Farrow is sentenced to hang for raping a 12-year-old girl in Vernon River. While a petition is being circulated in his favour, he attempts to escape, dooming any hope for clemency. His is the first state execution in the colony.

On 24 February, a group of Charlottetonians follow Donald McIntire as he is whipped at various locations in the town. His crime: petty larceny. His sentence: three sets of 36 lashes, delivered over the course of three weeks. Flogging persists as a punishment well into the 1840s.

On 28 January The *Royal Gazette and Miscellany* announces the marriage of the "very agreeable" Nelly MacDonald, sister of Capt. John MacDonald of Glenaladale. For the past 16 years she has been entrusted with the stewardship of her absent brother's extensive estate. In a society dominated by males, it is a singular achievement.

Charlottetown's *Royal Gazette and Miscellany* raises a polite eyebrow: "Was lately married, Mr. William Hunter of Richmond Bay, upwards of 70, to Miss Katherine McEachran, of 20 years."

1793

The *Royal Gazette and Miscellany* kindly supplies its readers with "A certain cure for Scurvey: 2 oz cream of tartar, 1 oz sulpher, pound them fine and mix with half a lb of treacle, taking half a spoonful an hour before breakfast, and the same quantity before going to rest. If this should purge too much, take only once every 24 hours."

"Last week was eaten in Charlottetown, in the course of 5 days, by a man belonging to Warren Farm, 10 lb beef, 8 lb pork, 6 dozen eels, 3 fine trout, 3 loaves of bread

— each weighing between 4 and 5 lb, 1 lb butter, 7 lb cheese, 2 gallons of milk, tea, etc."

On hearing news that France and Great Britain have declared war, Lt. Governor Fanning orders "A Day of Public Humiliation and Fasting."

1796

On petition of a group of Charlottetown women, Freelove Allen's death sentence for theft is commuted to expulsion from the Island. The sentence is delayed when Allen cannot get a passage out of the colony. Hers is the last sentence of exile the colony ever passes.

The Legislature passes *An act to prevent the robbing of gardens and orchards, potato and turnip fields*. "Whereas it has become necessary, in order to encourage the planting of orchards and gardens, to enact some regulation for the protection of fruit trees, roots and other vegetables against the predation of thieves and disorderly persons." Punishments are severe: one month in prison and a 40s fine for first offense, two months and a £4 fine for the second. If the crime is committed at night, the law demands an additional punishment of 50-100 lashes for the first offense, 100-150 for the second.

1797

St. John's Lodge of the Ancient and Honourable Fraternity of Free and Accepted Masons, Scottish Rite, is established in Charlottetown.

Charlottetown is treated to the sight of two of its most prominent citizens — Captain John "Hellfire Jack" Stewart and Captain John MacDonald — duelling in the street. The two own neighbouring estates, but are bitter political enemies. Though he later confesses to drawing his weapon first, MacDonald is older and lighter than Stewart, and is wielding a dirk against a broadsword. Luckily it is winter, and

Stewart is wearing so many clothes he can hardly swing his sword arm. The fight ends with no blood shed.

John Stewart
John "Hellfire Jack" Stewart was one of the Island's most prominent citizens from his arrival in 1770 to his death over 60 years later. Landowner, politician and sometimes duellist, he penned the first history of the colony in 1805.

Proprietor Col. John Robinson publishes *To the Farmers in the Island of St. John, in the Gulf of St. Lawrence*. Robinson is strongly in favour of a Court of Escheat to seize the estates of defaulting land holders.

On 5 September, Lt. Governor Edmund Fanning and a company of volunteer cavalry arrive in Princetown to suppress a militia mutiny. The mutineers are cowed into submission without bloodshed or punishment. Fanning's critics dub the episode the "Seige of Princetown."

1798

A census reveals the colony's population to be 4,372.

British cartographer H. Ashby publishes the first map to show "Prince Edward Island."

1799

On 1 February, Royal Assent is given a bill re-naming St. John's Island "Prince Edward Island." It's in honour of Prince Edward, Duke of Kent, commander-in-chief of British forces in North America. He's never been here. In fact, he once recommended the colony be re-annexed to Nova Scotia.

Father J-L-J Calonne, an aristocratic French priest driven from his homeland by the French Revolution, arrives on the Island to begin life over as a missionary in the pioneer colony. He stays until 1803, then moves to Quebec. Increasingly ascetic, he is revered by some as saint after his death in 1822.

1800

The erection of the first Anglican Church in Charlottetown begins. Located on the western end of Queen's Square, it will be finished the next year.

Between 1796 and 1800, Island shipyards launch 14 vessels.

1801

Thomas Cochrane becomes the Island's chief justice. He is said to be the youngest man in the history of the Empire named to so exalted a position. The Island is just a stepping-stone to bigger things. In 1802 he is promoted the Chief Justice for Upper Canada. There, later in his career, he has the poor judgement to drown en route to a case.

1803

On 1 August the *Polly*, one of three vessels bearing the "Selkirk settlers" arrives at Charlottetown, bound for Belfast. By the end of the month two other vessels, the *Oughton* and the *Dykes*, bring the rest of the 800 immigrants — all from the Highlands and Western Isles of Scotland. "This is the isle of contentment/ where we are now," one of the emigrants, poet Calum Ban Buchanan, will exclaim. "Our seed is fruitful here."

On 15 August Pierre Denaut, Bishop of Quebec, begins the first-ever visit of a Roman Catholic prelate to Prince Edward Island. He is not impressed with the "rough and ready" nature of religious observance in the colony.

1804

Col. Edmund Fanning retires with his reputation intact; of the Island's first four governors, he is the only one not recalled in disgrace. His secret? According to one historian, a combination of "geniality, deft duplicity, and judicious inaction." The former Governor stays on in the colony. He's now one of its biggest landlords.

The colony's new Lt. Governor is Joseph Frederick Wallet DesBarres. A flamboyant former military officer and surveyor, DesBarres is best remembered as creator of *The Atlantic Neptune* — the era's finest and most-detailed survey of the Atlantic seaboard.

James Bagnall begins the first of many publishing ventures with a newspaper, the *Royal Herald*. "Country produce and furs will be taken as payment from those who cannot make it convenient to pay in cash." Plagued by paper shortages and a lack of subscribers, the venture lasts a little more than a year.

1805

Cantankerous Irish barrister Caesar Colclough is appointed chief justice of Prince Edward Island, in part as reward for his loyalty during the Irish uprising of 1798. He is a reluctant appointee; it is over two years before he arrives on the Island. Once here, he will be in almost constant conflict with his boss, Lt. Governor DesBarres.

On 11 June, the schooner *Nancy* arrives from Greenock via Tobermory with 32 Scottish immigrants after a rapid passage of only 29 days.

Lt. Governor DesBarres orders a census. Four decades after becoming a separate colony, the Island has a population of only 7,041.

Thomas Douglas, Earl of Selkirk

The Earl of Selkirk publishes *The Present State of the Highlands of Scotland*. Population and other pressures are pushing the Highlands toward revolution, he argues. The only solution is to follow his example and assist Highlanders to settle in the New World.

Writing anonymously, John MacDonald, Laird of Glenaladale, publishes *Information for Proprietors on the Island of St. John*. Emigrant primers are becoming common, but only on Prince Edward Island will you find handbooks for prospective proprietors.

Britain's Royal Navy, led by Lord Nelson, destroys the navies of France and Spain at the Battle of Trafalgar. According to family legend, a 19-year-old sailor named William Cooper is on one of Nelson's ships. Thirty years later, Cooper leads the fight for land reform on Prince Edward Island.

On 3 June the snow *Favourite* is driven ashore on the bar near Malpeque Bay. She is neither the first nor the last vessel wrecked on the North Shore, but she's luckier than most. She gets off.

Between 1801 and 1805, Island shipyards launch 32 vessels.

1806

The Loyal Electors, arguably the first organized political party in Canada, return five members to the House of Assembly. Although motivated essentially by self-interest, they campaign on a platform of land reform, earning the ire of the ruling class and a reputation as the ancestor of the Island's subsequent Escheat, Reform and Liberal parties.

John "Hellfire Jack" Stewart publishes: *An Account of Prince Edward Island*. Aside from being a most detailed summary of the colony's natural and recent human history, Stewart's *Account* also provides all of his answers to the "Land Question."

1807

"Discouraged and disappointed in his art," architect John Plaw emigrates to the Island. Although the author of three respected works on architecture, Plaw has been unable to get enough commissions to make a living in England. The colony needs a whole slate of public buildings, and as soon as funds become available commissions Plaw to design a Court House and Market Hall for Queen's Square.

Lt. Governor J.F.W. Des-Barres orders his third census in three years. The colony's population has grown to 8,730.

Charlottetown's first Methodist minister arrives. The Rev. James Bulpit has been sent out by the London Missionary Society.

Lt. Governor J.F.W. Desbarres

1808

On 21 September the *Clarendon* from Oban, Scotland, lands with 188 immigrants.

Reverend John Keir arrives in Princetown to begin a 50-year Presbyterian ministry.

1809

On 29 August Lt. Governor J.F. W. DesBarres offers a 20-guinea reward for information about the "riotous and evil minded persons" who tore down Charlottetown's public stocks.

General Sir John Moore, beloved commander of the British Army in Spain, is killed during the Battle of Coruna. His dying wish is that he be buried on the battlefield. "Few and short were the prayers we said. And we spoke not a word of sorrow. But we steadfastly gazed on the face that was dead. And we bitterly thought of the morrow." Part of the burial party is a sergeant named William Johnstone. After the wars he settles at Cumberland Hill, near present-day Dundas. When he dies in 1856, nobody writes a poem about it.

On 3 April the colony loses its first established Presbyterian minister when Rev. Peter Gordon dies, aged only 36. Like other pioneer missionaries, he had travelled on foot, by boat and on horseback to minister a widely scattered flock in Covehead, St. Peter's and Bay Fortune.

1810

The *Weekly Recorder* is upset about the condition of Island roads. They're primitive enough to start with, but it doesn't help that some of the highways have been fenced across by local farmers.

Four years after the demise of the *Royal Herald*, King's Printer James Bagnall issues the first edition of the *Weekly Recorder of Prince Edward Island*. This latest publishing venture lasts about three years.

On 24 December, Thomas DesBrisay, Jr. announces that he has opened an apothecary's shop in Charlottetown at the corner of Grafton and Queen. He thus establishes a tradition; there will be a pharmacy on the site for another 175 years.

Francis Garrabo borrows £50 to begin building a grand hotel in Charlottetown. It will be several stories tall, span an entire block and will be topped with a cupola and larger-than-life gilded statue of the owner in a classical pose. When the partially-completed building blows down in a wind storm, Garrabo takes a job with the government, and later leaves the colony.

Despite being protected by law since 1770, the walrus is extinct here.

On 18 October the brig *Eliza*, bound from Portsmouth to Cascumpec, is driven ashore at Hunter Cape, near New London. Captain and crew reach shore safely. For one passenger, a Lt. Smith, it's his second wreck since setting out from England to rejoin his regiment in Quebec.

George and Pheobe (Cambridge) Wright establish the colony's first brewery at Bird Island, later known as Wright's Creek, in East Royalty. Although Islanders have a prodigious capacity for beer,

***Wright's Creek,** 1880*
Meacham's Atlas, 1880

the Wrights are unable to secure a constant supply of quality hops, and the brewery closes after several years.

Between 1806 and 1810, Island shipyards launch 25 vessels.

1811

On 6 January, the messenger sent to Halifax for the Mails makes it back to his "desponding family" after a harrowing journey through storms and ice floes lasting six weeks. Through sleet and storm and dark of etc., etc.

Fearing famine after an exceptionally poor harvest, Lt. Governor DesBarres authorizes a grant of £300 to purchase relief provisions in Halifax.

The London *Chronicle* publishes a letter from the Island dated 20 September. "We have four out of five vessels from Scotland, with emigrants already arrived, and for the sake of humanity, I hope the fifth may not. . . ." There is little food and no provision made for new emigrants, and growing conditions have been bad of late.

Islanders love the races. At an August meeting, "Mr. Jones Bay Mare Sprightly" takes on "Mr. Story's Bay Mare Lovely" in a race from "Mr. Rod's House on the East Road to the North end of Mr. Holland's fields." Lovely goes off a 3-1 favourite, but comes home a dismal second. The stakes are doubled for a re-match. "Our people," writes Father Angus MacEachern, "are extravagant in tea drinking, dress, grog and horse racing."

Only 13 years after Dr. Edward Jenner announced his smallpox vaccine, druggist Thomas DesBrisay Jr. advertises the cowpox vaccine for Islanders (free to the poor). Their fear of inoculation greater than their fear of smallpox, most Islanders pass on DesBrisay's offer.

"So great a scarcity of its productions has not been known for many years," laments the *Weekly Recorder* after a heavy spring snowfall worsens the food situation in the colony. The paper blames matters on too many farmers neglecting farming to work in the booming timber trade.

Alexander Crawford, Baptist preacher and author, arrives in the colony. Although the history of the Baptists on the Island dates from a visit from the great Henry Alline in 1782, it is really Crawford, a Scots Baptist, who plants the religion here.

On 30 September a tremendous gale pounds Charlottetown. In the harbour, several merchant vessels drag their anchors, and several pleasure craft are sunk. In the town, a building is blown off its foundation and the skeletons of two others under construction are blown down. One would hope this is a testament to the power of the storm and not the quality of Charlottetown's carpenters.

James Gibson of Charlottetown announces that he has imported "a complete set of Machinery for a Tobacco and Snuff Manufactory." It is unclear whether Gibson's Tobacco Factory ever gets off the ground.

1812

Charlottetown's new courthouse, designed by John Plaw, is used for the first time — by Bishop J. O. Plessis of Quebec to celebrate Mass. The building will see many other uses before it is torn down in 1972.

On 11 June, gripped by paranoia, Francis-Xavier Gallant of Lot 16 lures his wife into the woods and slits her throat. He is sentenced to hang, but dies first of cold and malnutrition in captivity.

Though they've been feuding for years, relations between Chief Justice Colcough and Lt. Governor DesBarres reach a low ebb. "The Governor," an outraged Colcough writes, "threw himself back in his chair and collecting all the foul Breath he could in his mouth puffed it full in my face." London has had enough. DesBarres is recalled; Colcough is sent to Newfoundland. DesBarres' enemies had charged that the 90-year old administrator had grown too feeble and senile to rule. By way of response, he is said to have danced a jig on top of a table to celebrate his 100th birthday. He dies in 1825 — a month shy of his 103rd birthday.

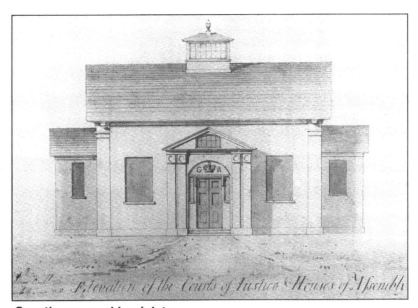

Courthouse and Legislature
Elevation by John Plaw

The influence of his famous brother, Admiral Sidney Smith, wins Charles Douglass Smith the appointment as the new Lt. Governor of the Island. Unfortunately, Smith has more confidence than competence and more energy than intelligence. Fortunately, war delays his arrival for another year.

With war just declared on the United States, Lt. Alex MacDonald of His Majesty's Canadian Regiment of Glengarry Sharp Shooters arrives from Quebec on a recruiting expedition. To bolster morale, he brings news and details of the American surrender at Detroit.

Island settler David Moore finds out about the War of 1812 the hard way. He is a passenger aboard the *Royal Bounty,* bound for Charlottetown from England. Off Newfoundland, his vessel falls afoul of an American privateer, and surrenders after a stiff fight. The passengers and crew are put ashore — after being robbed.

It has come to the attention of Governor DesBarres "that several French Prisoners of War are employed in different parts of the Island, without any permission or license having been obtained for that purpose." Anyone in possession of an unlicensed French POW is to return him immediately to Charlottetown.

On 21 July, Bishop J.O. Plessis of Quebec ends a 21-day visit to the Island. "In Canada," he writes, "we have little idea of the poverty of the Acadian chapels . . . and no idea whatever of the utter destitution of the Scottish churches." He is impressed with the Islanders' piety, though not with some of their practices. Scottish women, he notes, are unbecomingly immodest in their church-going attire.

1813

A modest, 18' by 26' building is erected on Queen's Square to serve as a Market House. Almost as soon as it is opened, it is judged inadequate.

On 3 March John Nicholson of Flat River and his son Samuel beat to death their neighbour John Ross. On 15 May they hang.

Insisting that the letter of British law be followed, Lt. Governor Smith cracks down on the colony's Catholics. Marriages performed by Catholic clergy will not be legally recognized and the colony's two Catholic Justices of the Peace are dismissed. Catholics weather the storm by appealing to the Governor-in-Chief in Quebec, who quietly pressures Smith to be a little less zealous.

A particularly severe mouse plague strikes the colony. It is said that a pit dug at night would be filled by morning and that cats, martens and other predators die from over-eating! Another outbreak in 1814, and a third in 1815 make these known for some time as "The Years of the Mouse." For reasons unknown, 1815 is the last of the outbreaks.

Faced with a chronic shortage of hard currency, the government offers two solutions. First, it decrees that bank tokens are to pass for their sterling value. Its second idea is more creative. It cuts the centres out of as many as 1,000 Spanish silver dollars. The centre plug circulates as a shilling; the outer ring as a five shilling piece. Thus is born the "Holey Dollar."

1814

Sancho Byers is sentenced to death for petty theft. There is little clemency for him, or his brother Peter, who gets the same sentence 12 days later for stealing a loaf of bread and a pound of butter. Both hang.

It was a good idea, but too easy to duplicate. Plagued by widespread counterfeiting, the government recalls the "Holey Dollar."

1815

James Bagnall publishes the first almanac devoted to the Island: *Prince Edward Island calendar for town and country.*

On 2 November, several Charlottetown militia companies are mustered on Queen's Square. Angered by the dismissal of their officers, four companies mutiny, refusing to obey orders. Bloodshed is avoided when the garrison commander declines Lt. Governor C.D. Smith's orders to fire on the mutinous militiamen. Smith is furious, and orders the rebellious commander arrested. Later, when Commander-in-Chief Sir John Sherbrooke hears of the incident, he removes the garrison from Smith's direct control.

British and Prussian forces end Napoleon Bonaparte's career as Master of Europe at the Battle of Waterloo. Among the British troops is a soldier named James Quinn, who later settles on P.E.I. No doubt his neighbours on the Georgetown Road get to hear about the battle many times before his death in 1873 at age 87.

"Holey" Dollar

Between 1811 and 1815, Island shipyards launch 80 vessels.

1816

Col. Harry Compton deeds 6,000 acres in Lot 17, including the site of Miscouche, to a group of his Acadian tenants.

Lt. Governor C.D. Smith

A former soldier in Napoleon's army, Charles Auffray arrives at the Acadian settlement of Cascumpeque. Although he has training as a silversmith, the fact he can read and write gains him a reputation as a scholar — and work as a teacher. His career lasts only three years. "He behaved in such a manner as to arouse suspicions," remembered one resident, "and soon his odd ways earned him the reputation as a sorcerer." In 1819 he moves to New Brunswick.

On 17 June a blizzard, the second of the month, sweeps over the Maritimes, a legacy of the eruption of a South Pacific volcano — Mount Tambora — the previous year. Throughout North America, this will be remembered as "the Year without a Summer." The Island's harvest is meagre but sufficient for survival — especially after Lt. Governor Smith bans the export of foodstuffs.

1817

On 22 March the *Valiant* leaves Hull, England for Prince Edward Island, bearing 196 emigrants. Included is Isaac Smith, future architect of Province House and Fanningbank.

1818

Henry Smith, the Lt. Governor's son, underscores his father's demand that the Assembly adjourn by putting his fist through one of the windows in the Assembly room. "I ups with my fist and slashed it through the window," he confesses. The Assembly is unable to punish either Smith for the assault on democracy.

On 9 May the *Dixon*, out of Kingston-upon-Hull, lands 28 English immigrants from the north of England at Charlottetown.

An article in London's *New Monthly Magazine* is perhaps a little too lavish in its praise for the Island. "Industry is not required," it cheerfully informs prospective emigrants, "amusement is the sole duty of the farmer."

A True Guide to Prince Edward Island attempts to rebut the excesses of the recent *New Monthly Magazine* article. "Poor people have been told of spontaneous crops in the wilderness," it warns, "and cleared land in places where they could hardly find their way 20 yards forward." For Islanders who believe "any publicity is good publicity," the exchange is a godsend.

In January, deaths from that dreaded but often mis-diagnosed killer, typhus, are reported in New London and Park Corner. Luckily, the real disease fails to appear.

On 17 November Queen Charlotte Sophia, the German-born wife of the mad monarch, George III of England, predeceases her husband. In all likelihood, she dies unaware that the capital of tiny Prince Edward Island is named in her honour.

In mid-December, trying to get in a final voyage before winter, the schooner *Sally* sets sail from "Crappo" for Plymouth. To avoid getting iced in the harbour, she sails without taking on provisions, hoping to load food and water in Charlottetown. Unfortunately, Charlottetown harbour is barred by ice, and while nosing about for a way in the vessel is overtaken by heavy seas and gales. Four die from exposure before the *Sally* is able to run aground at Blockhouse Point.

On 12 September the *PEI Gazette* reports: "a few days since a shoal of about 60 bottle nose whales swam into Cascumpeque Harbour." Trapped by the falling tide, only 20 escape.

1819

On 24 August, at Abell's Cape, Lot 56, tenant Patrick Pearce kills land agent Edward Abell. Determined to take possession of a fine black stallion in the tenant's possession, Abell refused to accept Pearce's rent payment. In a rage, Pearce stabbed Abell to death with a bayonet. Despite the huge price on his head — £20 — Pearce is hidden by neighbours until he can make good his escape the following spring.

A detailed account of the Island's potential as a colony — and its tangled political situation — appears in the *European Magazine*.

"A Late Resident" publishes *An Account of the Island of Prince Edward*. Hoping to be helpful to prospective emigrants, the author surveys the other colonies of British America and details the shortcomings of each one. By sim-ple process of elimination, the Island seems the only suitable emigration destination.

On 20 July Napoleon Bona-parte comes to town — well, at least his picture does. An 11' by 9' portrait by Mr. J.P. Drake, touring North America, is displayed at Col. DesBrisay's former house. "This picture is decidedly acknowl-edged by all who were personally acquainted with Bonaparte to be the most correct and striking likeness portrayed to the public since the bat-tle of Waterloo. Admission: 1s." Napoleon's portrait is probably the first art exhibition in the history of the colony.

"Slander is not uncommon in all small communities," de-spairs the *PEI Gazette*, "but in Char-lottetown it seems to rise spontane-ous from the soil.... Mothers initiate their children in it, and Miss and Master can neither be good, great nor fashionable without an ample share."

Angus MacEachern is cre-ated titular Bishop of Rosen. The "promotion" is the Bishop of Quebec's way of telling MacEach-ern he is now responsible for New Brunswick, Prince Edward Island and the Magdalen Islands. Later, Cape Breton is also added to the charge. For the 60 year-old MacEachern, the elevation merely means more responsibility without enhanced authority.

1820

As a guide for surveyors, Lt. Governor C.D. Smith orders that a meridional line be established to show proper magnetic north. The result is fixed in a series of stone markers and an upright cannon bar-rel placed in what is now Victoria Park. They're still there.

On 17 April the *Jessie* arrives from Dumfries, Scotland with 179 passengers.

James Christie burgles and burns John Hill's store at Cascumpeque. Hill's business never really recovers. Christie fares even worse. He hangs.

Itinerant teacher and bible salesman Walter Johnstone publishes *Letters from Prince Edward Island*, an account of his recent travels in the colony.

"The inhabitants of Crapaud and surrounding vicinity are anxious to open a market with Ramstag [Wallace N.S.] to exchange sheep for spinning wheels and chairs." Crapaud's exhibition is pos-sibly the first in the colony.

Between 1816 and 1820, Island shipyards launch 111 vessels.

1821

On 13 January, James Cash is hanged for rape. Cash is re-pentant on the scaffold, and does not ask for clemency.

Dr. John Mackieson, a young Scottish physician and sur-geon, arrives in Charlottetown. Dur-ing almost 65 years of medical prac-tice, he will see his profession trans-formed; his diaries and casebook are two important historical legacies.

On 11 October, the first Presbytery of Prince Edward Island is constituted in the home of Archibald Campbell in Belmont, Lot 16. The Moderator is Rev. John Keir.

Brig Jessie
Built by William Ellis in 1827, the *Jessie* was typical of the vessels being launched from Island shipyards. Between 1780 and 1920 close to 4,500 vessels were built on Prince Edward Island.

After 10 years of study in Quebec, Bernard MacDonald becomes the first native-born Islander to be ordained as a Catholic priest.

1822

In an effort to bolster his deteriorating political position. Lt. Governor Smith recommends that long-serving members of his Council be granted 1,000 acres each in consideration of their service.

John Holland, the Colony's Clerk of Ordnance and Stores, reports that Charlottetown's harbour defences are in a shambles. Fort Amherst, at the mouth of the harbour, has been incorporated into Warren Farm, and a local brickmaker has dug up a large portion of the earthworks. The Battery at the foot of Great George Street has been crowded out by a merchant's warehouse.

1823

On 1 November the new Market House in Charlottetown is officially opened. A lovely, 12-sided building with huge eaves under which vendors can shelter, the "Round Market" was designed by the late John Plaw.

On 3 December, one step ahead of authorities who have a warrant for his arrest, "Hellfire Jack" Stewart escapes for Britain bearing a petition demanding the recall of the intensely unpopular Lt. Governor, C.D. Smith. Tradition claims Stewart was smuggled out in a turnip barrel.

Printer James Douglas Haszard founds the Prince Edward Island *Register*. He publishes the *Register* until 1830, when he is appointed King's Printer and begins publishing the *Royal Gazette*.

On 27 December, two days out from Charlottetown, the brig *Jessie* goes aground on remote St. Paul's Island in the Gulf of St. Lawrence. By the time the wreck is discovered the following June, all 36 passengers and crew have perished.

1824

Lt. Governor C.D. Smith, as dictatorial as he is self-righteous, is summarily recalled. Against stiff competition, he has earned a reputation as "the worst governor in the history of the province." Incredibly, his brother, a much-esteemed naval hero, wins Smith a £500 annual pension — to be paid from the Island's annual grant. He collects it for 26 years.

On 21 October the new Lt. Governor, John Ready arrives in Charlottetown. That night, the city celebrates with its first-ever "general illumination." Ready will become the Island's most-popular governor. Transferred to another colony in 1831, he will go on to serve as governor of the Isle of Man, where he dies in 1845 after being accidentally poisoned with his own medicine.

Lt. Governor John Ready

Walter Johnstone, who toured the colony in 1820-21, donates 400 books to form the basis of a public lending library.

Nine lives are lost when the mail packet founders off Pictou Island on 30 October.

1825

On 30 August the *PEI Register* smugly announces: "Last week the doors of the gaol stood open, not a single prisoner in a population of 30,000."

With Royal Assent, *An Act to Repeal an Act Declaring That Baptism of Slaves Shall Not Exempt Them From Bondage*, effectively outlaws slavery on Prince Edward Island. Slavery will not be officially abolished in the British Empire until 1834.

The Benevolent Irish Society is organized under the patronage of Col. John Ready, an English governor with an Irish name.

Fearing the destruction of the fishery, the government bans the exportation of oysters for seven years. The law also has provisions to fine those who dig the shellfish to burn down for lime.

The *Register* reports that nearly 30 children in Charlottetown and vicinity have died of the croup between January and February.

On 15 July, the *Register* reports that smallpox cases have been reported in East Point, Orwell, Cherry Valley and Charlottetown and urges that those who have not been vaccinated do so immediately. Eight deaths are reported, the actual toll probably being higher.

"Timothy Testy" describes to the *Register* his brush with death on a snowy Charlottetown street. "I was returning from a short walk near the burying ground, plodding along wrapped in a brown study, when my reverie was suddenly interrupted by a loud giggle, apparently proceeding from a female voice immediately behind me; and on looking up, judge my terror on seeing the head of a chomping and foaming steed right over me. To start aside was, of course, the work of an instant, but not so quickly that I felt one of the shafts of the cariole graze my arm. In which a young couple, one of each sex, went whizzing along, apparently so completely wrapped in themselves as to take no notice whatever of me. What a mercy for me that the young ladies of Charlottetown are such loud laughers."

According to official statistics, the colony's 25,000 residents consumed 54,000 gallons of rum, 2,500 of brandy, and 2,000 of wine in 1825.

On 25 September the brigantine *True Friend*, bound from Quebec for Halifax, lands on East Point reef instead. Despite a violent northeast gale, passengers and crew are able to get ashore safely.

On 7 October an enormous, gale-driven forest fire rages through the Miramichi Valley, killing hundreds of people. The fire is so fierce it lights up the night sky in Charlottetown, while the wind blows charred pieces of wood as far as western Prince County.

Between 1821 and 1825, Island shipyards launch 147 vessels.

1826

On 17 March, the Benevolent Irish Society stages its first annual St. Patrick's Day celebration.

You can run.... A passenger on a brig from Newfoundland spots Thomas Clancy, alias Thomas MacKay. Now working in Alexander Cameron's Lot 16 shipyard, Clancy/MacKay is wanted in Ireland for murder; he allegedly killed a man during a hurley match by hitting him in the back of the head with his hurley stick. He is arrested.

From the *PEI Register*: "Pedestrian Feat. An Indian, named Francis Wilmot, about 10 days ago, performed a journey of 63 miles on foot, in the space of 12 successive hours. The object of his journey was to purchase a piece of cloth in Charlottetown to make a vest."

The 13 families of Covehead Settlement look on helplessly as a forest fire sweeps through their community. No lives are lost, but two farms are completely burned out, and five others lose most of their fences and crops. The fire also destroys several new bridges on the Prince Town Road.

On 17 October the *Prince Edward Island Register* is moved to comment on the unusually warm autumn. "A quantity of ripe strawberries, being a second crop, were picked a few days since in a farm on the York River."

1827

Charlottetown Justices of the Peace punish a rash of Sabbath-breaking wood-cutting with 10s fines. "We trust that these examples will have the effect of preventing in future such evil and illegal practices," comments the *PEI Register*.

The Legislature passes *An act to regulate the driving carts, carriages, sleighs and carioles on the Highways*. Islanders will drive on the left-hand side of the road (whip hand next to your neighbour) for the next century.

By a narrow, one vote margin, the House of Assembly rejects an act that would have extended full civil rights to the Island's Roman Catholic population. The failed reform bill is two years ahead of its time. Island Catholics will have to wait until Britain passes its own Emancipation Act in 1829.

Census results place the colony's population at 23,473.

"Any dogs found on the course will be destroyed," warns advertisements. On 4 October the annual horse races — a two-day event — begin at the new circular course near Bird Island [Wright's] Creek in East Royalty. The wrestling matches are strictly a sideshow.

Donald McDonald

Often called simply "The Minister," Donald McDonald forbad any photographs or paintings of himself. This portrait was painted by a follower from memory after McDonald's death.

A restless Presbyterian minister, Donald McDonald, experiences a profound conversion experience. An electrifying speaker, his fundamentalist, pentecostal teachings soon gather a large following. His followers become known as "McDonaldites," and within a decade they are one of the largest Protestant sects in the colony.

Highway at Mount Stewart, c1890
One of the oldest highways in the province, the St. Peter's Road connected Charlottetown to the eastern end of the Island.

Title Page, Holy Bible, J.H. White Edition, 1832 (detail)

On 22 January two Point Prim teenagers (and their dog) set out on the ice to hunt seals. The pan they are on begins to drift, stranding them. Two days later they are spotted off Wood Islands. Local farmers are able to rescue a badly frostbitten Archibald Kelly (and the dog), but no trace is ever found of his companion, a fifteen-year-old named McGrath.

Tragedy strikes Watson Duchemin, a Charlottetown block maker and soon-to-be-famous inventor. On 6 February he leaves his shop unattended for a few minutes and comes back to find the dead body of his five-year-old son — burned to death, apparently after brushing against an open flame. In 1828 Duchemin becomes one of the first members of the Charlottetown Fire Company.

On 28 August Islanders observe a meteorological rarity, a lunar rainbow, as the full moon shines through a shower of rain.

1828

On 12 November Wright's Mills, site of the Island's first brewery, goes up in flames.

John MacGregor publishes *Historical and Descriptive Sketches of the Maritime Colonies of British America*. Although his work is much imitated — and plagiarized — MacGregor dies bankrupt.

Publisher James Bagnall launches his last newspaper venture the *Phenix*. His first Island paper, the *Royal Herald*, lasted a little more than a year. His second, the *Weekly Recorder*, later renamed *Prince Edward Island Gazette*, lasted from 1810 until 1822. His third, the *Royal Gazette and Prince Edward Island Recorder*, was in print for a year and a half. The *Phenix* lasts until 1829, when Bagnall retires from the newspaper business. The main reason? His printing press is worn out.

For much of April, Charlottetown marvels at "Stewart's Pig." Raised by Peter Stewart of Hillsborough River, the pig is 9 1/2 feet long and weighs in at over 1,000 pounds. Size alone cannot save him. He is sold for £19 and sent to Halifax for exhibition.

Sylvain-Ephrem Perrey becomes the Island's first Acadian priest and first priest ever ordained in the colony.

1829

 A dozen settlers from East Anglia arrive on the *Minerva*.

George Thresher opens the colony's first art school. Students are scarce, so Thresher makes ends meet by painting carriages, sleighs and houses. He is also willing to glaze windows and hang wall paper.

The boat that wouldn't float. The hull of the 496-ton ship *Albion* is advertized for auction at New Chepstow, "as she now lies partly on her ways and partly in the sand, abandoned, by not going off when launching."

The *PEI Register* doesn't know what to make of Martha Jago, a female preacher of the Brienite sect newly arrived from Plymouth. Islanders don't know either. Letters to the editor will ponder whether or not what a woman says should be accepted as the word of God.

Rome creates the Diocese of Charlottetown, comprising Prince Edward Island, New Brunswick and the Magdalen Islands. The honour of becoming its first bishop naturally falls to Angus MacEachern, who has been the region's main (and often only) priest since 1790.

On 25 July a forest fire fanned by high winds threatens the tiny Island capital of Charlottetown. Four fire engines, the local garrison, and all able-bodied townsmen turn out to fight the blaze. The wind falters; Charlottetown is saved.

1830

On 25 August the cornerstone is laid for a new jail on Charlottetown's Pownal Square. Later generations will know it as "Harvie's Brig," after a long-time jail keeper. In 1911 it will finally give way to a new brick jail on Longworth Avenue.

On 12 April Michael White, 14, is flogged for stealing hams from a Charlottetown house and raisins from a store. Four months later, his 8-year-old brother is sent to jail for stealing a gunlock.

On 4 May a Committee sent to investigate finds over £1,400 — a fifth of the entire Colonial budget — missing from the coffers. The Colonial Treasurer, one Alexander Campbell, is dismissed.

Rev. John McDonald, a son of Captain John MacDonald of Glenaladale, brings out 206 Irish settlers to his Fort Augustus estate. The settlers were recruited in Ireland's county Monaghan, and their arrival touches off a large immigration from northern Ireland.

On 30 May the *Collina* arrives from Bideford, England with 74 immigrants from Devon and Cornwall.

James Douglas Haszard begins the *Royal Gazette*, later to become the government's official newspaper.

Madame Foriosa enlivens Charlottetown's summer season. Her show includes pantomime, fireworks and a tight rope walk. To cap her performance, she dances the fandango on stage blindfolded amid an unspecified quantity of eggs.

On 10 August the steamer *Richard Smith* docks at Charlottetown. It's the first steamship ever to visit the colony.

On 28 April, an Emancipation Act frees Island Roman Catholics from most civil disabilities. At last, they have the right to vote and hold public office. Although the original intent of the 1767 land grants was that the colony would be settled only by "Foreign Protestants," almost half of the Island's population is Catholic.

Between 1826 and 1830, Island shipyards launch 225 vessels.

1831

On 11 May, MLA Ewen Cameron moves that the seat of King's County MLA John MacDonald be declared vacant. MacDonald left for a trip to Halifax the previous November, hasn't been heard of since, and is presumed lost at sea. Ironically, Cameron's own seat becomes vacant first when he drowns while bathing below the battery at Fort Edward. Only 43 at the time of his death, Cameron was the Colony's leading reformer and its most popular politician.

In the by-election to fill John MacDonald's vacant seat, William Cooper, future apostle of Escheat, ends his campaign hiding from rioters in a St. Peter's loft. They fail to find him, and he is later declared elected. Once in the House, Cooper gradually takes over leadership of the colony's reform-minded politicians.

John Ready's replacement, Col. Aretas W. Young is sworn in as the Island's sixth lieutenant governor. He will be the first to live in Government House — and the first to die there.

On 13 July, the farmers and inhabitants of Three Rivers and Murray Harbour convene at St. Andrew's Point to form the Eastern Agricultural Society. Their host, John Wightman, is named president.

On 30 November St. Andrew's College, the first Roman Catholic college in the Maritimes, opens at St. Andrew's in the residence of Bishop MacEachern. Its goal: to educate young men for the clergy and the professions. The little school lasts 13 years.

1832

In his first major speech in the House, William Cooper — a former land agent — stakes out his political agenda: escheat (confiscate) the proprietors' estates and re-distribute them to tenants. His po-

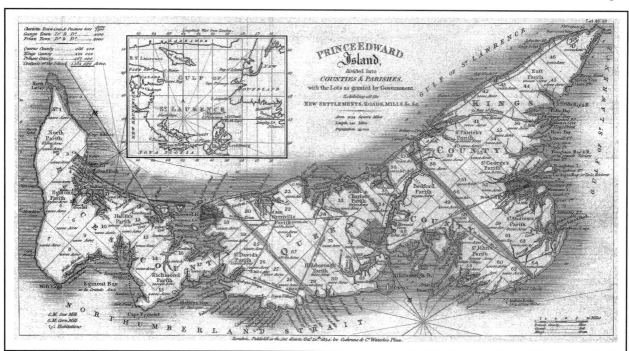

Map of Prince Edward Island, c1834
(James and Barbara Macnutt Collection of Historic Maps, PEI Museum and Heritage Foundation)

sition is immensely popular — though not with proprietors. Or land agents.

William Cooper
Assuming leadership of the colony's reform-minded MLA's after the untimely death of Ewen Cameron, William Cooper was a driving force behind calls for radical land reform.

On 8 May the *Pandora* arrives with 106 emigrants from southern Ireland. Sailing out of Waterford, Ireland, the vessel is a regular visitor to the Island.

On 27 May the *Calypso*, out of Bideford, England, arrives with 197 passengers, "chiefly mechanics and labourers."

J.L. Lewellin publishes *An Emigrant's Guide to Prince Edward Island*. Unlike many of his contemporaries, Lewellin's advice is actually helpful.

Joseph Boucette's *The British Dominions in North America* includes a chapter on the Island. The charitable might describe his book an *homage* to John MacGregor's recent *Historical and Descriptive Sketches*. Others might say he simply copied entire sections.

John Henry White launches a new newspaper: the *British American*. The paper lasts for nine months. In 1835 he gives up on the idea of making a living as a publisher and becomes a sea captain.

On 11 May the Island's first steam packet, the *Pocahontas*, makes her maiden crossing between Charlottetown and Pictou carrying mail and passengers.

The British American advertises possibly the Island's first hairdresser: "James Roue — Dresser, Peruquizer, Perfumer and Ornamental Hair Cutter." Mr. Roue stocks genuine Macassar Oil (Used by the King Himself!) and also promises to grind razors, table and pen knives "on shortest notice and in a superior manner." He will also purchase bear's meat "if delivered sweet."

J.H. White, publisher of the *British American*, advertises his edition of the *Authorized Version of the Bible*. It is the first *Bible* ever printed in what is now Canada — partly because it's actually against the law, since the Crown holds the copyright. In other eras, printers of unauthorized *Bibles* were imprisoned or executed. White simply fails to sell many copies.

On 23 June, according to local history, the *St. Domingo*, en route for Quebec with Irish immigrants, wrecks near East Point. Many of the passengers — Tierneys, Hughes, Prices, Pierces, Harrises, Campions, Drummonds — decide to stay.

The average temperature for February is -35 C°.

1833

 The land question begins to heat up. "Airsaig Mill" a mill belonging to Donald Macdonald, burns to the ground on 29 June. "A quantity of tinder and other combustible materials were found near the place, together with a file, which appeared to have been used in striking a flint." reports the *Royal Gazette*. "There is but too much reason to suppose that it is not the work of an incendiary." The Lieutenant Governor offers a £200 reward.

Artist William Valentine advertises his services as a portrait painter and miniaturist. Like the colony's other artist, George Thresher, Valentine is not too proud to accept commissions as a house painter.

Peter Fisher of Indian River does something unprecedented in the colony: he asks the Legislature for a divorce from his wife, who has left him for another. The House of Assembly eventually establishes a court of divorce in 1836. We don't know if it ever granted one to Fisher.

Between 12 and 13 August, "one of the most tremendous and destructive storms ever witnessed on this Island" flattens fields and barns throughout the colony. The new Anglican Church in Charlottetown is blown down. Roads are choked with windfall and hundreds of cattle are feared lost. Although 13 vessels are reported sunk or aground, only two seamen are lost.

1834

An official residence for the Lt. Governor is finally complete. Designed by builder Isaac Smith, the house is nicknamed "Fanningbank" after the estate it is built on.

An armed force of nine constables, led by Deputy Sheriff John Sims, sets out for Naufrage to arrest three men and two women charged with resisting an eviction order. They are met outside the settlement by a mob estimated a hundred strong and armed with muskets, pitchforks and homemade pikes. "Mr. Sims, finding all expostulation in vain, and that their numbers were rapidly increasing, deemed it prudent to return without attempting to use force which, there can be little doubt, would have been attended with fatal consequences to himself and his party."

On 1 April, slavery is officially abolished in all British possessions. It is doubtful that anyone on the Island actually owns a slave by this time.

On 1 August a schooner out of Quebec named *John Wallace* wrecks near East Point. Panic sweeps the community when it is learned that four of the *John Wallace's* crew had died of cholera on the voyage, and intensifies when three St. Margaret's residents die suddenly within a week. As physicians debate whether the St. Margaret's deaths were due to cholera or other natural causes, ports across the Island impose quarantines on vessels out of Halifax and Quebec.

1835

On 1 December, a year after moving in, Fanningbank's first resident, Lt. Governor Sir Aretas W. Young, dies. It is said his fatal illness started with a chill caught from the still-wet plaster in his new residence.

On 29 May the *Grace*, out of Belfast, Ireland, lands 221 immigrants (129 adults and 92 children) at Charlottetown.

On 1 November the *Acteon*, bound from Bathurst with a cargo of lumber, runs ashore and breaks up on the coast near Souris.

Between 1831 and 1835, Island shipyards launch 217 vessels.

1836

The *Royal Gazette* estimates that eight-year-old Mary Parry of Charlottetown is the youngest person ever to make the iceboat crossing. Determined to make it back to the Island after their vessel wrecked off the coast of Cape Breton, Mary and her father end a 300-mile overland walk with the jaunt across the ice. "Little Mary manifested a spirit of heroism and cheerfulness rarely surpassed by a grown person of ei-

Crossing Northumberland Strait"
Picturesque Canada, 1880

We were harnessed, with our faces to the bows, one hand firmly holding the gunwale, the body stretched slightly forward" and, at the word "Start!" each man equally drew the boat, and thus from a walking pace we got into a trot, then a canter, and, the speed once up, away we ran over the slippery surface of the ice, with the cheering "Pull hearty, my boys!" of our conductor, the boat gliding on the runners.

– B.W.A. Sleigh, *Pine Forests and Hackmatack Clearings,* 1852

ther sex... where the ice was good, she ran along, laying hold of the rope, to assist in drawing the boat, and could find cause of amusement, when her companions occasionally broke through the ice."

Just in case there were any doubts, the Legislature passes a law specifically excluding women from the franchise.

On 30 August, Col. Sir John Harvey arrives on board the *Emeline*. Harvey will fill in at the Lt. Governor's post for the late Aretas Young.

On 20 December, at the famous "Hay River Meeting" in northern King's County, over 700 tenants demand the establishment of a Court of Escheat that will confiscate proprietary estates and re-grant them to the tenantry. The tenants of northern and central King's are soon known as the most radical in the colony in their demands for land reform.

S.S. Empress, c1910
Beginning with ferries and river boats like the *Emo*, small steamers like the *Empress* were a feature of many Island rivers through the mid-1900s.

William Rankin starts a new newspaper: *The Prince Edward Island Times*. Devoted to the cause of escheat and land reform, the *Times* lasts only six months.

A "non-denominational" grammar school — Central Academy — opens in Charlottetown.

Charlottetown shoemaker William Fitzpatrick battles the currency shortage (and uses up his scraps of sheepskin) by issuing leather money redeemable at his office. The only leather notes ever circulated in Canada, they are soon suppressed by the Legislature.

Between 1836 and 1840 Island shipyards launch 287 vessels.

1837

On 6 June, Col. Sir Charles A. Fitzroy arrives from London to begin his term as Lt. Governor.

On 8 November, some 2,000 Islanders attend a noisy escheat meeting at George Sentiner's farm in King's County.

R. Montgomery Martin publishes *History of Nova Scotia, Cape Breton, the Sable Islands, Prince Edward Island, the Bermudas, Newfoundland, etc.* The few Islanders who read the book are grateful not to be relegated to the "etc." chapter.

The pro-tenant *Colonial Herald* begins a seven-year career supporting land reform in the restless colony.

Bernard Donald Macdonald, grandson of a prominent Glenaladale settler, is named the second Roman Catholic Bishop of Charlottetown. Not only the first Islander named to this position, he was also the first Islander ordained to the Roman Catholic priesthood.

On 7 July the brig *William IV*, bound from Halifax for Quebec with 10 soldiers of the 83rd Regiment, the regiment's baggage, and 21 women and children is driven ashore near Cascumpeque. The passengers are sent on to Quebec; the vessel is refloated using empty casks for added buoyancy and sails for Halifax.

William Graham's Farm, New London, c1860
Sketch by Henry Cundall

This is an excellent poor man's country.... It is the Englishman's and Scotchman's and Irishman's friend.... There is room for thousands yet; and if the poor in England did but know what advantages this island holds forth, they would not stay and starve as they do.

– *London Emigration Gazette*, 1843

On 7 September, a heavy frost decimates the Island potato and cereal crops, causing much hardship and food shortages by the following spring.

Stephen Bovyer of Charlottetown patents an improved treadmill for generating horse-power. Horses are not grateful.

On 3 April, there is so little ice left in the Hillsborough River that the ferry between Charlottetown and Southport is able to commence operations.

1838

On 12 May the *Emo*, the first steam ferry to operate between Charlottetown and Southport, commences service.

Lord Durham's famous report to the Colonial Office decries "the extreme improvidence, I might say the reckless profusion of the original decision in 1767 to grant the entire colony by lot."

The Escheat Party, led by former land agent William Cooper, wins control of the Legislature with 18 of its 24 seats. Their platform is simple. Repossess (or "escheat") estates where proprietors have failed to fulfil the terms of the 1767 land grant (i.e. all of them) and redistribute the land to resident farmers. Cooper is convinced he can persuade the Colonial Office in London to go along with this plan, and is soon off to meet them in person.

On 1 August, The Olympic Amphitheatre and Gymnastic Arena begins 10 days of "Horsemanship, Chinese, and Grecian Exercises." There being little enough to do on the Island, the writers of the circus ad apparently feel less need for hyperbole — or explanation — than will be the case in the future.

On 14 January, Mrs. Allen Shaw of Pinette gives birth to her 21st child. The other 20 are still living, a rather remarkable occurrence in 19th-century Prince Edward Island.

In a span of only three months, a Bedeque woman [Mrs. Daniel Silliker] lost her husband and then her son to shipwreck. Devastated by the twin tragedies, she lost her sanity. Now she loses her life; after several abortive attempts, she hangs herself in the family's barn.

Scots-born John Geddie is ordained to the ministry at New London. He will labour there seven years, but his passion is foreign missions. When he and his wife, Mary Menzies, depart for the New Hebrides in 1846, they become the first Presbyterian missionaries from the British colonies.

On 17 June, the barque *Sir Archibald Campbell*, bound from Miramichi to Sunderland, strikes hard on the North Cape reef in heavy fog. The crew reach shore safely, only to watch a Yankee fishing schooner plunder the wreck.

On 23 October, HMS *Malabar* runs aground off Cape Bear. After jettisoning her 36 guns, she is re-floated with the assistance of local shipowner Joseph Wightman. His feat earns him the nickname "Sir Joseph Malabar," and a gift of plate from the British government worth £500.

Though the winter was mild, the ice has overstayed its welcome. At the end of April, the Hillsborough River is still ice-locked. Only a year ago, navigation on the river opened by 3 April.

1839

The *Royal Gazette* announces a new stage coach for the run between Charlottetown and Georgetown. "It is calculated to carry eight to ten passengers, and is provided with an awning which can be let down or rolled up, according to the state of the weather." The two-horse coach makes its run twice weekly.

Government leader William Cooper returns from his mission to convert the Colonial Office to his plan for radical land reform. Unable to even get a meeting with the Colonial Secretary, Cooper is forced to admit his journey was a complete failure. With the main plank of their platform shattered, the Escheat Party quickly disintegrates, and Cooper himself fades off the political scene.

On 25 May the *Consbrook* arrives with 308 Irish immigrants, chiefly from County Monaghan.

Hugh Murray includes a chapter on the Island in his *An Historical and Descriptive Account of British America*.

S.S. Hill publishes *A Short Account of Prince Edward Island*.

J.D. Haszard's book store runs the Island's first documented Christmas ad in the *Royal Gazette*.

On 2 January, the inaugural meeting of the Mechanics' Institute is held. It is founded to promote self-education and the spread of "useful knowledge."

1840

In January, when Flora Townshend, owner of Lot 43 sues tenant James Douglas for arrears in rent, Sheriff Peter MacCallum seizes Douglas' cattle for auction. Douglas' neighbours attend the auction as a mob and keep the bids for the cattle – worth an estimated £8 each – to a high of 1 shilling 6 pence. For good measure they pelt MacCallum and his deputies with snowballs and frozen manure. Five are later charged with riot and assault and get fines of £20 and jail terms as high as ten months.

John Arbuckle

On 12 March, MLA John Arbuckle is censured by the House for his "unseemly insobriety."

On 2 June, the *Rose Bank* completes another crossing from Belfast to Charlottetown, this time with 208 Irish immigrants.

On 8 September the *Rother*, out of Tobermory, Scotland lands 229 emigrants from the Isle of Skye.

On 14 September the *Nith*, out of Tobermory, arrives at Charlottetown with 315 passengers from the Isle of Skye, the second contingent from there in a week.

On 25 September the *Heroine*, Stornoway, Scotland, brings 281 passengers from the Isle of Skye, making a total of 825 Skye settlers in three weeks.

Charles Worrell buys the smallest lot in the colony — undersized Lot 66. The purchase completes the huge estate he has been assembling in King's County since the 1820s. The London-based lawyer is now the master of Lots 39, 41, 42, 42, 66 and large parts of Lots 38 and 40. Unfortunately, the 100,000-acre estate contains some of the worst farmland and most unruly tenants on the Island.

Between 1836 and 1840, Island shipyards launch 287 vessels.

Ship in Ice

1841

On 13 November, Sir Henry Vere Huntley arrives in Charlottetown to begin his term as Lt. Governor. Erratic and controversial, he will flirt with Responsible Government without ever really understanding it.

The *Journal of the House of Assembly* publishes a genealogy lesson to prove there is indeed a Family Compact on Prince Edward Island. Executive Council President George Wright is father-in-law to the Colony's Prothonotary, who is a brother to Council Member Robert Hodgson, a cousin of Council Member John Brecken, who is a brother-in-law of T.H. Haviland, the Colonial Agent. Haviland is also brother-in-law to Donald Macdonald and James Peake, two of the Colony's most prominent land owners and agents. The Council also includes: Ambrose Lane, a brother-in-law to Hodgson, and J.S. Macdonald, a cousin of Donald Macdonald and brother-in-law to Peake, Brecken and Haviland.

On 17 May the *Margaret Pollok* and the *Thomas Gelston*, both out of Belfast, Ireland, disembark 824 Irish settlers, the largest single-day immigration in Island history.

On 31 July the *Ocean* arrives in Charlottetown from Portree, Isle of Skye, with 335 passengers. Another 551 Skye settlers will arrive within the next two weeks.

The adolescent colony is beginning a growth spurt. The census completed by 1 August counts 47,000 Islanders, double the 1827 figure.

Rev. Ronald Rankin publishes his collected works — in Gaelic. His is possibly the first Gaelic book published in the Colony.

On 24 July, the *Colonial Herald* advertises an "Immense Attraction." A troupe of performers headlined by Charles Freeman, "the strongest and best proportioned human being in the world" and Mr. O'Connell, "the wonderful Tattooed Man . . . the greatest dancer the world has ever produced."

Three years after they were jettisoned when the HMS *Malabar* ran aground at Cape Bear, 10 of the 36 guns from the British warship have been salvaged using a diving apparatus belonging to James Fraser of Pictou.

Over 200 St. Peter's Harbour residents turn out to watch as the schooner *American Lass*, salvaged after wrecking the previous autumn, is carefully winched onto a 62-foot-long sleigh and hauled by 82 horses a half a mile out to sea – "a sufficient distance to be out of danger of grounding when the ice breaks up."

Stephen Bovyer has 24 of his "Bovyer's Patent Horse Power and Threshing Machines" for sale. One of the earliest agricultural machines ever made on the Island, it only needs two horses, two men, and a boy to thresh 150 bushels of grain a day.

1842

On 28 May the *Thomas Gelston* and the *Morgiana* arrive with 425 emigrants from Northern Ireland.

The *Islander*, one of the colony's leading 19th-century newspapers, begins publication as the champion of Island Conservatism.

Ice boat service from P. E. I. to Mainland.

Iceboats Underway, c1900

The intensity of the cold I shall never forget: it chilled me to the very heart: my clothes became in an instant stiff and frozen, and had it not been for a glass of raw brandy, twice repeated, all round, nothing, I verily believe, could have caused our congealed blood to circulate again through our torpid veins.

– B.W.A. Sleigh, *Pine Forests and Hackmatack Clearings*, 1852

On 16 August, The Great Olympic Arena and New York Circus begins a three-day engagement in Charlottetown, enlivening Islanders' dull lives with their "equestrian exercises." It will be 22 years before the next circus comes to call.

Just three years after the process was invented, travelling daguerreotypist J.W. Wilmot offers Islanders an opportunity to get their photograph taken. William Valentine, a Halifax-based artist who lived for a while in Charlottetown, has also been advertising the new process.

The *Royal Gazette* reports a massive November gale. Mr. Tremaine's wharf in the Charlottetown area is severely damaged. A new barque is blown from its moorings but is undamaged.

1843

Construction begins on St. Dunstan's Roman Catholic Cathedral in Charlottetown. The wooden church will serve until 1907.

Poplar Island bridge at North River — "the greatest thoroughfare leading to the Capital" is carried away by drift ice. To their dismay, road overseers find the remaining pilings badly eaten by worms.

On 24 March, over 200 angry settlers from the Bear River area turn out to forcibly halt a survey of Lots 44 and 45. They send the surveyor packing and tear up his stakes. They also forcibly reinstate evicted blacksmith Martin Heaney to his house, which belongs to proprietor Samuel Cunard. Later, an unknown arsonist burns the house of a wood ranger named MacGuire. A furious Governor Huntley offers a £200 reward for the arsonist and despatches 30 troops and a number of constables to restore order.

On 20 May the *Rose Bank* arrives from Belfast, Ireland with 149 emigrants.

James Buckingham publishes *Canada, Nova Scotia, New Brunswick and the other British Provinces of America*. We appear under the category "other British Provinces."

Reprinting a paper recently presented to the Academy of Sciences of Paris, the *Islander* advises "that bleeding at the nose may be almost instantly checked by raising the arm on the same side as that of the nostril from which the blood flows. It is well known that such haemorrhages are often formidable and sometimes fatal."

Two iceboats and nine men are swept away by strong winds and current at Cape Traverse. Thirty-two hours later, exhausted and frostbitten, they make shore at St. Peter's Island. They were forced to abandon one of the boats and much of the baggage, including a "Daguerreotype Apparatus" belonging to passengers Hodgkinson and Butler.

On 2 November, caught in a heavy gale, the schooner *Maria*, of Ship Harbour, Cape Breton, goes ashore at De Gros Marsh. Her cargo of local produce is damaged and subsequently discharged.

A three-member government commission reports on the lamentable state of currency in the colony. Among other things, they recommend the establishment of a bank that would issue sound paper money, payable on demand. And a bank is founded — eleven years later.

On 4 August a hailstorm does heavy crop damage in Queen's County. Farmer and diarist David Ross writes: "...hail stones one inch in diameter destroyed potato tops, grain, etc., etc. Leaves of hardwood trees strewn on the ground as in fall. Window panes knocked in. Brackley Point Road great destruction. h—l of a country."

Charlottetown, c1845
Watercolour by George Hubbard
The further you go from Charlottetown, the more primitive and hospitable the people become; they warmly welcome a stranger and seem happy, moral and contented.
— Lucy Isabella Bird, *An Englishwoman in America*, 1854

1844

By custom, the steamer *St. George* signals its departure by firing a blank charge from a small swivel gun mounted on its bow. On 2 August, as the *St. George* prepares to leave Charlottetown the cabin boy decides to see what would happen if he plugged the muzzle of the gun with a piece of coal. When the charge is fired the gun bursts. No one is injured by the explosion, but the *Islander* gives no news as to the fate of the cabin boy.

Prince County sheriff John Morris suspects a schooner out of Halifax — the *Dart* — of smuggling oysters out of Bedeque Bay. When he and three deputies try to board the vessel the crew fire on them, wounding a deputy named George Tanton so badly he later dies. Two vessels, the Admiralty's survey sloop HMS *Gulnare* and the S.S. *St. George* are sent to track the smuggler down. *St. George* catches up to the *Dart* off Point Prim, dismasts it by ramming, then tows the disabled schooner into Charlottetown. The *Dart's* skipper, William Hiscox, is tried for murder but the jury convicts him of manslaughter only and recommends mercy. He is sentenced to three years' hard labour at the Prince County Jail.

On 7 January, there is a wild scene during Mass at St. Margaret's when local MLA John Macintosh, a radical Escheater, confronts priest-proprietor John McDonald, suspected by many of calling in troops to enforce property rights in the area. Macintosh concludes a loud argument by spitting on McDonald. McDonald sues Macintosh for disrupting Mass, but the Court has no law against it. According to legend, he curses him instead, vowing that the man who spat on him would nevermore be able to hold spit in his mouth. According to community legend, Macintosh was henceforth known for a slight propensity to drool.

On 26 July the *Independence*, from Belfast, Northern Ireland, disembarks 156 immigrants.

J.B. Cooper's reform-minded weekly, the *Colonial Herald* ceases publication after seven eventful years.

The Island is deemed too small for both bears and humans. Taking the initiative, the humans legislate a bounty on bears to hasten their destruction.

A correspondent from Pictou observes that 3,000 of the land's 15,000 Presbyterians are now followers of Donald McDonald. The rest are evenly divided between the Free Church of Scotland and the Nova Scotia Synod. He also notes that a Mormon missionary garnered a few converts during a recent visit.

Robert McKinlay announces the imminent opening of his Charlottetown tobacco factory, which will convert imported tobacco leaf into Island tobacco products.

Hard on the heels of Robert McKinlay, Charlottetown businessman Thomas B. Tremain announces the establishment of his own P.E. Island Tobacco Factory at the head of the Queen's Wharf. "Tremain's No. 1" is his staple product.

1845

On 4 December, the light is lit for the first time in Point Prim lighthouse, the Island's first. The circular brick tower (soon sheathed in wood) is designed by versatile Island architect Isaac Smith, who is already busy overseeing the erection of the Colonial Building.

On 12 February the *Morning News* boasts "lovers of curiosities can see at our office, a small quantity of new potatoes — the produce of the year 1845! Beat this, ye Blue-noses, if you can."

Radical concepts in geology are explained by William Heard at a meeting of the Mechanics' Institute. "The lecture presented . . . a somewhat novel theory which supposes the earth to be many thousands of years older than has been previously supposed by Philosophers."

The first Baptist Church in Charlottetown opens. The collection amounts to £12.11s. The building lies on the north side of Euston Street facing the centre of Prince Street.

On 9 June, six men drown at Rollo Bay when a sudden storm capsizes their fishing craft.

Donald MacLeod of French River makes an interesting discovery while digging a well. It's a rock that appears to have teeth in it. In 1852, after making its way to the Philadelphia Academy of Natural Sciences, it's named *"Bathygnathus Borealis."* Loosely-translated, this means "part of a jaw with teeth, found in a well up north." Bathygnathus is better known as a dimetrodon — a sail-backed reptile common 300 million years ago. MacLeod's find is probably the first dimetrodon fossil ever found.

Island shipbuilders sometimes have to resort to novel ways of getting their products into deep water. On 20 March, a large crowd watches as teams of horses drag two newly constructed vessels from the shipyard of John and James MacMillan a half mile out onto the ice at Covehead. When the ice melts, the vessels will automatically be launched.

Between 1841 and 1845, Island shipyards launch 359 vessels.

1846

Robert Bruce Stewart immigrates to Prince Edward Island with his family. Owner of some 67,000 acres, "the laird of

Strathgartney" will become the Island's largest resident proprietor.

When the *Morning News and Semi-Weekly Advertiser* hires Reformer Edward Whelan as editor, the paper takes a sudden swing to the left. After several months of suffering Whelan's attacks the local Family Compact buys the paper to shut him up.

On New Year's Eve geologist Abraham Gesner submits his survey of the colony to the Legislature. Gesner has found traces of copper on Governor's Island, coal at Gallas Point, and iron ore at Fortune Bay, but that's all they are — traces.

Potato blight is raging on both sides of the Atlantic. While Ireland starves, the Island legislature prohibits the export of potatoes from the colony to conserve the healthy stock.

Secretaries rejoice! Shorthand comes to the Island. "Mr. Hill respectfully announces to the young gentlemen of Charlottetown that he'll be conducting classes in Phonography or writing by sound." The editors of the *Islander* comment that the system, just invented by Isaac Pittman, is the best shorthand method they have ever seen.

On 19 June, Abraham Gesner lectures the Mechanics' Institute on caloric (heat). Here he unveils his newly invented lamp fuel, which he will later dub "kerosene."

1847

On 26 January, the Island legislature meets for the first time in the newly finished Colonial Building — now called Province House.

The Scottish settlers along the shore of Lot 30 decide it is time to name their community. Most of them are from Argyllshire. The choice is an obvious pun: Argyle Shore.

On 1 March, electoral, religious and ethnic tensions combine at a by-election in the Belfast district. As Catholic Irish and Protestant Scots voters clashed, a witness recalls: "The noise was like . . . the simultaneous driving of wedges when a vessel was about to be launched." At least three lives are lost; scores are injured. The "Belfast Riot" is the worst incident of electoral violence in Island history.

Donald Campbell is sworn in as the new Lt. Governor. He soon makes it known that he has little time for radical concepts like land reform and responsible government.

The Colonial Office in London is determined to extend Responsible Government to all of its North American colonies. The desire among the Island's conservatives to block Responsible Government is almost as great as the determination among its reformers to attain it. A stormy election night on 8 May sees Reform leaders George Coles, William Swabey, and Edward Whelan charged with rioting and causing a disturbance.

Edward Whelan founds one of the Island's greatest newspapers, the *Examiner*.

On 22 May the *Lady Constable* arrives from Liverpool with Irish immigrants fleeing the Great Famine. Of the 419 souls on board, 25 have died of typhus on the way out; eight more succumb before the vessel is finally placed in quarantine; 53 others are infected. Local health officials spend as much time squabbling as coping with the crisis.

On 10 March the body of schoolteacher Thomas Irwin, missing since 14 February, is discovered on the ice off Big Pond. For nearly 20 years, Irwin has championed the cause of the Island's Mi'kmaq, but he could not find a publisher for his Mi'kmaq grammar book.

In a daring mid-ocean rescue, William Douse and the five crewmen of the schooner *Jenny Lind* take 12 survivors off the wreck of the barque *Amitie*. As a gesture of thanks, the survivors commission a painting of the rescue, which survives to the present day.

William Douse

A Conservative candidate in the Belfast district, William Douse had to flee for his life during the bloody 1847 riot. Although his political opponents painted him as one of the most hated land agents in the colony, his death in 1864 occasioned one of the biggest funerals in Island history.

1848

On 18 November, after a nightmarish journey, 72 Scots immigrants arrive in Georgetown. They left Glasgow on the *Lulan*, part of a group of 121 Highlanders bound for Cape Breton and the Island. Smallpox broke out in mid-voyage, carrying off 24 of 186 passengers and crew.

Just one year after the opening of his most famous building, Province House architect Isaac Smith shifts his career focus. He moves to Nova Scotia and becomes a Methodist missionary.

Isaac Smith

The "Bog School" opens in a west Charlottetown slum. It has been inspired by Mr. Richardson, general secretary of the Colonial Church and School Society (Anglican) for British North America. Miss Sarah Harvie, daughter of the local gaoler, will spend the next half-century as its devoted teacher.

1849

On 12 November the *Fanny* sails from Charlottetown for the California gold fields with 43 eager Islanders aboard. Some stay. Most come back home. None find their fortune. Three weeks later William Cooper, frustrated apostle of Escheat, sails with his family for the gold fields in his brig, the *Packet*. Although he finds his way back to the Island, his sons and daughters decide to settle in California.

A branch of the Royal Agricultural Society is established in Georgetown. Its founding meeting subscribes £17 towards the advocacy of improved farming methods and better livestock.

The Legislature passes an act intended to establish a legal basis for the currency of the colony. Thus, order is finally brought to the Island's currency, a mishmash of coinage from a half-dozen countries.

1850

The results of the February election sees George Coles' Reformers winning 18 seats to the Tories' 6. Now that they control the Legislature, the next task for the Reformers is to persuade Lt. Governor Campbell the colony is ready for Responsible Government.

On 10 October, opponents to Responsible Government lose their greatest ally when Lt. Governor Sir Donald Campbell, a staunch opponent of the process, dies in office. His death facilitates an accommodation between Island Reformers and imperial authorities on the contentious matter of self-government.

Inspired by British examples and possessed of sufficient leisure time to pursue such sports, local citizens organize the Charlottetown Cricket Club.

Inspired by a speech from scientific farming advocate (and judge) James Horsfield Peters, the farmers around Princetown form an agricultural club, one of many organized across the colony to promote better farming practices.

The ferry between Canso Point and Charlottetown sinks "in a squall of wind." The ferryman — John Johnston — "his lad," Hugh Curry of West River and Neil Curry of Nine Mile Creek spent an hour in the water, clinging to the oars. Neil Curry decides to swim for shore, but drowns, "leaving a wife and small family to mourn his loss." The other three are picked up by a boat from Warren Farm.

"During a short but violent thunderstorm," on 3 October, "the electric fluid struck the house of Mr. George Aitken, Three Rivers." The bolt descended through the chimney, into the kitchen and through five farm workers who were sitting in a row on a bench. The five are unhurt, but unable to move for a little while. After exiting the farm workers the bolt smashes a rafter to splinters and punches a hole in the roof. As a parting gesture, it also blows a barrel in the yard apart.

Between 1846 and 1850, Island shipyards launch 428 vessels.

1851

When Archie Cameron of Lot 27 misses the iceboat, he decides to walk from Cape Tormentine to Cape Traverse. With a fencepole in hand for emergencies, he leaves around one in the afternoon. By 4:30 he is safely ashore on the Island. After an overnight stay in a Cape Traverse boarding house, he sets out for home the next morning.

On the morning of 25 July Donald McDonald, owner of the Glenaladale estate in Tracadie, is shot at his front gate by two unknown assailants. "So detested was he," Lady Isabella Bird later recounts, "that several persons passed by without rendering any assistance." McDonald is rescued by a tenant, who bundles him into a cart and takes him to Charlottetown for treatment. Bird maintains the kindly tenant was later forced to leave the colony "to escape the vengeance which would have overtaken the succourer of a tyrant." Despite a £100 reward, no one is ever charged for the attempted murder.

Crossing by ice boat, the new Lt. Governor, Sir Alexander Bannerman, reaches Prince Edward Island. He has been instructed by the Colonial Office to institute Responsible Government.

"Sketches Among The Mackerel Men"

Harper's Weekly, October 13, 1883

From the 1820s through the mid-1880s, hundreds of American schooners voyaged north to fish the rich mackerel stocks off Prince Edward Island's north shore.

On 23 April, Reform leader George Coles forms the first "Responsible" government in Island history.

Veteran newspaperman James Douglas Haszard founds *Haszard's Gazette* after losing his job as Queen's Printer to rival journalist — and favourite of the new government — Edward Whelan.

While the *Royal Gazette* concedes that football and hurley are good, wholesome winter sports, it requests that the young Charlottetown apprentices and labourers not take over lower Queen Street every mild evening to play them.

Edward Palmer

Regarded with respect but little affection, Edward Palmer was a force in the Conservative party for several decades in the mid-1800s.

On 21 June, Premier George Coles and Edward Palmer, Leader of the Opposition, duel with pistols in what is now Victoria Park. Palmer misses; Coles does not return his fire. The cause of the altercation remains unclear. Holding Palmer's coat is another future Father of Confederation, T.H. Haviland.

Beginning on 3 October and lasting three long nights, the "Yankee Gale" traps hundreds of American fishing vessels against the Island's north shore. At least 80 vessels and 150 fishermen are lost in the most deadly storm in Island history.

George Coles

A merchant, brewer and distiller by trade, "Jarge" Coles was the Island's first Premier elected under Responsible Government and one of the most popular politicians of his era.

1852

Robert Hodgson becomes the Island's first native-born chief justice.

"Light!" cries the *Islander*. A harbour light has been erected on Blockhouse Point to guide vessels safely into Charlottetown Harbour. Soon a lighthouse is erected, and the area becomes a popular picnic spot for local families.

John Lawson publishes *Letters on Prince Edward Island*.

Influenced by American examples, Premier George Coles sponsors the first free education act in the British Dominions.

On 15 October, a storm drives 21 American fishing vessels onto the shore at Souris. Losses are estimated at $50,000. A witness writes: "Two hundred destitute Seamen can be seen . . . strolling about in distress and want, many of whom escaped without shoes, hats or jackets."

On 21 October, four Miminegash men are lost when their fishing boat, loaded with a cargo of wheat, capsizes in a northeast gale. The wreck drifts ashore, bottom up, at Richibucto, New Brunswick.

On 3 December the brig *Britannia*, homeward bound to Sunderland, England, with a cargo of Miramichi timber, wrecks at Skinner's Pond. Only the mate, Anthony Alexander, reaches shore alive. His crewmates are buried at the Episcopal Church graveyard at Kildare.

Frederick Gisborne lays the first submarine telegraph cable in North America between Cape Tormentine, N.B., and Carleton Head, P.E.I. Complete by mid-November, it is a dress rehearsal for a much grander project: a trans-Atlantic cable.

David Ross writes on 14 December: "Betwixt last night and this morning a most awful gale of wind from the East unroofed and levelled houses throughout the Island, killing lots of cattle, horses, etc. No damage of any consequence done with me but there is not a neighbour around that can say so."

1853

The "battle" of the islands ends with Panmure being selected over Boughton Island as the proper location for a key lighthouse to guide vessels into Three Rivers (Cardigan Bay), the Island's finest harbour.

The Land Purchase Act empowers the Island government to buy the estates of consenting proprietors for re-sale to the tenantry. The measure has two flaws. The proprietors don't have to sell, and the government has too little to spend.

On 29 September, a vicious nor'easter drives 13 American vessels from their anchors and beats them ashore at Cascumpeque. There is no loss of life, but five of the schooners are destroyed. In the same storm the steamer *Rose*, engaged by the Admiralty to enforce off-shore fishing limits on American vessels, is wrecked at the east entrance to Rustico Harbour.

On 7 October, seven lives are lost in the sinking of the decrepit mail steamer *Fairy Queen*. In a shocking dereliction of duty, the captain and crew abandon ship leaving their 13 passengers to their fate. The drowned passengers' ghosts are seen entering the Kirk of St. James shortly after the steamer goes down.

The Newfoundland and Prince Edward Island Electric Co. is incorporated. Promoter Frederick Gisborne intends the Island to be a stepping stone for a submarine cable linking New Brunswick to Newfoundland.

A group of progressive local businessmen incorporate the Charlottetown Gas Light Co. Within a year 60 homes are being supplied with gaslight.

"We regret to have to record the most disastrous storm ever experienced in the Colony," the *Islander* writes on 23 December. Beginning shortly after dark, a southeast gale batters the Island with hurricane-force winds, felling trees and buildings by the score.

1854

The Reciprocity Treaty allows free trade between the U.S. and British North America. The treaty seems tailor-made for the Island's needs. It gives the Americans access to a fishery Islanders aren't using anyway and opens American markets to the Island's agricultural produce. Coupled with an increasing demand for the products of Island shipyards, the Treaty ushers in an unprecedented era of prosperity.

Upper Canadian politician Dominick Daly is sworn in as the Island's second Lt. Governor under Responsible Government. He is the first Roman Catholic ever named to the post.

A year ago, George Coles' Reformers lost to the Tories. But when a new Franchise Act enlarged the Island electorate, the Lt. Governor dissolved the House, claiming the new electorate should be heard. It is. Coles sweeps back into office with an 18 seat to 6 majority.

The Government hoped it would be a model of how well the Land Purchase Act could work, but scandal mars their purchase of the huge Worrell Estate, which encompasses Lots 38 to 42. Kept ignorant of the Government's interest by his trustees, Charles Worrell sold the property to one of them, William Henry Pope, for £14,000. A few weeks later, Pope gets £24,100 from the Government.

A. Munro publishe *New Brunswick, with a Brief Outline of Nova Scotia and Prince Edward Island*.

The British garrison is withdrawn from Charlottetown. Britain has just gone to war with Russia, but the Island capital doesn't seem in much danger of attack. On the other hand, the British regulars are needed in the Crimea.

On 19 November, the schooner *Susan Stairs* of Halifax wrecks on the reef at Flat River en route to the Miramichi. The schooner is a total loss, but the crew and much of the cargo is saved.

The Bank of Charlottetown, the Island's first home-grown bank opens for business.

New Brunswick's Westmoreland Bank announces the opening of a branch — the first ever bank on Prince Edward Island — in Charlottetown. The local agent is merchant James Purdie, who does his banking out of his store on the corner of Water and Pownal. The branch closes in 1856. The Westmoreland Bank goes bankrupt a decade later.

1855

Charlottetown is incorporated as a city. Robert Hutchinson is elected the first mayor. The old law courts building — recently serving as a flour market — has been renovated as a city hall. The civic seal is designed by George Thresher, who is paid the handsome sum of one shilling for his creation.

A Charlottetown Police Force is established with a complement of six officers.

On 14 September, a donnybrook between storm-stayed American fishermen and Georgetown locals ends with a gunshot that breaks one rioter's thigh. Georgetown is outraged, but the whole affair blows over.

On 8 June, the *Islander* reports on the hottest rumour in Halifax. Joseph Howe is about to be named the new Lt. Governor of P.E.I! The famous Nova Scotian reformer and publisher does come to the Island in an official capacity — in 1860 as a part of the Commission investigating the Land Question

The stream of immigration to Prince Edward Island has virtually dried up. There are only 57 names on Collector of Customs' "List of Emigrants" arriving on the Island during the past year.

Results from the third census in the past 14 years are in. The Island's population has climbed to 71,496; in 1841, it barely topped 47,000. It is the beginning of the Colony's "Golden Age."

Dr. John T. Jenkins sets up a medical practice in Charlottetown, becoming the Island's first native-born physician.

Haszard's Gazette marvels at an elaborate egg wagon built to handle thousands of eggs. They are to be collected across the countryside, then shipped to the U.S. How fresh will they be? The *Gazette* does not hazard an opinion.

Alive to recent scientific advances, Charlottetown druggist William R. Watson advertises the "Patent Lacteal Artificial Breast," the latest innovation for nursing mothers.

St. Dunstan's College opens near Charlottetown to educate young Catholic males for the professions and the priesthood. Total enrollment: 18.

On 28 September, Charlottetown shares vicariously in the only real Allied victory in the whole Crimean War, the fall of Sevastopol. The night after news of the surrender, the whole town is illuminated in celebration. On his return from the war Col. John Hamilton Gray, who served on the British Army Staff, will name his house "Inkerman" after the famous battle.

As the sun rises on 9 January, a sound like heavy-laden wagons rolls through Charlottetown. Buildings sway to and fro as two earth tremors, about a minute apart, shake the Island. Damage is minor.

On 10 March, a late winter storm overtakes an ice-boat crossing between "the Capes." A young medical student, Henry Haszard, dies of exposure before the party can reach safety. Despite the inherent dangers, the iceboats' safety record is remarkable. In 130 years of service, Haszard's will be the only death of a passenger during an iceboat crossing.

Winter is late. The *Examiner* for 8 January marvels that there is no ice in Charlottetown Harbour. The harbour doesn't begin to freeze over until early February.

Between 1851 and 1855, Island shipyards launch 435 vessels.

1856

The winter ice-boat service across the Northumberland Strait is sometimes risky, sometimes remarkably efficient. On 2 February, two boats leave Cape Traverse at 6:30 am for Cape Tormentine. Six hours later, they're back with the mails, ten passengers and the fastest round-trip on record.

Queen's Square, Charlottetown, c1855
Possibly by a student of Helen Bayfield, this colour sketch shows Queen's Square much as it looked when Charlottetown became a city.

Iceboats and Crews, c1890

The bags containing the mails were placed in the bottom of the boat, and my portmanteau in the centre, while the carpetbag was tied under one of the seats. Limited to freightage, these boats carry only what cannot possibly be avoided, as it is all-important, for passage on the surface of the ice, that it be light.

— B.W.A. Sleigh, *Pine Forests and Hackmatack Clearings*, 1852

This photo gives a very good view of how iceboats were being built by the late 1800s. Extremely light, their keels are shod with iron runners. The unusual lines of the bow and stern are ideal for sliding up onto – and over – snowbanks and ice.

The Island receives fairly gentle treatment in Lady Lucy Isabella Bird's *An Englishwoman in America*. She loves the countryside, but is ambivalent over Charlottetown. She concedes it is "the prettiest town in British America, next to Quebec." However... "Quebec is described as being the hottest and coldest town in the world; Paris the gayest, London the richest. But I think that Charlottetown may bear away the palm for being the most gossiping."

George Peake

Most of the Island's shipbuilding output was in the form of smaller brigs and brigantines that were built for immediate resale in Great Britain. But by the late 1850s many Island shipbuilders were launching larger vessels like the barque *George Peake* and operating them as freighters-for-hire.

Col. B.W.A. Sleigh publishes *Pine Forests and Hackmatack Clearings*, a memoir of his travels through British North America. Sleigh cut quite a swath through the colony in 1852 when he announced he was buying the massive Worrell Estate and intended to establish a bank and steamship line. Then his numerous creditors caught up with him and he had to flee the colony. Part of *Pine Forests* may well have been written from his cell in a Halifax debtor's prison. He lavishes three chapters of the book on Prince Edward Island, with very little good to say about it or its people. "The fame of Island lawlessness has extended to neighbouring provinces," he writes. "When one hears you are bound for Prince Edward's, you perceive an involuntary shudder, and are favoured with a commiserating caution, such as a traveller from Italy would receive on announcing his intention to enter some well-known banditti pass."

The William Critchlow Harris family, including future artist Robert and future architect William, arrive in Charlottetown from Wales.

The organizational meeting of the YMCA is held at St. Paul's Church School in Charlottetown, less than ten years after the movement was founded in London. Captain John Orlebar, RN, is named its first president.

Henry Cundall, land agent for Samuel Cunard, despairs of the tenants in Murray Harbour. "What is to be done with them is a puzzle — too proud to be servants and not fit for masters."

The government opens a Normal School in Charlottetown to train teachers for the Island's 268 schools. Of the 11,000 children eligible for basic schooling, only 2,200 attended classes in 1855. One of the problems with the

Water Street, Charlottetown, c1860

There is nothing attractive about the business part of Charlottetown. Most of the houses and shops are wooden and ordinary, and the streets are quite destitute of shade trees. There is a prevailing air of neatness, however, and the streets are clean except when the wind blows and raises a dust... The chief beauty of Charlottetown lies in the suburbs, and there the most fastidious taste cannot fail to be delighted.

— letter from Saint John *Telegram*, reprinted in the *Islander*, 9 Sept., 1864

system is a shortage of trained teachers.

On 26 October the *Henrietta*, bound for England with lumber from Quebec, grounds on the outer bar at West River, near East Point. Heavily damaged in an autumn storm, she breaks up in the heavy surf. A perilous rescue saves 10 of the 14 crew members.

1857

Outrage in the streets of Charlottetown. "In defiance of the law," writes *Civis,* "cows are now seen on every street within the city.... On Sunday last a ferocious animal, in the shape of a cow, attacked a very aged woman in my immediate neighbourhood, who has since been confined to her bed from the severe injuries she has sustained. The cow is still at large!! Where are the police?"

An aspiring Island journalist, Thomas Kirwan, announces his intention to publish a History of Prince Edward Island in four numbers of at least 50 pages

each. There is much history to tell, but apparently there are no subscribers. Kirwan's book never appears. Later in the year his pro-Liberal newspaper, the *People's Journal*, also folds for lack of subscribers.

In an atmosphere of rising sectarian strife, the Charlottetown *Monitor* begins a spirited, sometimes bigoted, advocacy of Protestant and Conservative interests.

1858

On 19 February, in an atmosphere of mounting sectarian tensions, the "Great Protestant Meeting" in Charlottetown demands compulsory Bible-reading in the colony's non-denominational public school system. The Island's Catholics consider this an attack on their religious beliefs. The place of religion in the school system swiftly becomes a bitterly divisive issue. In the following general election, the Liberals return to power, but with a slim, 16 seat to 14 majority.

Politicians in Canada float for the first time the idea of a union of British North American colonies. The Legislature here couldn't be less interested.

On 21 July, the barque *James Gibbs* arrives from Uigg, Isle of Skye with 300 Scottish immigrants. Theirs is the last large-scale emigration to Prince Edward Island.

On 29 November the *Prince Edward*, captained by Edward Nowlan, leaves Charlottetown with 92 emigrants bound for New Zealand. They are lured by the promise of good land and favourable reports about the new colony. Although it doesn't begin to gather momentum until the 1870s, outmigration from the colony has begun.

On 29 July, possibly the most bizarre advertisement ever to appear in an Island newspaper runs in the *Examiner:* "Notice to the public: Whereas a rumour has been circulated throughout the country that a dead child was found in a well on the Brighton Brewery premises, I beg distinctly to inform the public that such is not the fact. The circumstances of the case are these: That having rented for a servant man the premises at some distance from the Brewery, in cleaning out a neglected well on said premises, for the domestic use of the occupier, the body of a child was found, which circumstances originated the report."

Coroner Daniel Hodgson appends a note of his own supporting the fact that a dead infant was found in the well, but that there was no question of it being connected in any way with the Brewery, the servant or the previous occupant of the house. The mystery is never resolved.

On 20 July, some 3,000 well-wishers attend a giant tea at Princetown to celebrate the golden jubilee of Rev. John Keir, "father" of Island Presbyterianism. Two months later he is dead.

Charles Stanfield and W. W. Lord announce they are ready for "drying, fulling, and dressing cloth" at their new mill in Tryon. Stanfield later sells his share in the mill before setting up in Truro, Nova Scotia. There he starts making underwear. The rest is history.

Now working for Cyrus Field, Northumberland Strait cable designer Frederick Gisbourne completes the world's first trans-Atlantic telegraph cable. For a few, intoxicating months, messages flash instantaneously across the Atlantic. Then the cable breaks. It takes three more cables and another eight years before North America has a permanent cable link to Europe.

William C. Macdonald

A grandson of John MacDonald of Glenaladale (who left Scotland to escape the evil effects of capitalism) William Christopher founded Macdonald Tobacco and became one of the richest capitalists in Canada.

Tracadie-native William Christopher Macdonald and his brother Augustine set up a tobacco company in Montreal. Although Augustine gradually withdraws from the business, William C. goes on to make Macdonald Tobacco one of the richest firms, and himself one of the richest men in Canada.

On 1 August, Charlottetown merchant James Duncan launches the 1,795-ton ship *Ethel*, the largest sailing vessel ever built on Prince Edward Island. The marriage of ship and owner seems appropriate; "Wee Jamie" is said to stand seven feet tall.

1859

Lt. Governor George Dundas allows the citizens of Baltic to change the name of their settlement to "Dundas." Along with Howlan and Huntley River, Dundas is the only other community on the Island to be named after a Lt. Governor.

Although the change is yet to be officially made, the community of Green's Shore is becoming known more and more as "Summerside."

On 12 May, a ghastly murder occurs at Goblin Hollow: Ann Beaton of Lyndale is bludgeoned to death with a grubbing hoe by person or persons unknown. No one is ever convicted of the crime, but local people harbour their own suspicions.

George Dundas is sworn in as Lt. Governor. He will be the first Governor since the 1820s to serve more than five years in the post.

Campaigning on an anti-Popery platform, the Conservatives, led by Edward Palmer, topple the incumbent Liberal government. The Tories, who fiercely resisted Responsible Government, seem to have mastered the new political game. As long as they can split the electorate among religious lines and maintain the Protestant vote, their hold on power seems assured.

Lt. Governor George Dundas

Lt. Governor George Dundas officially recognizes John Sark as "Chief of the Indians of Prince Edward Island."

On 15 April, newly-appointed Queen's Printer Duncan MacLean succumbs to pleurisy. As editor of the Tory *Islander*, he was been a worthy rival to the great Edward Whelan, editor of the Liberal *Examiner*. John LePage, the colony's unofficial Poet Laureate, later muses: "Both trained to vigorous intellectual strife/ They WROTE — as Roman Gladiators FOUGHT — for life!"

Ross's Weekly begins a short, spectacular career. John Ross's newspaper becomes the chief organ of the radical Tenant League movement; when it fails, so does *Ross's Weekly*.

On 7 July General Sir William Fenwick Williams, Inspector of Fortifications and Crimean War hero, gets a grand welcome from Charlottetown. He is careful never to deny the persistent rumour that he is the bastard son of Prince Edward, for whom the Island is named. Queen Victoria never acknowledges her alleged half-brother.

Father Georges-Antoine Belcourt, a pioneer missionary in the Canadian West, arrives in Rustico to become parish priest. His energy and leadership galvanize the Acadian community.

On 24 July the lights — gas lights — come on along Queen Street.

On 4 August a rare tornado tears up trees and swamps boats as it twists across the Island.

The *Sela*, a brigantine built for James Peake Sr., is launched from Cranberry Point. An otherwise ordinary boat, the *Sela* will become the last survivor of the over 4,500 vessels built in Island shipyards in the 1800s. Sold to owners in Britain, she sails until 1919 when she is beached in Wales. As late as the 1970s, her hull is still intact and visible above the sand.

1860

When a drunken crowd disrupts the trial of an unlicensed American rum-seller in Dundas, a battle royal erupts between the local Sons of Temperance and the tipplers.

The Duke of Newcastle, Colonial Secretary, names a three-member Land Commission to investigate the Island's thorny Land Question.

On 9 August Albert Edward, The Prince of Wales, gives the colony its first taste of royalty when he arrives for a two-day visit. Islanders are dazzled.

Prince of Wales College

Central Academy is raised to the status of a college and named for Albert Edward, the Prince of Wales, whose visit to the colony is imminent.

Peter McIntyre, a native of St. Peter's, is named Bishop for the Catholic Diocese of Charlottetown. By the end of his influential, 30-year reign, he will be known simply as: "The Bishop."

Albert Edward, Prince of Wales, at Government House, 1860
The Prince is standing third from the right in this early photograph.

It is an inventive age; John Nelson Burns of Lot 25 patents a lath-making machine. He doesn't get rich — but he probably has the last lath.

Making Hay, Martinvale, c1925
The first wave of farm mechanization came in the 1860s, when horse drawn machinery like the hay mower being driven by Samuel Finlayson replaced hand tools like the scythe being wielded by Daniel MacInnis. This photograph was taken early in the 20th century.

George Jenkins of Lot 49 patents an improved potato digging machine.

Temperance Hall sponsors a lecture on the idea of a railway between Charlottetown and Bedeque. "Rather a visionary scheme," records Henry Cundall, "which was picked to pieces by [David] Laird, who showed the absurdity of it all." Construction begins in 1872.

William McKenzie of Lot 48 announces that his newly patented potato digger can dig 500 to 600 bushels a day. Rival inventor George Jenkins of Lot 49 claims his "Prince of Wales" digger can handle two-and-a-half to three acres a day.

Southport native David Smallwood decides to settle in Newfoundland. One of his grandsons — Joey — will do quite well in politics there.

Between 1856 and 1860, Island shipyards launch 395 vessels.

1861

Three years before it receives a charter, a confident Father Belcourt erects a building for the Bank of Rustico. The handsome, sandstone building outlives its original purpose and is declared a National Historic Site in 1970.

A Commission struck in 1860 to investigate the Land Question recommends the Crown lend the Colony £100,000 to buy out the absentee proprietors. Failing that, the Commissioners favour compulsory conversion to freehold. Sensitive to the "rights of property," the Colonial Office disallows the Award.

The colony's population has risen by nearly 10,000 to reach 80,857. Eighteenth century prognosticators had predicted the Colony's population would exceed 500,000. Islanders are working on it.

Reverend George Sutherland covers all possible markets with *A Manual for the Geography & Natural & Civil History of P.E.I., for use of Schools, Families and Emigrants.*

C. Birch Bagster publishes *The Progress and Prospects of Prince Edward Island.*

Rev. Henry Crawford delivers a lecture in Souris on "Light Literature." He adopts a warning tone. "Light literature (not immoral) is useful, to a certain degree, in awakening dormant facilities, and also in refining the taste. At the same time, an overindulgence in its perusal is highly dangerous." The Reverend advises moderation and caution in its use at all times.

On 13 July, the Island welcomes its second Royal in less than a year. Prince Alfred, Prince Edward's younger brother arrives for a brief, unofficial visit while serving as a Royal Navy officer.

The more things change. . . The *Halifax Morning Journal* reports: "The Hon T. H. Haviland has been re-elected Mayor of PE Island without opposition." An outraged *Examiner* recommends "our respected contemporary to learn something of the geography of this colony."

On 20 May, Rev. George Nicol Gordon of Alberton and his wife, Ellen Catherine Powell, Presbyterian missionaries to the island of Erromanga in the New

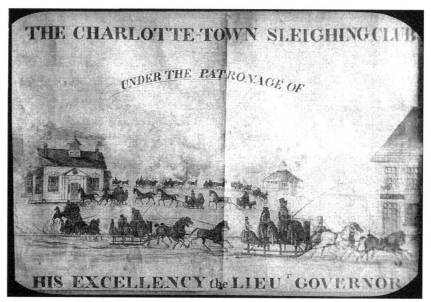

Charlottetown Sleighing Club, Queen's Square, c1840
In the winter it was so lovely. Such good snow roads and we all had good sleighs to drive about in with very handsome buffalo robes to keep warm, for it was very cold out there.

– Diary of Francis Hale Orlebar, c1920

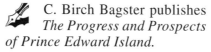

Howatt Farm, Tryon, c1895

The farms are well tilled, with comfortable homesteads and nicely kept fences, and it is doubtful in America there is a district of like area where the people are more uniformly thrifty and where poverty is so little known.

– J. Heber Hastam, *1896*

Hebrides, are murdered by natives. Gordon's brother will meet exactly the same fate 11 years later.

On 12 May the 690 ton barque *Royal Bride*, owned by William and James Yeo, strikes an iceberg on a voyage from Swansea to Montreal. Hitting at 8 mph, the starboard bow is caved in, and the crew have barely enough time to launch their boats before the vessel sinks. All get away safely and six hours later are picked up by the *Prarie Flower* and taken to St. John's.

On 17 August, an unnamed vessel leaves Malpeque for Cascumpeque with a load of shingles. Crewed by two brothers and a cousin, all named Branders, all from New London, it is hit by a sudden squall near Hog Island. The boat capsizes. All drown.

Elisha Weatherbie, Lot 49, exhibits a new reaping machine he is manufacturing. Local newspapers are enthusiastic. "Farmers... unhesitatingly agree that this machine in a trial was decidedly superior to the imported ones in several respects."

On 8 February, a terrific thunder and lightning storm breaks over Charlottetown, followed by torrential rain on what

is remembered as Black Friday. That night the temperature plunges to -33.9 C°.

1862

Basking in a glow of Victorian patriotism, a meeting of local residents name their southern Queen's community "Alexandra," after the Prince of Wales' beautiful young bride. None of Bertie's many paramours will ever be accorded the same honour.

The Scots around the Belfast Cross Roads choose a new name for their long established community; the public meeting opts for "Eldon."

Local residents decide to rename their West Prince community "Wellington," after the Anglo-Irish conqueror of Napoleon. It is a nobler title than the former name, "Quagmire." The decision is toasted with host A. Allan's potent homebrew.

Ross's Weekly reports on the first — and last — run of the season for the accident-prone steamer *Emo*. She takes 16 hours to make the round-trip from Charlottetown to Mt. Stewart. A female passenger remarks she would rather walk. It's likely faster.

A Charlottetown jury notes that "the young men belonging to St. Dunstan's College are frequently seen playing at batt and ball on the Lord's Day, on the college grounds." They could get a 10s fine, if charged.

On 3 December, the Elective Council Act is proclaimed. Henceforth, the Legislature's upper house will be elected, not appointed.

Elizabeth Lockerby-Bacon publishes an anthology of poems, *The Wild Brier: Or Lays By An Untaught Minstrel.* Her most ambitious poem, an epic involving the Yankee Gale entitled: "George and Amanda," consumes 60 pages of the anthology.

"Fabruis Cassius Funny Fellow" lampoons the Island's political situation in *An Address to P.E.I.*

A 17 June cricket match pits "the Lawyers against all comers." "All comers" win with five wickets to spare.

The Royal Agricultural Society holds an Industrial Exhibition of Domestic Manufactures and Agricultural Productions in Charlottetown.

Dentist C.F. Hubert advises: "Parties suffering from indistinctness of speech occasioned by loss of their teeth, can have both restored by the insertion of artificial masticators — in either gold or silver plate." Dr. Hubert will be delighted to supply both.

Alma resident Maurice O'Connor enlists in the Union Army at Houlton, Maine. Other Islanders have joined up, but O'Connor's zeal is remarkable; he walked all the way from Prince Edward Island. He will survive the bloody Civil War and return to the Island.

The Island issues its first postage stamps, bearing a likeness of Queen Victoria; they are in denominations of 2, 3, and 6 pence.

1863

Lt. Governor Dundas lays the cornerstone for the a new brick Methodist Church (Trinity United) on Prince Street.

The Conservatives defeat the Liberals 18 seats to 12 in a bitterly-contested general election fought almost solely on religious issues. "No Popery" is the Tory war cry. As long as they can persuade the electorate to vote along religious lines, their hold on power is secure.

Although fresh from electoral victory, Edward Palmer, premier for the last four years and Conservative leader for a generation, resigns. He's been pushed out, not by the Liberals, but by his own colleagues. Palmer is bitter, but not too bitter; he stays on as Attorney-General in John Hamilton Gray's cabinet.

William Henry Pope

Seeming to believe in adding insult to injury, William Henry Pope enrages Catholics by choosing St. Patrick's Day to introduce legislation incorporating the Island's Grand Orange Lodge. The ferocity of the debate that follows is unrivalled in Island history.

Horse-Drawn Road Grader, c1910

Each spring or early summer four residents of each district was supposed to take a team of horses each and work with the machine for a day. One team was hitched to the pole, then two teams abreast and the fourth in the front. The only man having a seat was the driver of the pole team and there was great rivalry for the position. Some men who were always late for other work would appear first, hoping to be the chosen one, but the operator of the machine usually reserved this seat for the oldest man or one who might be lame.

— *Historical Sketch of Eastern King's,* 1972

On 23 December, the *Pakeha* sails for New Zealand, bearing 34 Island emigrants.

Hutchinson's Directory of Charlottetown goes on sale at 9s. per copy. The first known directory in Island history, it will become a useful guide for contemporaries — and a treasure trove of information for later historians.

On 30 September, the Society for the encouragement and revival of the Ancient and National Music of Old Scotland stages a noisy bagpipe contest before 600 spectators in Charlottetown. Although he finishes third, Donald McFadyen wins a 10s bonus for wearing the kilt. Although its use is fading, Gaelic is still the second-most common language in the colony.

On 10 March, Lt. Governor Dundas and his Lady host a "Prince's Wedding Ball" at Government House. It's in honour of the Prince of Wales' marriage to Princess Alexandra of Denmark.

The act of incorporation for Charlottetown's Union Bank receives Royal Assent. The Bank commences operations the next June. Soon it becomes the Island's largest bank. The Bank of Rustico also receives a charter. It will become the smallest chartered bank in Canada.

On 14 April a mud-spattered pedestrian writes to the *Islander*. "It was ludicrous as well as painful to see on last Sabbath, ladies of all ages . . . floundering about in the mud like swine in a hog sty." He recommends sidewalks.

1864

With the closing and imminent sale of the barrack grounds in Charlottetown, the city will lose its main signal flag mast. On 6 June a replacement is erected in the front yard of Province House.

After a trip down the frozen Hillsborough River, St. Andrew's Chapel reaches Charlottetown and is set in its new place on

"Read All About It!"
Daily Examiner *paperboys*, c1910

Pownal Street. The building almost never made it. With five miles down and seven to go, it had crashed through the ice at Appletree Wharf and spent a night on the bottom of the river. Saved by a combination of prayer and sweat, it will become St. Joseph's Convent.

On 17 December, somewhere on the highway connecting the Georgetown Road and the Cardigan Road, Terence MacInnis, a farmer from Lot 66, is murdered. Although a £100 reward is offered for information leading to the conviction of the murderer, no one is ever arrested for the crime.

On 1 September the historic Charlottetown Conference, which will conceive the Dominion of Canada, opens with a discussion of Maritime Union. Islanders seem more interested in Slaymaker & Nichols' Olympic Circus, the first to visit the colony in some 22 years.

On 6 September, at 9:30 am the Charlottetown Conference delegates assemble at Government House for a photo opportunity before convening again. The result is the most famous photograph ever taken on Prince Edward Island.

On 8 September the Charlottetown Conference ends with a grand ball at Province House. Fine food and dancing are not conducive to the speechmaking that ensues, but the remarks show that Confederation has become a distinct possibility. The delegates agree to meet again to discuss the details.

On 10 October the second Confederation Conference, this time hosted by Quebec City, convenes to hammer out the terms for the union discussed at Charlottetown. Terms are made, but four of the Island's seven delegates have become anti-Confederates. Most Islanders will agree with them.

On 16 December, anti-Confederates within the Conservative party force the resignation of Premier John Hamilton Gray, a passionate supporter of union with the other British North American colonies. Shipbuilder James College Pope (a closet Confederate) is the compromise candidate selected to succeed him.

The "Tenant League" is founded in Charlottetown.

Members pledge to withhold rent in order to force proprietors to sell their holdings to the tenants. Gradually, civil disobedience drifts into violence.

The first issue of Edward Reilly's *Herald* is published. It becomes a fixture in the Island publishing scene, lasting until 1923.

The *Evening Patriot* begins existence as the *Patriot*, a Liberal organ. Its run as an Island newspaper will last until 1995.

The Island's first Highland Games highlight the second annual Scottish Gathering, sponsored by the Caledonian Society.

On 7 September, Thomas D'Arcy McGee takes time out from Charlottetown Conferencing to deliver a lecture on "Robert Burns and Thomas Moore" to the Young Men's Catholic Institute at St. Andrew's Hall. "The price of admission being 3s, the audience was not large."

The Legislature approves a closed season on partridges and tree grouse (January to October) because the "very great destruction" of them "has tended to render them scarce."

Minnie Cochrane MD, an Allopathic Physician trained in New York, arrives in Charlottetown. By giving you a little bit of some other problem, she can treat anything, including "rheumatism, scrofula, dyspepsia, cancers, croup, dropsy, etc." She also delivers and extracts teeth.

So *that's* why they came to Charlottetown! The *Monitor* for 19 May proudly reports the Toronto *Patriot's* recommendation "that the Legislature of Canada take pattern by the Legislature of Prince Edward Island, a province that can justly boast the best Legislative Assembly, the best Legislative Council and the best Executive Council in the British

Dominions." Please. We blush!

On 24 August two of the Island's communication mainstays —S.S. *Commerce* and S.S. *Heather Belle* — collide off Point Prim. The *Commerce* is able to continue on its way, but *Heather Belle* needs major repairs.

The Prince Edward Island Savings Bank, operated by the Colonial Treasurer, opens for business. By 1871, deposits top £68,000. After Confederation, it becomes the Dominion Government Savings Bank.

Old Store Point Light, c1925
The first light was erected at Old Store Point in 1869 to guide vessels into the tricky anchorage at Beach Point.

1865

Responding to years of lobbying, the Island government allocates $2,000 for construction of a proper lighthouse at North Cape, the dangerous northwest tip of the colony. The 63-foot-high, octagonal tower opens in 1866 — at a cost of $5,000.

As a great procession of radical Tenant Leaguers March through Charlottetown in a St. Patrick's Day show of strength, the Deputy Sheriff tries — and fails

— to arrest League leader Sam Fletcher. Justice has been flouted; the authorities grow alarmed. Three weeks later a huge *posse comitatus* slogs through the mud to Alberry Plains to arrest Fletcher. But Sam isn't there, and the posse has to slog home again. Story and verse will ensure that the whole farce becomes an Island legend. Within a month, Lt. Governor George Dundas issues a proclamation condemning the Tenant League as an "unlawful association" On 18 July, Deputy Sheriff James Curtis and his bailiffs are attacked by Tenant League sympathizers near Milton. Fearing the situation is getting out of control, and not sure where the sympathies of the local militia might lay, Governor Dundas asks for a company of Regular Army soldiers be sent from Halifax to garrison the Island.

"A confederate screw unfairly put upon us." London informs the Island Legislature that it will no longer be sending funds to cover the Lt. Governor's salary.

Summerside's first newspaper, the *Journal*, begins publication; 135 years later, it is still operating.

Prince Edward Island is now the only colony in British America that is not on a decimal currency system. If pounds, shillings and pence are good enough for the Mother Country, they're good enough for us!

Patrick Reilly announces the opening of a tobacco factory, the first in Prince County, in the fast rising town of Summerside.

Queen Victoria graciously assents to the act of incorporation of the new Summerside Bank. The little Island bank will last 36 years before being swallowed up by the Bank of New Brunswick.

Between 1861 and 1865, Island shipyards launch 497 vessels.

Although the total number of vessels launched (132) will be slightly larger in 1866, this year ranks as the high water mark for tonnage built by the Island's shipbuilding industry. One hundred and thirty vessels totalling over 35,000 tons come down the slipways.

1866

The *Islander* publishes E. W. Hales' report on the feasibility of constructing a canal linking the Hillsborough River to Tracadie Bay, in effect making two islands out of P.E.I. Hales

After The Fire, Charlottetown, 1866
Though a large portion of the downtown business district was destroyed, Charlottetown's Great Fire of 1866 might have been worse. If the flames had managed to set St. Dunstan's Cathedral alight there is no telling where the fire might have stopped.

sees no engineering obstacles that cannot be overcome. The question, of course, is not "how," but "why" and "who?"

Horseless Carriage, c1865
Made by the same firm in New Jersey, this steam-powered carriage is very similar to the one debuted by Father Georges Belcourt at the 1865 St. Jean Baptiste Day picnic in Rustico.

Father George Belcourt debuts his horseless carriage at a St. Jean Baptiste Day picnic in Rustico, thus becoming the first Canadian motorist, the first to buy a car, and the first to import one. He is also the first to have a car accident when he fails to negotiate a turn and goes off the road. The machine is retired.

After a two-year extension, the United States cancels the 12-year-old Reciprocity Treaty with British North America. Although not immediately felt, it is a damaging blow to the Island economy, which has prospered by supplying duty-free foodstuffs to industrial New England.

Still nervous after a year of civil unrest among radical land reformers, the Island government panics at rumours that Fenians might invade and the annual St. Patrick's Day parade occasions extraordinary security precautions. The Fenians want to ransom Canada for Ireland. There is no telling what they might ask in return for P.E.I. In an extraordinary move, the government passes acts to prevent "the clandestine training of persons to the use of Arms," and "the concealment of Arms or munitions of war." Almost half of the colonial budget is diverted to equipping dozens of new, suppos-

edly trustworthy volunteer militia companies.

Echoing a similar motion in the House of Assembly, the Legislative Council denies that any terms could induce Prince Edward Island to enter Confederation.

Arson is suspected after the "Great Fire" of Charlottetown destroys four city blocks and some 200 houses. The office and presses for *Ross's Weekly* are lost. Another casualty is Liberal leader George Coles, a Captain in the Fire Department. He never recovers from the physical and mental toll of fighting the fire.

Hard on the heels of the Great Fire of Charlottetown, a very suspicious fire breaks out in a carriage shop next door to George Coles' brewery — obviously the work of "foreign incendiaries." As Charlottetown is gripped with terror and paranoia, the Governor offers a £300 reward and the police are given special powers to arrest "suspicious vagabonds and vagrants."

On 4 October, only two years after ferrying the Canadian delegates down to the Charlottetown Conference, the S.S. *Queen Victoria* is caught in a hurricane and sinks off Cape Hatteras. Only her ship's bell survives.

On 27 October, a severe storm causes a flurry of shipwrecks shipwrecks off Island shores and heavy damage to local wharves.

Buoyed by an era of prosperity, local merchants in Souris and Alberton succeed in having acts of incorporation passed for banks in their respective towns. In the end, neither materializes.

1867

Cabinetmaker and City Councillor Mark Butcher turns his hand to architecture and designs Charlottetown's new Market

building — "The largest and the best building of its kind in the Lower Provinces" — at least in the *Patriot*'s humble opinion.

On 29 March, Queen Victoria assents to the British North America (BNA) Act, creating the Dominion of Canada. Prince Edward Island maintains a policy of splendid isolation from the union.

After nine years in office, the Conservatives are unseated by the Liberals in a general election. The electorate seems to think the Tories are soft on Confederation, and send the Liberals to Charlottetown with a 19 seat to 11 majority. Only five of 30 members in the new House support union.

Edward Whelan
Journalist and newspaper publisher Edward Whelan was one of the driving forces behind the movement for political and economic reform in the 1850s and '60s.

The year of Canadian Confederation is very hard on Prince Edward Island's older politicians, especially its "Fathers of Confederation." On 10 December, 43-year-old Edward Whelan dies. A recent by-election defeat in St. Peter's, a seat he held for 21 years, was a crushing blow which some felt caused his death. George Coles, though still serving as leader of the Liberal party, enters into a swift and catastrophic physi-

Matthew and Maclean, Souris, c1900

With financial backing from Charlottetown businessman Benjamin Heartz, Uriah Matthew and John McLean opened a store in Souris in 1869. The business incorporated as Matthew and McLean in 1908, and at its peak in the 1920s included fish stands, wharves, lobster canneries and this fine store.

cal and mental decline. Almost forgotten, William Cooper, the controversial founder of the Escheat Movement, dies on 10 June at his home, Sailor's Hope.

What's in a name? Everything, in the case of Charlottetown's newest newspaper. The *Presbyterian*'s reverend editor scorns secular issues.

The first event in Charlottetown's new Drill Shed is an Industrial Exhibition. The affair will evolve into the Provincial Exhibition and Livestock Show and, ultimately, Old Home Week.

"Beggars are becoming a nuisance in Charlottetown," bemoans the *Patriot*. It's obvious that the City needs a poorhouse for the "helpless poor" and a workhouse for the merely indolent.

On 27 June the garrison of British soldiers, called in nearly two years earlier to quell the Tenant League disturbances, fi-

nally leave for Halifax. Charlottetown and London have a difference of opinion over who should pay for their upkeep while in the colony. To emphasize the point that staying out of Confederation might get expensive, the Colonial Office insists the Island pay.

On 21 February, Rev. Donald McDonald, founder of the Island's "McDonaldite" Presbyterian sect, dies in Southport. He leaves behind some 10,000 followers, one-tenth of the colony's population. Known today as the Free Church of Scotland, McDonald's church is still active.

On 24 November, while bound for Le Harve, the *L.C. Owen* sights through the spray of a heavy gale a ship named the *Norwood* sinking in the North Atlantic. After a difficult, 30 hour rescue, the *L.C. Owen* is able to bring all 25 crew safely on board.

1868

Intent on re-naming their community, a public meeting replaces the names Sconser and County Line Road with the poetic name for Scotland: Caledonia.

Working from the deck of the *Heather Belle*, workers struggle through May to repair the submarine telegraph cable between Cape Traverse and Cape Tormentine. The link was broken in four places by a rogue harbour buoy that escaped from the Mirimachi.

Speed *and* comfort. The new steamer *Princess of Wales* makes the passage from Pictou to Charlottetown in 3 hours, 49 minutes. "One of the fastest as well as most comfortable passenger boats plying in the waters of the Lower Provinces," estimates the *Halifax Reporter*.

On 20 August, the *Patriot* reports that Premier George Coles has tendered his resignation "on account of ill health." Hopefully, a change of scene "will return him to his wonted health." Unfortunately, Coles has succumbed to a severe mental illness that will only end with his death in 1875.

Henry Lawson

Lawson's *Patriot* was one of the longest-lived papers on the Island, remaining in print for 15 decades.

On 29 August, the American revenue cutter *Hugh*

Mussel Mud Diggers

From a sketch by Robert Harris

In the estuaries were beds of decayed shell fish, 10 feet thick. When the ice formed, huge diggers were set up, operated by horses. A hole was cut in the ice; a long beam armed at the end with a tripfork was forced by a rude pawl and rack into the face of the bed. The load was lifted by a capstan, and came to the surface, white shells and black mud dripping with seawater. The treasure was hauled on sleighs far inland and placed in piled upon the snowy fields to be spread in the springtime. For 20 years this shell would dissolve slowly and supply the soil with lime. Assiduity in hauling "mud" was a sign of success, a rite; and it was often put upon land which had no need or could not be improved. One boy, seeing these piles upon an exhausted and abandoned farm, made the judicious observation, "I do not know whether to praise this man for his industry or reproach him for his folly."

— Andrew Macphail, *The Master's Wife*

McCulloch docks at Charlottetown. On board is a semi-official Delegation from the United States Congress, here to talk free trade. London will not be amused when it discovers the Island flirting with the Americans.

The celebrated Tom Thumb and his troupe appear at Charlottetown's Market Hall. "They are undoubtedly the most astonishing and delightful wonders of the Age!," say the ads.

A typical late winter scene. An estimated 500 mussel mud diggers are at work on Island rivers. Before spring break-up they'll have moved over 100,000 tons of mud from river bottoms to farm fields. The decomposed shellfish found in the mud is a rich source of the lime demanded by the Island's acidic soil. Although brutally hard work, it is estimated that a good dressing of mussel mud on a field will last 20 years or more.

Despite an early spring, Island farmers are feeling the pinch of last year's poor hay crop. Many are being forced to feed seed stock to their cattle. A Malpeque farmer reports 500 bushels of oats stolen from his granary. "This is certainly one of the most daring robberies we have heard of," reports the Summerside *Journal*. But the paper is confident the gang responsible will be found out. "When rogues fall out, honest people get their own."

On 22 June, Alexander Beaton of East Point reports a plague of flying ants. He describes "a windrow of ants, or pismires, in some places 3 feet deep and as many wide, extending along the North Shore many miles from East Point."

A correspondent to the *Patriot* describes Charles Stanfield's new woolen mill in Tryon. The facility is 150 feet long, 30 feet wide, three stories tall and houses 12 power looms. Its 30 employees will turn out over 100,000 yards of cloth per year.

Based on the results of a field test in Charlottetown, George Millner's new Double Grain Sowing Machine "bids fair in a short time to rival the best grain sowers of modern times."

Mowing machines and horse rakes "of Prince Edward Island Manufacture" can be had at Beer & Sons Seed & Implements

Charlottetown From the Southport Wharf, c1910

The aspect of Charlottetown from the water is particularly pleasing, rising in an amphitheatrical ascent from the water's edge, composed of gay and lively buildings, separated from each other by groves and gardens, whilst the quality of the land assigned to each house gives it the appearance of nearly twice its natural size.

— Joseph Bouchette, *The British Dominions in North America*, 1832

Warehouse in Charlottetown. Despite the urging of the press to "buy local," Island manufacturers cannot compete in the long run with the large manufacturers in Canada and the U.S.A.

George W. Williams of Charlottetown patents an improved grain sowing machine. He fails to sew up the market.

During a 23 July thunderstorm, lightning strikes - through a bedroom window in Summerside, hitting "the steel hoops of a ladies' skeleton skirt." The skirt was uninhabited at the time, but "ladies take warning. Hoops may render your appearance attractive, but when they attract lightning there is not so much fun in the matter."

Cycling Party, c1910
Debuting in the 1880s, "safety bicycles" like those being ridden by these well-dressed couples quickly supplanted the "velocipedes" of the 1860s.

John Yeo
The youngest son of the powerful Port Hill shipbuilding family, John Yeo was best known for his political career. As an MLA, MP and Senator, he represented his Prince County constituency for 66 years – a record of service considered unequaled in the British Commonwealth.

On 25 August, shipbuilder and merchant James Yeo dies at his home in Port Hill. A West Devon immigrant, he rose from nothing to become one of the colony's richest and most powerful individuals and head of its most productive shipbuilding families.

Yeo, his sons: William, John and James Jr., and his son-in-law built or owned shares in over 500 vessels.

1869

The residents of one section of the O'Leary Road vote to rename their community Unionvale.

At a public meeting held for the purpose, the people of Big Cape" exchange that name for the more euphonious "Monticello."

With a MacDonald in the chair and a MacDonald as secretary, a meeting of residents of Fork's Settlement, at the head of the Vernon River, unanimously renames their community Glencoe. (It is not known if any Campbells were present.)

The community of Darlington, just south of Hunter River in Queen's County, chooses its name at a public meeting.

St. Peter's Anglican Cathedral is consecrated in Charlottetown's rundown west end. The "Bog Chapel" becomes a bastion of "High Anglicanism" in the province.

On 6 April, George Dowie's becomes the last public state execution in British America. It is a grisly affair. After a much-publicized trial and repentance, Dowie is dropped through the scaffold. The rope breaks and Dowie falls

to the ground, dazed and bruised. His executioners try twice more before they succeed in killing him. The crowd boos. The *Patriot* hopes the citizens of the colony never have to witness such a thing again.

James Yeo Jr.
The middle son of James Yeo, James Yeo Jr. — or "Hunchback Jemmy" — was a well-known shipbuilder in his own right. He was also one of the Island's most successful federal politicians, winning his Prince County seat six times between 1873 and 1891.

The Island's first bank robbery is abortive. On 17 June, two gentlemen notice one of the Bank of P.E.I's iron shutters has been wrenched open. They alert bank officials. The robbers are evidently frightened off.

J. H. Fletcher founds the *Island Argus*, a Charlottetown newspaper. The *Argus* doesn't last long. Fletcher goes on to become Lt. Governor of South Dakota.

"The introduction of the Velocipede into this City," notes the *Islander*, "though only of recent date, is rapidly developing itself. Already several of our young men are decidedly expert and graceful velocipedists."

On 3 March, while hunting ducks at St. Peter's Harbour, William Henderson and his son come across "a large sea serpent." They row out to the animal and, after three volleys from their shotguns, are able to tow it to shore. "On the animal being measured, he was found to be 29 feet three inches long, and his greatest circumference, 29 inches; his colour was a dark brown. On being opened, it was found to contain several trout and salmon, besides three geese and two ducks, in a putrefied condition."

The Island's first native-born chief justice, Robert Hodgson, becomes the first native-born Islander to be knighted.

On 22 August, while on his way to join his regiment in Quebec, Victoria's third son, Prince Arthur, pays his second visit to Prince Edward Island.

On 22 October, a small earth tremor lasting 15 to 20 seconds gently shakes Islanders awake.

Rev. James Burns of Pownal patents an improved, all wooden carriage spring.

1870

The Sisters of the Congregation of Notre Dame celebrate the opening of their new brick convent/school on Sydney Street with a student concert.

The Legislature votes £400 to clear title to Lennox Island and turns it over as a reserve for part of the colony's Mi 'kmaq population.

Lt. Governor William Robinson

Robert Poore Haythorne's Liberal government falls when George Howlan and Andrew A. Macdonald lead the Catholic members of the Liberal caucus across the floor to join James Pope's Conservatives. Howlan and Macdonald are angry over the Protestant Liberals' opposition to grants for Catholic schools. Despite the fact the Conservatives had campaigned as an "anti-Papist" party throughout the 1860s, Howlan and Macdonald are willing to believe they will support the Catholic cause.

William Robinson is commissioned to succeed George Dundas as Lt. Governor. Robinson is secretly instructed to use every means at his disposal to promote the Island's entry into Confederation. He does.

D.H. MacKinnon, proprietor of the New York Clothing Store on Great George Street, publishes a proclamation renaming the street "Broadway" — "A name which will give new life and vigour to the artistic skill and mechanism displayed on so successful a street." MacKinnon's play fails to impress the critics.

On 8 July, Sir John A. Macdonald, Prime Minister of Canada, arrives at Falconwood House to convalesce for the summer after suffering a gallstone attack. Unkind pundits blame his

Simpson's Mill, Hope River

The custom was to take the wheat to the mill in the winter, on the ice along the shore and across the rivers. In that year of early need [c1840] her uncle put a bag of four bushels on the back of a horse, and walked alongside, through the woods by the head of the rivers, to the mill, a distance of 27 miles. He returned the next night with the flour. The Master's wife often told us that the taste of that bread never left her mouth.
— Andrew Macphail, *The Master's Wife*

low spirits on spirits not gall-stones. Macdonald takes time to visit the Legislature and sign its guest book. Under "Profession" he writes: "Cabinetmaker."

Ads celebrate Angus Gregor's Carriage Factory and Agricultural Works at New Glasgow Bridge, "fitted up with Steam-power and all kinds of labour-saving machinery."

The Island's approximately 170 water-powered mills provide a ready potential market for William Biggs' new invention. The Tryon resident patents an improved water wheel.

Between 1866 and 1870, Island shipyards launch 416 vessels.

1871

The cornerstone is laid for the YMCA building on Charlottetown's Richmond Street. It is allegedly the first building erected in North America exclusively for YMCA purposes.

The Legislature incorporates a company intending to build a toll bridge across the Hillsborough River at Charlottetown. Tolls are set, but the whole project hits troubled water, and there is no bridge until 1905.

The Island government awards Schreiber & Burpee the contract to build a provincial railway. The price per mile is fixed, but not the distance, which begins to grow as railway builders seek the cheapest — though not the straightest — route across the Island countryside. When the first sod is turned on 5 October the *Patriot*, a hostile observer, calls it "a sad and sorry affair. We believe there was never such a fizzle in the history of the colony."

The arguments for a rail-road are dazzling. The Island will become an industrial power as factories spring up along the route. More land will come

S.S. Harland, *West River*
Even after the coming of the railroad, small river steamers like the *Harland* were crucial to the Island's transportation system.

under cultivation. There would be more jobs, higher wages, higher prices for exports. There will even be an influx of American tourists worth £300,000 per year. Who could say no to such a grand undertaking? Agreeing with the majority that the Island cannot prosper without a railroad, the Assembly decides to build one. Lt. Governor Robinson is delighted. "The heavy taxation which will be occasioned by railway construction," he writes his boss in the Colonial Office, "[will] eventually lead the people to consent to enter into Confederation." He's right.

One of Island history's more whimsical newspapers, the *Broad-Axe* begins satirizing the government and other Island institutions. Islanders might laugh, but they don't buy the paper. It soon vanishes.

The Mammoth Empire City Circus and Menagerie comes to Charlottetown. In addition to

Snowshoeing Party, c1890
We often coasted a great deal on bob-sleighs. Going to any hills close by. It was splendid exercise. Snow shoeing was also great fun but more tiring, I found it.
– Diary of Francis Hale Orlebar, c1920

regular circus fare, the Empire offers: "A gratuitous balloon ascension. Professor Reno, the renowned French aeronaught, will fly his monster balloon *Tallulah* in a journey across the clouds." The gratuitous ascension is cut short by stronger-than-anticipated winds.

 J. W. Dawson submits to the Island government the report of his geological survey of the province. Not much has changed since Abraham Gesner's report of 1846. Among the natural resources Dawson identifies are peat, building stone and brick clay. He cannot resist adding an appendix on fossil finds.

Jason Barry ploughs up a large church bell on his farm at Stookley, near Morell. Hidden by the Acadians of nearby Havre St. Pierre at the time of their Expulsion in 1758, the bell is recast and given to the Roman Catholic church in Rollo Bay.

The Wesleyan Day School, an imposing brick structure four storeys high, opens on Upper Prince Street. In 1877, it is taken over by the province as a public school and re-named after its location.

The Merchant's Bank of Prince Edward Island, the Island's fifth home-grown bank, opens for business in offices on Water Street in Charlottetown. Although its existence is by times precarious, it will outlast all of its contemporaries.

The Decimal Currency Act introduces currency based on dollars and cents. Since 1865, the Island has been the only colony in British North America not on a decimal system. William Cundall is authorized to procure £1,500 worth of pennies. A Birmingham mint turns out 2,000,000 "Tree Cents" — the only currency ever officially minted for the colony — but Confederation will make them obsolete.

North River Bridge, c1893

The *Semi-Weekly Patriot* reports on what Thomas Huestis, lightkeeper at Seacow Head has been up to in his spare time. He's invented an improved version of the mitrailleuse (an early machine gun). "We may be wrong, but we believe Mr. Huestis is a made man."

Abraham Gill the Younger of Lot 32 patents a hay carrier.

George W. Millner of Charlottetown patents his version of an improved milk pail, designed to keep the milk in and other barnyard substances out.

Watson Duchemin receives a U.S. patent for his egg carrier design. His "Patent Egg Carrier" will be used as a model for the modern egg carton.

On 25 November, "One of the most terrible storms which has visited this locality for many years" sweeps through the Island. "Houses, fences and trees were laid prostrate before the gale," reports the *Patriot,* "Wharves were broken up by the surging of the billows, vessels were torn from their moorings and cast adrift and disasters are reported from all quarters."

The keel of the Crapaud-built schooner *Snow Squall* was laid in a snow storm, and later launched in a snow storm. On 15 October, she is lost in a snow storm on a trading voyage to Newfoundland, taking all hands with her.

1872

The Island is beginning to show the strain of carrying a heavy and ever-growing railway debt. With costs spiralling out-of-control and the road only partially built, the Legislature is unable to raise the funds to complete the project. Suddenly, Confederation begins to look like an attractive alternative.

The Island's first indoor ice-skating rink, the Charlottetown, opens on the eastern shore of Government Pond. The round building soon proves impractical for ice hockey or speed skating.

Rev. S. E. Perrey of Mont-Carmel, the first Roman - Catholic priest ever ordained in the colony, makes a novel donation to the Miscouche Convent: a 200-pound pig!

When his missionary brother George was murdered by natives on the South Seas island of Erromanga, James Douglas Gordon of Alberton vowed to follow in his brother's footsteps. He does. On 7 March he, too, is murdered by the natives of Erromanga.

$ The government hires Robert H. Crawford to supervise collection of the hundreds of thousands of copper tokens in circulation as money. The exchange rate is 16 cents a shilling.

Mussel mudders take note! William MacKenzie of Lot 48 patents an improved mud fork, to replace the scoop with which mussel mud diggers are equipped.

From swords to ploughshares... In January, *The Island Argus* announces that Thomas Huestis, the Seacow Head lighthouse keeper who invented a machine gun in his spare time, has also invented an improved potato planter. Unfortunately, he is unable to invent a method for changing his political stripes. In July, after a change of government, he loses his job.

Potatoes are already a staple crop. Soon they will be an industry. To harvest them, George Millner of Charlottetown patents an improved potato digger.

Neil Taylor of Brooklyn, Lot 61, announces his patented invention, "Taylor's Treble Purchase Stumping Machine."

Daniel MacKinnon and William Fraser of Charlottetown patent "MacKinnon and Fraser's Reversible Extension Carriage."

1873

The North River Bridge was scheduled to be completed by September. However pile drivers will still be at work and interfering with shipping well into November.

Summerside's Island Park Hotel, built on Holman Island, now offers a ferry service to the mainland. The new steamer *Frank* will make a regular run.

A petition bearing 4,000 signatures is delivered to the House of Assembly. It demands an immediate ban on the production or importation of spirituous liquors.

Robert Poore Haythorne
When the mounting railway debt threatened to bankrupt the colony in 1873, Premier Robert Haythorne was forced to negotiate the Island's entry into Confederation.

On 2 January, driven to desperation by an enormous railway debt, Premier Robert Poore Haythorne's cabinet decides to ask Ottawa for terms of union. Haythorne comes back with a surprisingly generous offer. The Conservatives under James Pope win the subsequent election by claiming they could negotiate an even better deal. Pope comes back with further — minor — concessions, which the Legislature votes to ac-cept. On 1 July, accompanied by the rattle of musketry and the roar of cannon, the Island officially joins Confederation. Sheriff Watson reads the union proclamation with a flourish, but his audience — three people — doesn't even bother to cheer.

On 17 September, the Island elects its first federal MPs — six in all. They make quite a splash in Ottawa. Arriving at an almost deadlocked House of Commons at the height of the Pacific Railway Scandal, David Laird declares their intention of voting against Sir John A. Macdonald's Conservatives. His speech is regarded as the death blow for the government. Within the week he's sitting in Alexander MacKenzie's newly-formed Liberal cabinet.

A Boston newspaper gives an enthusiastic review of a recent exhibition by a new Canadian artist, Robert Harris. Buoyed by this success, Harris returns to the Island. He is quickly commissioned by the Legislature to do a series of portraits of members who have served as Speaker of the House.

The first issue of *The Island Hero* is published. It does not appear that Messrs. Graves and and McMurtry's small monthly lives to see a second issue.

Victoria Park, **c1900**

A men's choral society is organized. It is intended to be "free of sectarian bias."

Captain Martin Van Buren Bates, the Great Kentucky Giant and his wife, Anna Swan, the Nova Scotia Giantess, appear at Market Hall. Captain Bates is slightly under, and Anna Swan is slightly over, seven feet six inches in height.

Officials in Souris report a smallpox epidemic. Six die from the deadly disease.

Flattered, we're sure. The *Quebec Chronicle* compares Prince Edward Island to the fashionable Isle of Wight, and praises the high state of culture here.

The question of Temperance is discussed by the Young Men's Institute. They agree to disapprove of the use of intoxicating liquor in any form.

Messrs. Eaton and Frazee open a commercial college at the corner of Queen and King Streets.

On 9 June, three boys try to cross a creek near French River on a homemade raft. The craft capsizes, drowning two. Only the quick reaction of Thomas Pillman saves the third.

Peaking on 24 August, one of the deadliest storms in the history of the Maritimes, the "August Gale," wreaks havoc on the fishing fleets along the Island's North Shore. There are few survivors from the 40 wrecks.

The Island's colonial currency becomes officially worthless when the Lt. Governor signs a law recalling and cancelling all Prince Edward Island coins and banknotes.

It may just be a pipe-dream, but Robert Longworth Fox, Charlottetown marble cutter, patents "Fox's Improved Hot Air Apparatus" — "a new and useful improvement on the method of heating apartments now used in Canada."

According to the *Argus*, Jacob Carvell is off to Winnipeg, where he'll become head of the Manitoba Mounted Police.

The launch of the S.S. *Prince Edward Island* indicates that Island shipbuilders are willing to change with the times. The ocean-going steamer is one of the largest on the Island Registry.

1874

Title to 40 acres of Government Farm is transferred by Ottawa to the City of Charlottetown to be used as a public park. With admirable loyalty, it is named after Queen Victoria.

Reflecting the harmonious relations between the various ethnic groups that live there, a meeting of the people along the Line Road between Lots 13 and 14 decide to call their community "Harmony."

Stanislaus Perry

The first Acadian ever elected to the Prince Edward Island Legislature and the first Acadian to serve as its Speaker, in 1874 Stanislaus Perry became the first Acadian ever elected to the House of Commons.

Demanding the erection of more lighthouses along Island coasts, MPs J.C. Pope and

Whistle Stop at Travellers' Rest, c1900

I take a jaundiced view of this railway. I only traveled on it once, and then I was two and a half hours late in a journey of 40 miles. In the first place, a herd of cattle belonging to a personal friend of the engine driver, notwithstanding the frantic screams of the whistle, insisted on remaining on the track until the functionary before named, assisted by the conductor and some passengers, got off and drove them home. Then at a wayside station, a picnic party of about 20 young people got in and were altogether too much for our locomotive. As my friend, the driver (who spent a good deal of time cruising up and down the line on foot) remarked: "she was kind of balky at the hills."

— John Rowan, *The Emigrant and Sportsman in Canada*, 1876

Northern Light, 1880
Picturesque Canada
Designed as "winter steamer" to keep the Island in communication with mainland, the *Northern Light* had a specially reinforced wooden hull. Unfortunately the small, under-powered vessel was rarely up to challenging the ice that ruled the Northumberland Strait every winter.

A.C. Macdonald claim that in the past year "about 200 boats and schooners were reported to have been lost and nearly 200 lives." They decide not to mention that most of the damage was caused by a single storm — the August Gale.

Sir Robert Hodgson, the first Islander ever to be named chief justice and the first Islander ever to be knighted, becomes the first Islander ever to be appointed Lt. Governor.

P.R. Bowers launches a new weekly newspaper. His *New Era* passes rather quickly.

Two lobster factories pack $10,500 in product. This represents 3% of the provincial fishery.

The *Summerside Journal* marvels at the house being erected by plasterer James Smith "on a plan entirely new in this country." The building material consists of mortar mixed with pebbles to form "a sort of compost." Builders call it concrete.

1875

Charlottetown's new Law Courts building features a town clock — illuminated automatically every evening.

The *Island Argus* reports a petition to the federal government for a post office from the people around Hope River Wharf. Ever practical, the meeting also renames its community Bayview.

"Back Settlement, Lot 52" becomes "Lorne Valley" in honour of John, Marquis of Lorne, Duke of Argyll and Canada's new Governor General.

Slated for 4 January, the opening of the Prince Edward Island Railway is delayed by a succession of snowstorms. The PEIR doesn't begin service until 12 May.

When its first attempt is disallowed, the Assembly modifies the bill requiring the compulsory sale of proprietary estates larger than 500 acres. Once again, the Lt. Governor holds assent for the Governor General's consideration, but this time the Act is allowed, and the Land Question resolved. Ottawa loans the province $800,000 to cover the costs.

Robert Hodgson
An able administrator, Robert Hodgson was the first native-born Islander to be named Chief Justice. In 1869 he became the first Islander ever knighted and in 1874, the first to be appointed Lt. Governor.

Summerside, 1880
Picturesque Canada
This little seaport is intended to be attractive and it would give these travellers great pleasure to describe it, if they could at all remember how it looks.
— *Charles Dudley Warner,* Baddeck and That Sort of Thing, *1874*

On 27 September, the first civic elections are held in Summerside.

As the debate over denominational schools drags religion through the political mire yet again, the *Presbyterian and Evangelical Protestant Union* begins its career. It's primarily a religious paper, but it knows what it doesn't like — separate schools for Catholics.

Historian Duncan Campbell publishes *A History of Prince Edward Island*. The volume is long on the recent details of the Land Question, and short on pretty well everything else.

On 19 August, a great Highland Gathering is held on the grounds at Government House.

Off New London, a huge tuna fights fisherman John Pidgeon for the same mackerel. The tuna wins. It flies completely over the boat, striking Pidgeon on the shoulder, and carries off the gunwale on the opposite side. No wonder the huge fish are known as "horse mackerel."

On 29 May, five fishermen drown when their boat sets on the bar outside Rustico harbour. To prevent similar disasters in future, a new range light is erected.

It will go down as the coldest winter on record, with an average temperature of -10.4 C°.

Between 1871 and 1875, Island shipyards launch 351 vessels.

Falconwood Hospital, 1926

Canada's first mental hospitals were founded in the 1830s as places of refuge – or asylums – where kindness, discipline, fresh air and exercise could allow the mentally ill to heal. Built between 1877 and 1879 on a large estate overlooking the Hillsborough River, the Provincial Asylum at Falconwood was a modern, up-to-date treatment facility. By the time this photo was taken in 1926 the building was growing over-crowded and showing its age.

1876

The *Island Argus* announces a new name for the locality where the Souris Line Road intersects with the Shore Road at Black Bush. "Hermanville" evidently honours the community's first settler, Herman MacDonald.

The *Island Argus* reports that the inhabitants of Tracadie Sandhills have chosen a new name for themselves. A century later, "Blooming Point" will become one of the few Island communities ever to have a novel named for it.

The newly-constructed lighthouse at West Point goes into service along a coast known for phantom ships, sea monster sightings and rumours of buried treasure. It is said the flashing light from the 67-foot tower can be seen in Shediac, N.B.

Another Island landmark is born when the lighthouse at Wood Islands goes into operation. The square tower is 50 ft. high, and the attached dwelling house contains eight finished rooms.

James Peake, c1870

Emigrating from Plymouth, England in the early 1820s, merchant and land agent James Peake was one of the first to make it big in the Island's shipbuilding industry. He left one of the most prosperous firms in the colony to his three sons: George, Arthur and James Jr.

James Peake and his wife, Edith Haviland, hire William Critchlow Harris to design their grand home on West Street. It's Harris' first commission for a private home and he has evidently been told that money is not a concern. When Beaconsfield is finished two years later, it will be the most expensive private residence on the Island. The $50,000 price tag will be instrumental in driving the Peakes into bankruptcy in 1882.

Lobster Smack, Colville Bay, c1910

One of the terms of union with Canada was a guarantee of steam communication with the mainland in winter. Ottawa hopes to fulfil this pledge with the "winter steamer" *Northern Light*. More "ice-resister" than "ice-breaker," she will be icebound an average of 64 days per winter.

Even though they were abolished in England in 1837 and the rest of Canada in 1869, the pillory and public stocks are still in use in Charlottetown.

The Prince Edward Island Law Society is established in Charlottetown.

A 22 November by-election in Queen's County gives Islanders their first experience in voting by secret ballot. It's physically safer than the old, verbal method, but many campaign managers are unhappy. How can they make sure the voters they bribe stay bought? The government is also concerned over the expense of secret balloting and decides not to adopt the system.

The *Pioneer* begins life in Alberton. Two years later, during a smallpox epidemic, subscribers start sending the paper back unopened, afraid it may harbour the deadly germ. The epidemic forces the paper to Montague and, eventually, Summerside.

Islanders flock to "John H. Murray's Great Railroad Circus." It might not be "The Greatest Show on Earth," but it does claim to be the "Oldest, Largest, Best, and Only Legitimate Circus in America."

On 7 September, some 4,000 Islanders attend the Railway Employees' Picnic at Park Island in Summerside Harbour. William Dean takes home Lord Dufferin's medal for his third consecutive victory in the single sculls rowing match.

Charlottetown, from Fort Edward, c1870
From a sketch by W.O. Carlisle

Edwin Proctor of Kensington introduces his "Proctor Potato Digger" to West Prince farmers in the advertising columns of the Alberton *Pioneer*.

Charlottetown-born William Nelson LePage has discovered that it's not enough to merely make the best glue in the world — you also have to tell people about it. His innovative advertising campaigns are making "Lepage's Glues" a household name.

David Laird is named the first Lt. Governor of the Northwest Territories. Though sparsely populated, the territory is huge, including northern Quebec, Ontario and most of western and northern Canada. Laird will serve until 1881, neatly avoiding the 1885 Rebellion.

1877

The inhabitants of Dock Road have agreed on a new name, Elmsdale.

The new lighthouse at New London is completed.

School at Canoe Cove, c1860
Sketch by Robert Harris

On the road I passed a country schoolhouse at recess time. The children were playing in the road but when they saw the carriage approaching they ranged themselves in a row, and as we passed the girls curtsied low and the lads bowed in a most respectful manner. It was a quaint and pleasing sight.
– Harper's New Monthly Bazaar, 1876

Main Street, Souris, c1910

In winter, which begins in November and lasts until May sometimes, PEI offers special inducements to those who enjoy six months of snow and unlimited opportunities for sitting by the fireside o' stormy nights and listening to the furious din of sleet and hail beating against the ringing panes.
— Harper's New Monthly Bazaar, 1876

On Christmas Day, with his stone episcopal palace almost complete, Bishop Peter McIntyre invites the workmen employed in its construction to a banquet in their honour; 43 sit down to dinner.

The cornerstone is laid for the new Kirk of St. James in Charlottetown. Designed by William Harris and David Stirling, it is to be built of stone and wood.

After their annual 12 July march, Charlottetown Orangemen are besieged in their hall on Upper Queen Street while Catholic rioters pelt the windows with paving stones. Next day there is a run on small arms at local hardware stores as combatants prepare for the worst, but the worst never comes.

Two years after incorporation under a general act of the Legislature, Summerside's own Act of Incorporation passes into law. The Island's second-largest town has its charter.

The Island makes the big time with a feature article in *Harper's New Monthly Magazine*. *Harper's* is one of the most popular periodicals on the continent. By and large, it seems to like us.

W. L. Cotton's Charlottetown *Examiner* goes daily, giving the province its first daily newspaper. For good measure, it publishes a weekly edition as well.

Work begins on the new Prince Edward Island Hospital for the Insane at Falconwood, near Charlottetown.

In Lot 55, Donald Clark's son arrives home infected with diphtheria. Within two weeks, he and five of his siblings have succumbed. A few years ago, it is said, the family lost five children in another epidemic.

The local school board rents the former Wesleyan Methodist chool on Upper Prince Street for use as a public school. It buys the building in 1890. Today Prince Street School occupies the site.

Get 'em while they last. While buffalo are being hunted to near-extinction on the Great Plains, Fenton Newbery & Co. is doing a roaring business in buffalo robes. On 8 December a bale of them go on auction in Charlottetown.

29 January is the coldest day ever recorded in Charlottetown. The temperature plummets to -32.8 C°.

1878

"South Wiltshire" becomes "Kingston," by vote of a meeting of its residents.

Kirk of St. James Presbyterian Church, Charlottetown, c1900

The new stone Kirk of St. James, designed by (David) Stirling and (W.C.) Harris, opens for divine worship on Pownal Street. The old Kirk, supposedly haunted by the ghosts of the *Fairy Queen* disaster, is hauled next door.

A correspondent for the *Daily Examiner* is bullish about growth along the western line of the new P.E.I. Railway. One of the most noticeable changes is the rapid development of Barrett's Cross into the new town of Kensington.

W. L. Cotton
W.L. Cotton made Edward Whelan's *Examiner* into the Island's first daily newspaper.

Mystery surrounds the 26 October disappearance of Edward Lyons, a well-to-do farmer, while riding home to Souris River from Souris. His horse arrives without him, and his saddle is recovered from a nearby river. Lyons had been drinking and spending money freely. Foul play is widely suspected, but never proved.

After outlawing daytime swimming in Victoria Park, a city ordinance adds: "Nor shall any person indecently expose any part of his or her person . . . nor shall the plea of answering the call of nature be considered a palliation of the offense."

The Canada Temperance Act gives counties and municipalities the right to hold plebiscites on the prohibition of alcohol. Within a year, Prince County goes "dry" — in law if not in fact.

The *Examiner* for 14 May reports an "ill-bread" attack on an Italian waffle vendor! "The gentlemanly proprietor . . . asked Mr. C[oyle] if he desired to invest in his delicious edibles when, to our Italian friend's dismay, his shop was suddenly overturned by Coyle."

George Kelly, a 16-year-old mulatto from Charlottetown's West Bog district, is murdered by two young white men. Two local "swells" are arrested, then acquitted after a controversial trial. One is later lynched in the American West — for murder.

Albert Ruger, itinerant bird's-eye view-maker, begins sketches for his panoramic views of Charlottetown and Summerside.

The first incarnation of the *Island Farmer*, published by Schurman Bros. lasts less than a growing season.

Times are hard, for artists as well as tradespeople. Still, young Robert Harris is hopeful. He is advertising "Portraits Painted from Life, etc. during the next Six Months" at his studio in Full's Brick Building on Charlottetown's Queen Street.

Cricket still rules on Prince Edward Island, but an upstart American game is making inroads. The St. Lawrence Base Ball

***Christmas,* c1890**
This is the earliest known photograph of a Christmas tree on Prince Edward Island.

Club takes to the field today at Victoria Park for a practice.

It's a Christmas idyll as skaters glide over Government Pond in Charlottetown. Well, it's almost idyllic. "It was pleasing to note," notes the *Daily Examiner*, "there was not so much drunkenness as in former years."

On 22 November Captain Koenig, a Newfoundland fishing captain, lands in Alberton feeling most unwell. A few days later, his illness is diagnosed as smallpox. For the next four months, an epidemic preys on Alberton's citizens; meanwhile, surrounding areas cut off all communication with the stricken town.

The students at Mount Stewart school are having a tough time finishing their year. In May, an outbreak of mumps closed down the school. In early June diptheria strikes. It's hard on teachers, too; they don't get paid for the days they don't work.

A vice-regal visit from the Governor General, Lord Dufferin enlivens a summer overshadowed by a sharp commercial slump.

The *Daily Examiner* reports that William Coffin, Bay Fortune, has turned up the solid-gold handle of an urn while digging in his garden: "If reports prove true, Mr. Coffin will have his garden well dug for next season." Tales of Captain Kidd's treasure abound in the area.

Henry Cundall confides to his diary, "Took Miss Palmer to Temperance Hall where saw Edison's phonograph." The invention is travelling fast. Edison patented it just the year before.

Christmas has become a commercial event as well as a holy day. "Decorate your Homes with Artificial Vines — the Latest Novelty," commands Bremner Bros., who have, of course, an

excellent variety, along with 200 designs of Christmas Cards, "including the New Canadian Winter Scenes." The *Examiner* notes a new tradition that is taking root: "Tomorrow night the refulgent Christmas Tree will blaze in many homes, and happy hearts will dance for joy as its particular glories are revealed." Geese are going for 40-60¢ apiece at Charlottetown's Christmas Market. Turkeys start at 75¢; the biggest ones cost $1.40. "Though not in accordance with Presbyterian practice," writes Henry Cundall to Rev. John Jenkins, "I venture to enclose a Christmas card for Mrs. Jenkins & wish you both a Happy Season."

 Lt. Governor Robert Hodgson lays the cornerstone for a large brick school in Charlottetown's west end. Today, government offices occupy the site of the original West Kent School.

Ruined by the collapse of the shipbuilding market, James Duncan & Co., a leading Island mercantile firm, declares bankruptcy. The firm's liabilities exceed $329,000, most of it owed to the Merchants' Bank of P.E.I. and Duncan's Liverpool agent, Sir James Malcolm. Malcolm skips town; Duncan is arrested for debt.

Originating from 20 different locations, official weath-

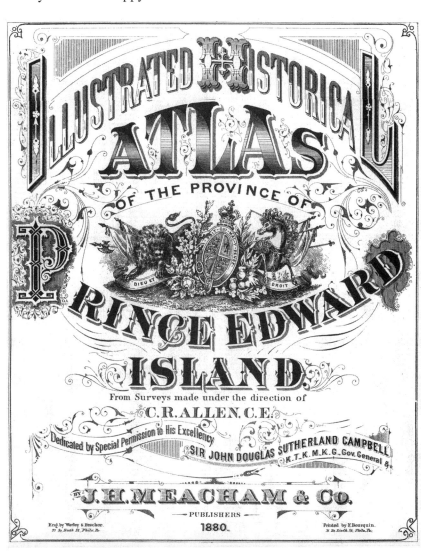

Title Page from *Meacham's Illustrated Atlas of P.E.I.,* 1880

Meacham's Atlas has been one of the most popular and sought-after books ever published about Prince Edward Island.

Princess Louise and the Marquis of Lorne

Meacham's Atlas, 1880

The visit of the Governor General and his Royal wife was the social highlight of the 1870's.

er forecasts are issued for the first time in the Maritime provinces.

1879

The Grand Jury, having visited the Charlottetown jail, recommends that prisoners be taken outside for at least one hour each day since there is no ventilation in the prison.

The Island's second native-born Lt. Governor, T. Heath Haviland Jr., is sworn in. Haviland's route to Fanningbank has been unusual — he resigns from a seat in the Senate to take the appointment.

W. W. Sullivan's new Tory government gets a ringing endorsement from the people in the election it called after taking office a month earlier. The Conservatives' 26 to four win is a record majority. Sullivan is the first Roman Catholic to serve as Premier.

The *Daily Examiner* announces that J. H. Meacham & Co.'s long-awaited atlas of P.E.I. is at the printers. Five presses, in New York, Philadelphia, Summerside, and Charlottetown, are busy at the task. The plates are deemed both accurate and beautiful.

Organized curling has been around in Canada since at least 1807, but it's still a novelty on P.E.I. On 5 March the Hillsborough Curling Club has what the *Examiner* describes as a "roarin' game" on the harbour ice opposite the Railway Depot in Charlottetown.

On 19 June, a large crowd at Upton Park near North River watch Stephen McNeill's horse French Sporter trim A.N. Large's mare Fairy in a controversial best of five match race. The total purse: $400.

He's no Ned Hanlon, but Charlottetown business-man-cum-sculler John Joy is more than a match for fellow townsman Frederick McKay. He rests on his oars a number of times during their five-mile race and still carries off the $50 purse.

General Tom Thumb and his troupe delight audiences during their first visit to the Island since 1868. The local press comments that the celebrated Lilliputian has gained weight since his last visit, but that his wife, Lavinia Warren, is as lovely as ever.

Lt. Governor T.H. Haviland, Jr. opens the Prince County Exhibition in Summerside's drill shed.

The King's County Exhibition opens in Georgetown.

Bishop Peter McIntyre opens the Charlottetown Hospital, the province's first, in his former residence on Dorchester Street. It has 14 beds and is open to all, except those with "incurable or contagious" disease.

Diphtheria, the deadly child-killer, strikes in a province-wide epidemic. In a particularly tragic instance, the MacArthur family of Tryon Road lose all five of their children in less than two weeks.

Lorne Hotel, c1890

Meacham's Atlas, 1880

By the latter half of the nineteenth century, tourism was becoming part of the Island landscape.

The ship's bell from the Island barque *Moselle*, reports the *Examiner*, could tell quite a tale (if it could talk.) Cast in 1674, it was sent from Rome to the chapel in Louisbourg in the 1730s. When the fortress was destroyed in 1758 the bell was thrown into the sea. About 50 years later the sea threw it back, and a local fisherman sold it to a Pictou tinsmith, who in turn sold it to Captain Carew of the *Moselle*.

On 14 August Canada's Governor General, the Marquis of Lorne, and his royal consort, Princess Louise, daughter of Queen Victoria, arrive for a four-day visit.

On 16 August, two Miminegash fishermen are chased by a 200-foot sea monster while hauling their trawls. They escape.

Captain John Sampson of the schooner *Louisa Montgomery* reports seeing a sea monster 10 miles west of Pictou Island. "The monster showed about a hundred feet above the surface, and the body was as large around as a barrel. It had a long tapering head similar to that of a land snake and its back was black. It was going straight along, at a rate of about seven knots — the foam breaking on each side as when a schooner is under way."

Prince of Wales College admits female students for the

Charlottetown, 1880
Picturesque Canada

It has the appearance of a place from which something has departed; a wooden town, with wide and vacant streets, the air of waiting for something.
— Charles Dudley Warner, *Baddeck and That Sort of Thing*, 1874

first time.

Pownal's new, two-room schoolhouse is complete. The school includes a novel innovation — a playground. "In most country districts, the children have no other playground than the highroad," comments the *Examiner*.

On 6 July, the ferry *Southport* is raised from the bottom of ferry wharf. After a diver from Pictou plugs the leak in the dead light which sank the boat in the first place, the city fire department steam engine "Rollo" pumps the vessel to the surface.

Business is bad, and at its annual general meeting, the Bank of P.E.I. writes off debts totalling $11,084, as a world-wide depression stretches out its tentacles to the Island province.

C.W. Smallwood demonstrates his newly-patented potato digger at James Pempraise's farm on the Malpeque Road near St. Dunstan's College.

On 29 October a heavy gale washes the front range lighthouse tower at New London some 200 yards westward down the shore. The same gale knocks the

John Robertson's Farm
Meacham's Atlas, 1880

range light at Sandy Island, Cascumpec off its foundation.

On 22 February, Islanders pick up the pieces after a snowladen nor'easter huffs and puffs and blows down trees and buildings, including the Roman Catholic chapel in Cardigan. The winds also fanned a serious fire in downtown Summerside.

1880

J.H. Meacham & Co. sue John Robertson of Long Creek for the cost of an engraving of his farm that he commissioned for the company's *Historical Atlas of Prince Edward Island*. Robertson is upset because the picture is not the agreed size and does not include his cows or his wife hanging out clothes. Meacham wins.

When Charlottetown resident Alex Campbell sees "a number of street arabs" attacking a little boy he intervenes. When "the ruffians" set upon him instead, he pulls a revolver from his jacket and fires in the air to scare them away. He is arrested for discharging a firearm but the judge is sympathetic. Campbell is fined five cents plus costs.

Although its been going on for over a decade, the exodus of Islanders to the "Boston States" has begun to reach alarming proportions. "Whole families are weekly emigrating to the US," the *Patriot* notes. "The movement is not confined to any particular class of the community — Farmers, Mechanics, Labourers, Clerks and Bookkeepers all furnish their quota to swell the tide."

Twenty cents for adults, ten cents for children: that's the price to attend the tea at the Point Pleasant Hotel. Proceeds go towards the new Presbyterian church underway at Stanhope.

The *Patriot* announces that Dr. McNeill of Stanley

Bank of Prince Edward Island Banknote, c1870
One of five Prince Edward Island banks created in the 1850s and '60s, the Bank of PEI was the biggest. Its collapse in 1882 was the end of the Island's "Golden Age."

Bridge has raised a crop of sugar cane, 1,000 lbs. of sugar to the acre. Despite McNeill's success, a new industry does not develop.

The Prince Edward Island Pottery Company opens at Mt. Edward in Charlottetown's Royalty. The company is managed by Fred W. Hyndman and employs eight men and seven boys, making 13,000 bricks per day as well as everything from flower pots to bean crocks. The firm's history is short, but chief potter Oswald Hornby's products will become valued artifacts.

Between 1876 and 1880, Island shipyards launch 194 vessels.

1881

Thomas H. Munn is appointed keeper at the just-completed lighthouse at Cape Bear on the southeast tip of the Island. The 46-foot high square tower cost $1,374 (significantly under budget!).

A bullish public meeting decides the area around Barlow's Mill in the valley below Wellington should be called Progress Town. The name — and the boom — are fleeting. The public prefers Wellington Station, where the railway passes.

"The boys who . . . catch them."

Lobsters . . . are despised by the older settlers. They should never be permitted to appear at dinner, and should not be eaten for breakfast or supper above once a week. After many years observance of this rule, I left the Island with as powerful a relish for them as ever. They are in great plenty in the harbours, but are best caught at sea. When brought to the wharf at Charlotte Town, the boys who usually catch them sell them for a halfpenny or a penny apiece.

—S.S. Hill, *A Short Account of Prince Edward Island*, 1839

The census reports just under 109,000 people on Prince Edward Island. The Island is not yet "Canada's Smallest Province" — at least in terms of population.

British Columbia's population is reported as 49,000.

🌀 Inspired by Nova Scotia's example, a group of eminent Islanders establish the Prince Edward Island Historical Society. The first president is Lt. Governor T. H. Haviland, Jr. History is obviously for the well-to-do. Entrance fee: $5. Annual subscription: $2. The Society operates for one year.

🚜 In 1874, there were only two lobster canneries on the Island. They packed $10,500 in product — 3% of the provincial fishery. Now the number of lobster canneries has exploded to 118. Lobster brings $1.2 million into the economy — 63% of the total fishery. Although the value of the catch quickly declines from this peak, the fishery remains an integral part of the provincial economy.

🚜 The government announces that of the 844,000 acres acquired since the Compulsory Land Purchase Act, 624,000 have been resold to resident farmers.

🏛 "How gratifying it is," writes the *Examiner*, "to observe that a taste for flowers is being steadily developed in Charlottetown. Twenty or thirty years ago, flowers could be procured at but one or two homes." It is a sign of progress towards "a higher level of refinement and culture" in the Island's capital.

🏛 In an editorial calling for new civic regulations to improve sanitation, promote commerce, and enhance the built environment, the *Examiner* lists the principal features of early Charlottetown: "log houses, blueberry barrens, spruce trees, and an old earth fort."

💲 On 21 November, the Bank of P.E.I.'s general manager, Joseph Brecken, leaves Charlottetown for Saint John, N.B. "on business." He keeps going. Suspicious

Wreck of HMS Pheonix, 1882
The London Graphic

Box Sleigh

In this season of snow lie pleasures and employments impossible at other times. Nature showers upon the roads the voiceless material that makes the means of travelling smooth and accessible to all... Nature bridges over the rivers with her far-reaching and trackless sheets of ice, and the woods disgorge their fuel and their timber ware by tons, to glide over the ice king's acres towards the homes of families and the haunts of industry.

– C. Birch Bagster, *Progress and Prospects of Prince Edward Island*, 1861

bank officials discover a catastrophic cache of bad loans and false accounts. Brecken's dishonesty ruins the Island's oldest bank. A week later, the Bank suspends payments. Five months later, after trustees sort through the mess, the Bank declares bankruptcy. As both depositors and Directors scramble to cover their losses, the economy reels from the body blow.

"Mr. Hubert Haszard, at the foot of Queen Street, has just had a telephone erected establishing a connection between his bookstore on the first floor and his bindery on the third. It works well."

Summerside's Thomas Hall wins first class honours at the Dominion Exhibition in Halifax. "Tho quiet and unassuming in appearance and manner, [he] occupies now the proud position of standing at the head of all mechanics in his line throughout the Dominion." Hall has been manufacturing and patenting improvements to farm machinery since 1860.

"The ice on our coasts is without precedent," Henry Cundall confides to his diary on 17 April. The regular steamer service between Summerside and Shediac still cannot begin its season. There is too much ice.

1882

Tryon's handsome new Methodist Church is formally opened.

"We saw his intense look of pre-Rafaelite wonder as he viewed the walls, gazed on the beauty of the platform, and sniffed the redolent smells of stale eggs, butter and cabbage." On 11 October, Oscar Wilde's North American lecture tour makes a stop at Charlottetown's Market Hall. Wilde preaches that even ordinary objects should be made beautiful, but the audience seems more interested in his knee breeches. He goes on to fame and scandal;

Marco Polo

Engraving by Russel Peirce

"The Fastest Ship in the World." Built in Saint John in 1851, the *Marco Polo* was one of the most famous vessels in Canadian history when it ended its career on a Cavendish sandbar.

Charlottonians start painting their houses brighter colours.

On 12 September HMS *Phoenix,* one of the Royal Navy's newest and most sophisticated warships, wrecks on East Point Reef. The crew gets ashore safely, but the ship is lost.

The Tryon Woolen Manufacturing Co. is incorporated. It takes over from the pioneer mill established by W. W. Lord and Charles Stanfield.

It's one of the worst winters in living memory. On 12 May, in eastern King's County, there is so much snow people are still using sleighs to get around.

New Glasgow's Cornelius O'Brien is named Archbishop of Halifax.

1883

New lighthouses girdle the Island like a string of Christmas lights. The new, square tower at Cardigan River is 32 feet high.

The winter steamer *Northern Light* spends most of the winter bottled up in harbour by heavy ice. Islanders are wondering: "What good is a winter steamer that can't operate in winter?"

The launching of Summerside's *P.E. Island Agriculturalist,* a weekly newspaper catering to the interests of Island farmers, underscores the increasing importance of the province's number one industry.

"The gold fever is striking hard here," a West Prince observer writes the *Examiner*. Traces of gold and silver have been found at Cape Wolfe. Now everybody thinks they've found more: at Souris, in Tignish and on Robertson's Island.

The *Daily Examiner* reports that the Colorado potato beetle has reached Prince Edward Island.

On 21 January, Peter Fraser and Nathan Squires set out from Bangor for Lot 65 on a hunt-

62

ing expedition. Trapped by a weeklong blizzard, they succumb to starvation and exposure. Their bodies — and Fraser's diary — are found the following spring.

"Old Hatch, The Charlottetown Crier"

Sketch by Robert Harris

Town crier John Hatch was a frequent sight on Charlottetown streets in the mid-1800s. In his old age, after his sight failed, he was guided on his rounds by his adopted son Johnny, who got to ring the bell.

MacDonald and MacDonald's lobster factory at St. Columba burns down. Building and contents, insured for $4,000, are lost.

On 22 July, ten-year-old Johnny Hatch burns most of the block on the northwest corner of Queen and Grafton Streets, including the police station and his adopted parents' lodgings. "Little Johnny" was well-known around town as the assistant to his father, town crier John Hatch. He is sent off to Boston's "Home for Little Wanderers."

On 25 July, the *Marco Polo*, once touted as the fastest ship in the world, is intentionally run ashore at Cavendish — to avoid sinking in deep water. Also dubbed "Queen of the Seas," the vessel's fame is long past. The first notice of the wreck reports that a "Norwegian barque named *Mark Apollo*" came ashore.

On 30 August, a rogue wave capsizes the Lunenburg fishing schooner *Welcome* off Campbell's Cove. Nine men are drowned; one survivor clings to the rigging for a night and a day before being rescued.

Financially stable but feeling a trifle anxious after the recent collapse of the Bank of Prince Edward Island, the Union Bank of Prince Edward Island (established in 1864) amalgamates with the Bank of Nova Scotia.

A Bell telephone representative, Robert Angus, signs up 11 subscribers at $30 per year. Although a telephone exchange needs at least 25 subscribers to be viable, Angus is hopeful the service will catch on.

An Island emigrant warns the *Patriot*'s readers that smallpox is ravaging the Colorado mining town of Leadville, a magnet for Islanders hoping to cash in on the state's silver bonanza. Although the "boom" has departed Leadville, at least one Islander is doing well there. Years later, George F. Campion of Souris reputedly leaves $15 million to each of his three children.

1884

On 15 August, the second annual National Acadian Convention is held in Miscouche. The delegates adopt an Acadian flag (the French tricolour with a gold star in the blue section) and a national anthem ("Ave Maris Stella"). New words are intended for the latter, but they never materialize.

Ex-politician Andrew A. Macdonald, the Island's postmaster general and a Father of Confederation, is commissioned as Lt. Governor.

The Prince Edward Island Hospital formally opens in a building on Longworth Avenue. Two homes and nearly a century later, it merges into the new Queen Elizabeth Hospital. The P.E.I. Hospital's first home survives as an apartment building.

"Beat this who can!" In the midst of a bragging war about big eggs, the *Examiner* for 7 May crows about a "champion" egg belonging to A. Herman exhibited at its office. The monster is 71/2" around and weighs 51/2 ounces. Poor hen!

Kilmahumig
Meacham's Atlas, 1880

The *Patriot* for 20 May reports: "there are very large quantities of ice off West Point, some parts being covered with blood. The ice is supposed to be from the Newfoundland coast, and probably has been part of a field on which the seal fishery was prosecuted"

On 24 May, Charlottetown observes its first Arbor Day. Volunteers plant hundreds of trees in a valiant attempt to beautify the City. Arbor Day quickly becomes a local tradition.

On 18 October, Robert Houston Horne of Bloomfield makes a chilling entry in his diary: "Peter Cain's little child stolen out of the house by a woman."

On 12 May, heavy pack ice crushes the coal steamer *Tunstall*, sending her to the bottom a few miles off Covehead. Most of the crew walk to shore; the rest use a boat.

On 20 February, the south side of Queen's Square along Richmond Street is razed by fire. Over the next decade the street, once called "Cheapside," is rebuilt in fine style, becoming "Victoria Row" — one of Canada's architectural jewels.

26 January is the coldest day ever recorded on Prince Edward Island. James Hunter, observer for the Meteorological Service, reports a low temperature of 37.2 C° at his farm, Kilmahumaig, near Alberton.

Stanhope-born (but Boston-raised) Henry Havelock Oxley becomes the first "Islander" to play major league baseball. He catches several games for the New York Gothams before returning to a semi-professional league.

1885

The newly formed Telephone Company of Prince Edward Island holds its first board meeting.

George Howlan

A long-serving MLA from Prince County, George Howlan was named to the Senate in 1864. He resigned in 1879, was re-appointed in 1880; resigned again to run in the 1891 General Election and was re-appointed for a third time after losing the contest. He resigned for the third (and final) time in 1894 to become the Island's Lt. Governor.

Senator George Howlan has the perfect solution to the problem of winter communications to the Island. Instead of trying to go over the ice by steamer or flimsy iceboats, he suggests going *under* the Strait by tunnel or subway. Estimated cost? Around $15,000,000. Howlan incorporates The Northumberland Straits Tunnel Railway Co. and offers to build the structure. All that Ottawa has to give him is the winter steamer subsidy, the P.E.I. Railroad and a bit of cash to get things started. Islanders think he's onto something.

The community of Pownal greets is first, and only, newspaper. The *Pownal Argus* isn't even typeset. The handwritten monthly lasts two issues, writer's cramp presumably having crippled the publisher.

The roller skating craze sweeping North America reaches Summerside as Mr. Muttart opens his Roller Skating Rink on the upper floor of Montgomery's Hall. "It is oval in shape, and laid with narrow pine flooring. It is a little over 90 feet long and 30 feet wide. The walls and ceilings have been plastered and white washed and gaily decorated with Chinese lanterns, oil paintings, chromos and bunting. Every afternoon is set aside for ladies only."

A smallpox epidemic strikes Charlottetown and fear stalks the city. Of 119 people infected, 53 will die.

On 27 January, a sudden storm traps three ice-boats, containing 22 crew and passengers, on Northumberland Strait. Huddled under a shelter made of two overturned boats, the party burns the other for warmth as they drift down the Strait for two days. They finally come ashore near Argyle Shore. Loss of life is narrowly averted; frostbite and pneumonia aren't.

The first electric lights are switched on in Prince Edward Island as Charlottetown debuts a string of electric streetlights. "There is no doubt that ere long electricity will become as familiar to us as gas or kerosene," the *Examiner* forecasts, "and it behooves us to keep pace with the times and not remain forever in our sleepy hollow."

Ex-meteorological observer Henry Cundall writes: "We have had the most beautiful season ever remembered here. . . ." The memorable weather persists well into fall.

Between 1881 and 1885, Island shipyards launch only 77 vessels. Although Islanders hope the industry will rebound, its glory days are over.

1886

"A blue-eyed calamity, waiting to strike," Trout River's Larry Gorman has settled in Maine. Although he makes much

Gardens at Holman House, Summerside, c1880

Watercolour by George Ackerman

of his living cutting timber in the lumber woods, he'll be remembered for his satiric, often caustic folk songs.

On 8 January, death ends the career of John LePage, "the Island Minstrel." Published in newspapers, sold in broadsheets, and collected in two anthologies, his occasional poems and local satires have earned him a reputation as the "Island's Poet Laureate."

On 24 May the Island's pioneer rugby team, the Abegweits, play their first game, against Pictou. They win.

On 1 July 7,000 spectators crowd a racing oval in Summerside to witness the first harness racing meet ever held in the town. Tremendous interest has been generated in the contest, a match race between Robert McLeod's imported speedster

Hernando and the Island-bred trotter Black Pilot. Black Pilot wins in a blazing time of 2:35 1/2.

1887

The cornerstone is laid for Charlottetown's new brick city hall on the corner of Queen and Kent Streets. The Romanesque Revival building, designed by Phillips and Chappell, is ready by the following year.

At a "Great Tunnel Meeting" in Charlottetown's Market Hall, Senator George Howlan announces that Prime Minister John A. Macdonald has promised to build a tunnel to the Mainland. It is, after all, election time.

The *Summerside Journal* warns: "Counterfeit $2 notes of the Union Bank of Prince Edward Island are in circulation in New Brunswick. Watch out for them."

The Charlottetown Water Works Act establishes a Commission of Water and Supply and lays the legislative foundation for supplying clean water to the Island's capital from the Winter River basin. The following year, a brick pumping station will open on the Malpeque Road. It's still there.

City Council resolves that city houses should be numbered "that the addresses of our citizens may be more easily found and also that postal delivery may be secured." The resulting addresses are used until 1907.

The *Summerside Journal* notes: "Mr. Holman's garden is looking its best, and it is no wonder that persons delight to linger around it. When will Summerside have a public garden, even of the moderate dimensions of Queen's Square garden in Charlottetown?"

Owen Connolly

💲 On 27 December Owen Connolly, reputedly the richest man on Prince Edward Island, dies, leaving much of his estate to charity. Connolly is an Island "rags to riches" story. Arriving without a penny to his name, he built a mercantile fortune during the boom years and managed to hold on to it after the collapse.

1888

🍁 Charlottetown's Council and civil administration move out of their quarters in the Market Building and into their new City Hall.

🧭 Instead of a tunnel, Ottawa orders a new winter steamer for the Island. *Stanley*, built in Glasgow and named for Canada's new Governor General, is built of steel and boasts 907 horsepower. Unlike the old *Northern Light*, *Stanley* can actually break through light ice. Unfortunately, she also has a habit of riding up on thicker ice pans and, sometimes, staying there.

⚖️ On 12 October, stranded in Souris harbour by bad weather and worse catches, drunken American fishermen tangle with local citizens. In the ensuing riot, one of the fishermen, a Nova Scotian named Joseph Strophe is killed. On hearing the news, the dead man's distraught wife is said to have cursed the women of the community. "May you all die widows, like me!" Given the general tendency of husbands to die before their wives it was, you must admit, a pretty canny curse to impose.

⚖️ After a sensational trial, William Millman is found guilty of murdering Mary Tuplin of Margate. Still protesting his innocence, he is hanged.

 Although it is not known when the first individuals arrived, by this year several families from southern Lebanon have settled in the Charlottetown area. By the early 1900s, a small but thriving Lebanese community is established.

🖋️ Frederick's Publishing Co. advertises in the Charlottetown *Herald* for "ten reliable men to canvas for Prince Edward Island Directory; big pay to the right men." Frederick apparently finds them; the Directory appears in 1889.

🏇 On 30 August nearly 6,000 spectators crowd Green Brothers' new racetrack in Summerside for a rematch between Hernando and Black Pilot. Black Pilot wins again, shaving almost three seconds off of his previous time.

Dr. Roderick Macdonald
Born in 1858, "Dr. Roddie" was named "The Dean of Canada's Physicians" in the 1950s. He practiced for 70 years, lived to be 103 and attributed his vigour to buttermilk and boiled potatoes.

⚕️ Fresh from the University of Toronto medical school, Dr. Roderick Macdonald comes home to St. Peter's to establish a medical practice. Seventy years later, at the age of 100, he decides to retire.

 Santa Claus makes one of his first personal appearances in

S.S. Stanley, c1895
Built in 1888 as a "winter steamer," the *Stanley* spent many frustrating days – and months – confined to port because of ice conditions during her tenure here.

Seaside Hotel, Rustico, c1875

In traversing this Island and visiting the private houses and living in the hotels, one is pleasantly reminded of the Old World; there is not much bustle and there is much more comfort.

W. Fraser Rae, *Newfoundland to Manitoba,* 1876

Charlottetown — accompanied by his son! — at the Diamond Bookstore. Santa's appearance fails to inspire the *Examiner's* editorial staff. "It is hard to write or say anything new about Christmas," they write, displaying a singular lack of imagination. "It comes to us year after year, bringing with it joy and gladness and often reconciliation to severed friends."

1889

Stanhope's Seaside Inn, later known as the Stanhope Resort Hotel, opens for business. Built by a local farm family, it hopes to take advantage of a new but promising industry — tourism.

Merchant Jebediah S. Carvell is named Lt. Governor. The Newcastle N.B. native sought his fortune in Australia, California and Oregon before settling in Charlottetown in 1860. Like T. Heath Haviland, he resigned his seat in the Senate to take the appointment.

The Island Farmer is revived by the Pioneer Publishing Co.

The Charlottetown Driving Park and Provincial Exhibition Association, incorporated in 1888, stages its first race card at the still-unfinished Charlottetown Oval. There are two events, each a best-of-five series of dashes.

McLeod & Stewart of Charlottetown cause quite a stir

when they exhibit a sample bale of prepared peat moss from their peat bog on Lot 48. Envisioned as a substitute bedding for livestock, the peat bale fails to replace straw.

Some people have dogs or cats; merchant and lobster packer Caleb Carleton of Souris has a golden eagle. Three feet high with a wingspan of seven feet, it was found on the shore at Little Harbour — totally exhausted — after a southerly gale in October.

Despite widespread opposition — "Local time," thundered one Liberal opponent of the measure, "meets the aspirations of local people" — Prince Edward Island adopts Standard Time. On 9 May, in the quiet of night, the Commissioner of Public Works climbs to the clock tower at the Law Courts building and adjusts the hands ahead 12 minutes and 29 seconds.

Forest fire rages through West Prince County. Between 24 and 26 September, communities from Portage to Bloomfield lose more than 30 houses, barns, mills and other buildings. Hundreds of acres of woodland are consumed. Hundreds of telegraph poles disappear

Charlottetown Driving Park, c1890

A growing passion for harness racing began to grow on the Island in the 1880s. Racing ovals sprang up around the province, but the most elaborate track was in Charlottetown. The wooden grandstand seen here was completed in 1890. This may be a photo of the 1893 Provincial Exhibition and Harness Racing Meet, which offered a total purse of $1,300.

Water Street, Summerside, c1893

The brick building being constructed on the left is R.T. Holman's new department store – the biggest on the Island. To the right is the clothing store operated by John MacKenzie. A MacKenzie suit won honourable mention at the Paris Exhibition of 1878 and "knocked the spots off everything" at the 1880 Dominion Exhibition.

and it takes several days to get a train over burned stretches of track.

🔬 The *Summerside Journal* reports that Laurent Doucette of Kildare Station "says that he has his flying machine now completed." Doucette is charging 10¢ a look. Neighbours nickname him "L'Oiseau" — "the Bird." He's better remembered as a folksong writer.

🔬 Beecher Crosby of West River shows off his new invention, an improved brake for wagons, at the Provincial Exhibition.

☀ A vicious nor-easter topples over the lighthouse at North Rustico by undermining the bank on which it was erected. The light is subsequently moved back onto safer ground.

1890

🌹 The grandstand of the newly constructed Charlottetown Driving Park is completed just in time for the grand opening of the first combined Provincial Exhibition and harness-racing meet.

⚖ Neil MacLeod's Tories secure a narrow two-seat majority in the provincial election. Within a year, victory is converted into defeat by a series of by-election losses, ending eleven years of Conservative government.

🖋 Dedicated to defending the Roman Catholic cause, a new weekly newspaper called *The Watchman* begins publication.

Lucy Maud Montgomery

🖋 7 December—"...the proudest day of my life!" writes a young L.M. Montgomery in her journal. Living with her father and stepmother in Prince Albert, Saskatchewan, she has just received word that the Charlottetown *Patriot* has printed her first publication, a poem on the legend of Cape Leforce.

🖋 The Charlottetown *Guardian* begins "covering the Island like the dew."

W.R. Bovyer's Milk Wagon, c1910

Butter was most precious. To provide in the short summer a supply for the winter demanded resolution against children clamouring for milk and cream. In later years when it became the habit of some to send the milk to the factory, the children were stinted; they were deprived of the by-products, the skimmed milk, the buttermilk, the whey, the curds; and the Master's wife always protested that she could discover the families that sent milk to the factory by the starved look of their children.

– Andrew Macphail, *The Master's Wife*

George "Budge" Byers emigrates to New England. His 100-bout boxing career will include matches with the top heavyweights of the day.

On 7 February, the Hillsborough Hockey Club stages the first men's hockey game ever in the province. Played in the Hillsborough Rink, the game ends in an 8-8 tie.

Prime Minister Sir John A. Macdonald, the Grand Old Man of Canadian politics, pays a complimentary visit to Summerside as part of an Island tour. It is his third visit to the town — and his last. Within a year he is dead.

The Island welcomes the Rt. Hon. Sir Frederick Arthur Stanley, Governor General of Canada, and Lady Stanley on an official visit. Islanders already know Sir Arthur as the namesake of their valiant winter steamer, S.S. *Stanley*. Canadians will later know him as the donor of the Stanley Cup.

On 18 September, ten hours of torrential rain deluges the Island with 5.5 inches of rain — an unprecedented downpour.

Between 1886 and 1890, 52 vessels are launched from Island shipyards.

1891

Supreme Court judge James Horsfield Peters retires from the bench, ending a 43-year term, the longest in Island history. A former land agent, he has never been popular, but he is a very good jurist. Two of his sons will serve as premier and a grandson will win the Victoria Cross.

A series of by-election victories puts Frederick Peters' Liberals in power.

It is census day on Prince Edward Island. The province's population reaches a new high of 109,078 but it is an in-

Water Street, Charlottetown, 1894
The blizzard of 15 January, 1894 was considered "the worst for many years." This photo was taken shortly after it ended. In an era before automobiles, care was taken to shovel sidewalks but streets were left snow covered, allowing easy passage for horse and sleigh.

crease of only 287 people in the last decade. As the tide of outmigration gains strength, the total will soon begin to fall.

Naturalist Francis Bain publishes *The Natural History of Prince Edward Island*. Authorized as a textbook in Island schools, it is still considered the best general description of the Island's geology, botany and zoology.

The Charlottetown Athletic Association, precursor of the famous Abegweit Amateur Athletic Association, is formed. The Abegweit Club will be the dominant multi-sport club in eastern Canada.

Harness racing is seizing the popular imagination and tracks are springing up all over the province. On 26 September a crowd of nearly 2,000, swelled by arrivals on a special train from Charlottetown, attends the opening card at the new trotting park in Souris.

When the species becomes extinct in 1914, it will be remembered that this was the last year a passenger pigeon was sighted here.

On 16 October, Charlottetown native William Turnbull of the S.S. *Baltimore* is attacked by an anti-American mob on the streets of Valparaiso, Chile. When he dies on 25 October, his murder sparks an international incident that will bring the United States and Chile to the brink of war.

1892

Supporters of a fixed link stage a great "Tunnel Tea" at Cape Traverse. Special attractions include boat tours to where test bores are assessing the seabed under the Northumberland Strait and "the great wonder of the age," the phonograph.

Of the seven newspapers thought to have been published in Souris during the 19th century, only one issue of one paper, the *Souris News*, remains extant.

The New Perth Dairying Co., sponsored by Dominion Dairy Commissioner James W. Robertson and formed by local farmers, opens its cheese factory. Within a year 10 more incorporate, and New Perth has inspired the emergence of the Island dairy industry.

Shipwreck, location unknown, c1890
There were upwards of 700 shipwrecks off the Island's coastline between 1750 and 1950.

The Island becomes the last province in the Maritimes to pass a Medical Act calling for the examination and licensing of physicians.

Lumberjack Jerome Maillet from Palmer Road dies in Bethel, Maine, a few months after being crushed by a falling tree. A ballad composed in French on his tragic death by Laurent Doucette of St. Louis, P.E.I., will be sung throughout all Eastern Canada.

On 22 August the worst gale in 20 years, a rare sou-easter, savages the Island with 60 to 100 km winds. At Souris, 100 feet of breakwater is washed away, while a 1,000-ton barque, the *Gazelle* is driven ashore near Wood Islands. All over the province, buildings and trees are toppled.

Jacob Gould Schurman of Freetown is named President of Cornell University. He will later become a diplomat, serving as American Ambassador to China and Germany. Once touted as a Republican candidate for President, he is probably the only Islander to have a street in a town in Germany (Heidelburg) named after him!

Island-born James Jeffrey Roche is commissioned to write the poem that will be read to dedicate the Gettysberg War Memorial.

1893

The Masonic Temple Opera House, the finest and most elegant of Charlottetown's theatres, opens on Grafton Street, just west of Queen, with a performance of *A Russian Honeymoon.*

Prince Edward Island loses its upper house when the Legislative Council is merged with the House of Assembly to form the Legislative Assembly. The new arrangement is unique in Canada: 15 dual ridings each elect one "Councillor" and one "Assemblyman." Premier Frederick Peters leads the Liberals to power in the reformed House, winning 23 seats to the Conservatives' seven.

L'Impartial, the Island's first French-language newspaper, is launched in Tignish by the Buote family.

On 4 March, the first womens' hockey game is played in the province.

The Charlottetown Club is established. In later years a local wit, noting the Club's proximity to Province House, Queen's Square School and St. Dunstan's Basilica quips: "On Great George Street you'll find legislation, education, salvation and damnation!"

A puzzled *Patriot* reports on 21 December: "The ice up the East River yesterday was ripped up for about 200 yards in length, and large pieces thrown a considerable distance in the air, by some unaccountable eruption." Several peo-

Composing Room of L'Impartial, c1900

ple and a team of horses had just been on the spot. "This is the second phenomenon of this kind within the last few years on the East River."

The first Acadian school inspector, Joseph-Octave Arsenault makes his inaugural report.

The P.E.I. Acadian Teachers' Association is founded in Charlottetown.

On 16 January, in a desperate attempt to make safe harbour at the island of Miquelon, the Alberton-based schooner *Gracie M. Parker* drives onto the rocks in a blinding snowstorm. All seven crewmen are lost, plunging Alberton into gloom and inspiring a well known folk song.

A 31 May fire in Georgetown begins in a stable on Main Street and consumes five houses and their outbuildings, plus the Salvation Army hall before residents wrestle it under control.

Income tax is levied in Prince Edward Island for the first time; the rate is 1% on incomes over $350.

1894

Merchant and political war horse, George W. Howlan, is commissioned as Lt. Governor. Never shy, Howlan has been lobbying for the appointment since 1884.

Charlottetown marvels at an early Chinese immigrant. Two years out from his homeland, he has arrived from Montreal intending to open a laundry. He does.

The O'Leary Trotting Park opens to a public absorbed by harness racing.

Only three years after the game's invention, the first basketball match is played on Prince Edward Island.

Robert Olton forms a partnership with Charles Dalton.

Both are interested in breeding silver foxes in captivity. Silver foxes — so-called because of the silver tips on their black fur — are one of the rarest animals in nature. In a society where being rich means wearing fur, silver fox pelts fetch extraordinary prices. When Oulton succeeds in creating a stock that will breed true in captivity, he and Dalton create an industry that will make a handful of Islanders wealthy beyond their wildest dreams.

Charles Dalton

Charles Dalton was a mildly-prosperous Alberton merchant when he teamed up with Robert Oulton in the early 1890s. In a world mad for exotic furs, their aim was to create a method to breed the rare and precious silver fox in captivity. They succeeded, and Dalton become one of the Island's richest individuals. He was honoured with the Papal Knighthood and an appointment as Lt. Governor later in life.

The Charlottetown *Examiner* reports that the Vernon River cheese factory is receiving 14,000 lbs. of milk daily from local farmers. In June, 318 cheeses were made at the factory, one of dozens established in the province during this decade.

On 26 September General William Booth, founder of the Salvation Army, lectures in the Methodist Church — now Trinity

United — in Charlottetown.

A spring snowstorm on 26 April catches lobster fishermen by surprise. At least two schooners are lost at sea, and lobster factories across the province report boats missing.

On 8 December, a major fire devastates the village of Mount Stewart.

The smallest chartered bank in Canada closes its doors as the Bank of Rustico's charter expires.

A major snowstorm grips the province over 14 and 15 January. A northwesterly gale whips the heavy snowfall into 20-foot drifts; rail lines are blocked; and the winter steamer *Stanley* is stranded out on the Northumberland Strait.

In the swan song for shipbuilding at Mount Stewart, once the Island's busiest shipyard, Angus MacDonald of Pisquid launches the *Hillsborough*, a side-wheeler commissioned by the Island government. She plies the Charlottetown Rocky Point ferry route for the next 40 years.

1895

Duncan Marshall organizes a provincial off-shoot of the Patrons of Industry on the Winsloe Road with 12 members. The reform-minded farmers' party contests one by-election — and comes third.

Joseph-Octave Arsenault makes history when he becomes the first Island Acadian to be named to the Canadian Senate. A successful merchant and lobster packer, he is a 27-year veteran of the Island legislature and father of a future premier.

"West Wind blow from your prairie nest. . .": Critically acclaimed Canadian Mohawk poet E. Pauline Johnson gives a reading at the Charlottetown Opera House on 7 August. Charmed but not entirely won over, the *Examiner* praises her "high poetic and dramatic talent if not genius."

The Hillsboro Dairying Co. opens at Mount Herbert.

The Hazelbrook Dairying Co. Ltd. is incorporated with shares divided among participating farmers. It soon becomes one of the largest wholesale and retail cheese and butter factories in the province.

Government statistics reveal that lobster and oats top the Island's list of international exports. Two old trading partners, the U.S. and Britain, receive the bulk of P.E.I.'s $1,037,947 worth of exports.

A Halifax newspaper describes the perfectly-proportioned woman — at least according to the *New York Weekly*. A 5'5" woman should weigh between 138 and 148 pounds with a 34" bust and a 24" waist. The perfect face should feature a round head, large forehead, small ears, large eyes and narrow eyebrows!

On 7 July James Peake, Jr., once one of the richest individuals on the Island, dies in poverty in Vancouver, B.C. His fortune was wiped out by the collapse of the economy in 1880 and the heavy debt incurred while building his luxurious home, Beaconsfield. Leaving behind his wife and family, the bankrupt merchant had emigrated from the Island in 1884 in search of employment. His is not the only death his wife, Edith (Haviland) Peake has to deal with. On 11 September her father, Thomas Heath Haviland, Jr. dies in Charlottetown after a distinguished career. A leading Conservative politician, he has also been a Senator and Lt. Governor.

Cannery Crew, Murray Harbour, c1900

On entering the first thing you see is the immense round boilers, built around with brick and cement. Into these boilers the lobsters are plunged when they come from the boats. . . . Long tables are provided, on which they are placed when taken out of the boiler, and after the 'cracker' has done his work, the meat of the tails and claws is picked out by girls and placed in cans of different sizes; but usually they hold about one pound.
— *Charlottetown Examiner*, 1890

Ada Johnson, c1895

The invention of the "safety bicycle" in 1885 helped free Victorian women like Charlottetown's Ada Johnson from fashionable inactivity.

"BICYCLE BLOOMERS have not yet become fashionable in Charlottetown, but we are daily taking orders for KNICKERBOCKERS from many of our wheelmen," boasts tailor D.A. Bruce. For now, it appears women will continue to ride the new safety bicycles clad in dresses.

 On 30 March a major fire destroys six buildings in Summerside's business core.

Summerside Electric Co. presents the town with its first electric bill — $6.92.

In sharp decline since 1880, the shipbuilding industry

hits historic low production figures. Between 1891 and 1895, Island shipyards launch only 18 vessels — mostly small fishing schooners. From a peak of 35,000 tons in 1866, the industry now struggles to launch 600 tons per year.

1896

The *Daily Examiner* reports a name change by Islanders with apparent Tory sympathies. At the suggestion of Seymour Young, they have called their community Earnscliffe after Sir John A. Macdonald's Ottawa residence.

St. Paul's Church, Charlottetown, c1860

Our church had high pews so when the Children were young they were allowed to sit on a Hassock and look for pictures in the Prayer Book.

– Diary of Francis Hale Orlebar, c1920

The first services are held in the new stone St. Paul's Anglican Church, one of architect W.C. Harris' most beautiful creations.

American oil magnate Alexander McDonald builds Dalvay-by-the-Sea — so-called to differentiate it from his main mansion in Cincinnati, also named Dalvay.

The Legislature approves construction of a roadway leading from West Street along the harbourside to Victoria Park.

The Patrons of Industry of PEI launch their official organ. The *Patron of Industry*'s causes include votes for women, reduced government spending, abolition of the Senate, fairer tariffs and taxes. It is slightly ahead of its time.

On 1 September, a devastating fire sweeps through Tignish, reducing 70 buildings to ashes.

1897

Premier Frederick Peters leads his Liberal government to re-election with a 19 seat to 11 victory. Shortly afterwards, Peters decides to move to British Columbia, turning the Premiership over to A.B. Warburton. Sometime in 1899, Peters remembers to resign from his seat in the Legislature.

On 6 March, William Grant & Co. sponsor a free magic lantern show. The entertainment consists mainly of views from New York City, but includes a number of local scenes as well. The captive audience is also subjected to introductory remarks extolling the business virtues of Grant & Co.

On 31 March, the Charlottetown Abegweits beat the Summerside Stars 4-3 to become the first Island Senior Hockey champions.

On 6 June, the great John Philip Sousa's Band performs in Charlottetown to an appreciative audience. In their honour, the band plays "The Charlottetown Gallop," presumably composed for the occasion.

On 22 June over 10,000 Islanders gather in Victoria Park to celebrate Queen Victoria's Diamond Jubilee.

The Abegweit Grounds are opened at the northern end of Upper Prince Street. It is the Island's first outdoor athletic complex.

1898

Bishop J. C. Macdonald lays the cornerstone for the new brick Notre-Dame-du-Mont-Carmel church.

The Acadian community mourns the death of its two most influential politicians. Just two weeks before the new year, Joseph-Octave Arsenault, the first Island Acadian named to the Senate and one of the leading figures in the province's Acadian "Renaissance," died at his home in Abram's Village. Then, on 24 February, the community lost Stanislaus Perry. A native of Tignish, Perry was the first Acadian to sit in the Island's Legislature and, in 1874, became the first Acadian ever elected to the House of Commons.

The Dundas Dairy Association turns out its first cheeses at a factory in the King's County

Dalvay-by-the-Sea

village. The plant will operate into the 1950s.

The Charlottetown Sewerage Act provides for construction of a modern sewage disposal system for the Island capital. The result pollutes the Hillsborough River, but Charlottetown's streets and backyards certainly smell better.

"The whole scene is indescribable and there is none finer this side of Boston." In James Paton & Co.'s "immense" Charlottetown store, "six magnificent arches with spruce and other garlands, studded with [151!] electric lights span the centre of the store."

1899

On 11 January, strong tides undermine the base of the Rustico lighthouse, toppling it into 12 feet of water

Ottawa sends a powerful new winter steamer, *Minto*, to help the beleaguered *Stanley* maintain winter links to the mainland.

In a letter to Liberal Premier Donald Farquharson, Liberal Prime Minister Sir Wilfrid Laurier rejects P.E.I's claims for increased federal subsidies. A quarter century

of Confederation has seen little but economic hardship and population decline for the Island.

Dr. Peter A. McIntyre of Souris, a Roman Catholic, is commissioned as Lt. Governor after considerable intrigue, including an alleged promise from the Bishop of Charlottetown that he will endorse the Liberals during the forthcoming federal election.

W.H. Crosskill publishes *Prince Edward Island, Garden Province of Canada: With Information for Tourists*. With the tide of immigration long past, the emphasis in descriptive literature has shifted to information for visitors.

"There ought to be a Prince Edward Island Magazine," cries the *Guardian*, "and here it is!" Charlottetown printer Archibald Irwin publishes the first edition of the *Prince Edward Island Magazine*, inviting submissions "on any subject likely to prove interesting." He gets history, short stories, poetry, literary reviews and essays galore. His new venture prospers.

The Prince Edward Island Hockey League is formally organized.

In an age that is not delicate on the subject of weight, a local newspaper reports that the five Bearisto sisters have weighed in at a combined total of 1,169 lbs. It makes no mention of their brothers' weight.

Offering reduced fares to the Prairies, Canadian railways sponsor the first Harvest Excursion. The trip out west to work on the grain harvest becomes an annual event for many young Islanders.

On 27 November Charles Coghlen, founder of an actors' colony at Fortune, dies in Galveston, Texas. Some years later, a great storm washes his coffin out of his Texas cemetery. The *Daily Examiner* reports its recovery, but Ripley later claims Coghlen floated clear back to Fortune. Believe It or Not!

An omen for the coming century? A meteor flashes over the Island an hour before midnight on New Year's Eve. A phone call from Souris reports the meteor falling to earth "a short distance in the rear of the town, exploding as it fell with a report that equalled the loudest thunder."

An amendment to the education act allows women to sit on school boards.

On 25 October, the first of three Transvaal Contingents is given a heroes' send-off by 4,000 well-wishers as it departs Charlottetown en route for South Africa. One hundred and twenty-five Islanders will end up serving in the Boer War. Two will die in battle.

An estimated 7,000 American tourists visit the Island. A decade ago tourism was a trickle. Now it's becoming a stream. Soon, it will be a flood.

James Curtis Shaw of Stanhope is named Principal of Vancouver College. Under his leadership the college forges an affiliation with McGill University, and in later years will be known as the

"S. S. MINTO" ENTERING GEORGETOWN HARBOR, P. E. ISLAND.

S.S. Minto, c1900

Built to assist the *Stanley* in providing winter steamer service, S.S. *Minto* was a larger, more powerful boat. Unfortunately it, too, was often confined to port because of heavy ice conditions.

University of British Columbia.

1900

Central Christian Church opens on Charlottetown's Kent Street and the cornerstone is laid for St. Mary's Roman Catholic Church, Indian River. Both are W. C. Harris designs.

The first automobile since Father Belcourt's ill-fated vehicle arrives on the Island. Steam powered, seating 12, the monster is imported by a local business syndicate, who offer 10¢ rides.

The provincial Prohibition Act is passed. Prohibition will go into effect in each county when a majority of voters choose to repeal the more permissive Canada Temperance Act.

Even though they've experienced three leaders in as many years, the Liberals are still able to win the Provincial election 21 seats to nine and retain power. The new Premier is Donald Farquarson, who replaced A.B. Warburton as leader the year before. Farquarson himself will resign in 1901, to be replaced by Arthur Peters, former Premier Frederick Peters' brother! The Premiership has become little more than a stepping

Fishing Stand Near Souris, **c1910**
Water for the cannery on the left was piped in across the inlet from a well on the hill to the right.

stone to more lucrative appointments.

On 4 August Mr. Ward, formerly of the 1st Leicester Regiment, gives an illustrated lecture in Georgetown on the war in South Africa.

The number of lobster canneries in the province peaks at 246. The lobster industry, recovered from near-collapse in the late 1880s, contributes an average of $500,000 per year to the provincial economy.

Alexander Gillis of Grandview finds a stalk of wheat 5'2" tall growing in his six acre grain field.

The P.E.I. Hospital moves into handsome new quarters on Kensington Road. The setting is marred somewhat by a noisy railway crossing and a nearby rifle range ("the Butts"), but the facilities prove adequate for the next three decades.

Imperial sentiment peaks on 2 November as Charlottetown welcomes home the 1st Transvaal Contingent from the Boer War. "It was the sight of a lifetime," wrote one observer. "As [the procession] passed along the street, the people all broke ranks to shake hands ... such a crush you never saw."

On 18 February, Roland Taylor of Charlottetown becomes an "Imperial Martyr" when he is killed at the Battle of Paardeberg. Eight days later one of his comrades, Alfred Riggs, also of Charlottetown, is killed in the same battle. They are the only Islanders killed in action during the Boer War.

It may be that the anxiety of entering the last century of the millennium has heightened some Islanders' sense of the miraculous. Legends and miracles cluster around the memory of Father Francis McDonald — for 60 years the pastor in Roman Catholic parish of St. George's — after his death on 9 July. On 15 September, the body of Father James Duffy is exhumed, 40 years after his death, for re-burial near the new church at Kelly's Cross. To the astonishment of those

"Pastoral Scene, Prince Edward Island," **c1900**
Although P.E.I. shares not the wild extravagancies and romantic scenery which characterizes her neighbours, the Traveller will be delighted with her milder and more feminine beauties and grace."
— C. Birch Bagster, *Progress and Prospects of Prince Edward Island,* 1861

75

Wedding Scene, St. Dunstan's Cathedral, 1900
The second St. Dunstan's Cathedral was little more than a stone shell when it hosted this fashionable wedding on 31 July, 1900. The groom is William Lewis Scott; the bride, Alice May Sullivan, daughter of the Island's first Roman Catholic Premier, W.W. Sullivan. This version of St. Dunstan's was begun in 1896, completed in 1907 but destroyed by fire in 1913.

present, his body is found to be almost perfectly preserved. For decades afterwards, parishioners use clay from his grave as a balm for small hurts.

On 25 August, while en route to Charlottetown from Summerside, Engine No. 6 derails near the Blueshank Road, killing engineer David Pound.

There'll be lots of coal for North Lake stockings this Christmas. A coal boat, the *Citizen*, comes ashore on 3 December in a snow storm just below the farm of Stephen MacDonald.

Ambrose Monaghan of Kinkora defies doubters of his home-manufactured farm equipment, promising 100 testimonials to its excellence on request.

On 1 August, Daniel McMillan and his horse are killed by lightning as they ride along St. Peter's Road.

On 11 October, a furious gale blows over the range lights at Tracadie, Brighton Beach, and Annandale.

Between 1896 and 1900, 16 vessels are launched from Island shipyards.

1901

On 22 January, Queen Victoria dies after a 64-year reign, the longest in British history. The Island was named after her father, her son was the first Royal to visit, but Victoria never strayed far from home. Most Islanders alive cannot remember when she was not the monarch.

On 8 February, the steamer *Stanley* frees her sister steamer *Minto* from the ice near Pictou, only to get stuck herself. The ice rafts her clear out of the water, and she spends the next month stranded on top of the floes.

The Island welcomes the new century with a decline in its population. The census reports the province's population has shrunk by almost 6,000 to 103,000.

On 18 August, Island-born George Godfrey dies in Boston, aged 49. Fighting as "Old Chocolate," he was one of the world's top heavyweight boxers in

Hillsborough Bridge Workers, c1903
These construction workers, nicknamed "sandhogs," are actually standing on the bottom of the Hillsborough River. They're working in one of the caissons that will support the second-hand railway bridge bought to span the Hillsborough River.

the 1880s, but racial prejudice cost him any chance at a world title.

In his first competition as an Abegweit, Bill Halpenny sets a Maritime record of ten feet, one inch in the pole vault. He will become one of the best vaulters in the world.

The Provincial Department of Agriculture is created. The first minister is the Hon. Benjamin Rogers.

The Children's Aid Society is organized. After a half-century of good works, it will be dissolved in 1954.

On 5 December Ambrose Atkins, night watchman on the Hillsborough Bridge construction project, is presumed drowned when workmen arrive to find only a trail of footsteps and his lantern. His body is not found; legend suggests he was accidentally buried in one of the bridge piers.

Charlottetown's *Daily Patriot* boasts that the Island hasn't had a divorce in over 30 years. Of course, it's easier to stay unhappily married than to get a divorce here, where the government refuses to constitute a divorce court. There won't be one until 1945.

The venerable Hickey & Nicholson Tobacco Co., in business since the 1850s, builds a new factory off Prince Street in Charlottetown. Employing 32 hands, it guarantees that Hickey & Nicholson will be a household name to generations of Island chewers and smokers.

Small fish swallow smaller fish. A special general meeting of the shareholders of the Summerside Bank agrees to a merger with the Bank of New Brunswick, ending 35 years of Island-based banking.

George Wightman, scion of a prominent shipbuilding family, launches the three-masted schooner *Empress*. At 349 tons, she is the largest vessel ever built at Montague. Her Island career lasts only 12 years, but she lingers on in local memory.

1902

On Christmas Day, amateur naturalist John McSwain conducts the Island's first Christmas Bird Count, one of the earliest such counts carried out in Canada. Problem is, he can't find any birds, and concludes they've all been driven south by the cold.

"While a great many people who leave this Island come back with their heads on right side up, quite a few come back seemingly with their brains topsy-turvey to everything but bright coloured dresses and slang grammar." So warns the *Daily Examiner*.

1903

Amid mild controversy, City Council considers a name change for the section of the Malpeque Road leading into Charlottetown. In the end "Elm Avenue" wins out over the early favourite, "Hooper Avenue." Decades later, "University Avenue" has the last word.

Soldier's Monument, Charlottetown

Dedicated to the memory of Alfred Riggs and Roland Taylor, the only two Islanders killed in action during the South African War, this monument was the first war memorial on Prince Edward Island.

On 6 July the Boer War Memorial, a bronze sculpture by Hamilton McCarthy of Ottawa, is formally dedicated on Queen's Square.

Market Building, Charlottetown, c1905

The market here is a unique institution that fails not to please and interest visitors. Semi-weekly come in from the surrounding districts market gardeners and women laden with the luscious products of this great garden, which they display temptingly in the two floors of the market building.
– U.S. Consul in Charlottetown, 1905

One of the most embarrassing episodes in the history of the winter steamer service begins on 13 January when the *Stanley* is stranded on an ice floe off Sea Cow Head. The *Minto* sails out to transfer the mails and passengers, delivers them to Georgetown then sets out to free her stranded sister ship, which continues to drift quietly down the Strait on its iceberg. On 25 February, after the *Minto* succeeds in bashing a path within a half mile of the *Stanley,* its propeller falls off. With both winter steamers stranded the Island is forced to rely on the iceboats for its main contact with the mainland. Explosives experts are brought in to blast the ice away, and on 17 March the *Stanley* breaks free and takes its erstwhile rescuer in tow. Nine weeks after setting out from Summerside, she enters port in Georgetown. Calls for an alternative to the winter steamer service intensify.

The P.E.I. Fish & Game Protection Association, promoted by Albert E. Morrison and E.T. Carbonell, is organized with the Lt. Governor as honourary president. Their aim is conserve fish and game for anglers and hunters.

The Farmers' Institute of Urbainville holds an agricultural exhibition which will eventually become the annual Egmont Bay and Mont Carmel Agricultural Exhibition.

Locals in Eastern King's call mid-January "Pig Day" — the day farmers ship hogs to the local pork packing plant. This year, much concern is expressed about "fish-fed hogs," and about renegade porkers running at large in the countryside.

A ghost is reported in a vacant house across the street from the Summerside Post Office. Hundreds of Summersiders gather to see if they can catch a glimpse. Perhaps bashful before large crowds, the ghost fails to appear.

***Sawmill, O'Leary,* c1910**

McAlpine's Directory for 1909 listed 200 mills of various sorts in 129 locations across the Island.

On 5 February, King's County residents are startled by a heavy thunder and lightning storm, the second in a week. An intense cold snap follows.

May is one of the coldest on record; local prognosticators estimate spring is nearly two weeks behind the previous year.

On 23 April, the *Examiner* reports the death of variety star Percy C. S. Paul in St. Paul, Minnesota. He was born in Charlottetown, the son of Capt. R. Paul. Today, he is, of course, totally forgotten.

1904

Charlottetown's fourth Market House, a beautiful stone building designed by William C. Harris, opens for business on Queen's Square. In Souris another Harris building, St. Mary's Roman Catholic Church is also officially opened.

Buoyed by the federal Party's re-election earlier in the fall, Arthur Peters' provincial Grits sweep to another electoral victory, taking 22 of 30 seats.

D.A. MacKinnon is named Lt. Governor.

A three-member Forestry Commission warns of "a timber famine" unless government takes steps to improve the quality and the acreage of the province's dwindling forests. The government acts; 25 years later it establishes a tree nursery.

Dr. Eliza Margaret Mac-Kenzie of Flat River comes back from medical school and sets up a practice in Charlottetown. Her time here is short. Within a year she has moved on.

On 12 April, the *Guardian*'s eastern correspondent reports another recurrence of the mysterious lights far out on the ice off East Point. It is a rare winter incidence of the mysterious phantom ship of the Northumberland Strait.

John McInnis and his family live on the Miminigash Road near Alberton. In early January they hear strange knocking noises outside their house, which they first dismiss as the wind or a neighbour playing a prank. But the knocking

78

Prince Battenberg's Squadron, 1905

continues, on calm nights and when they can find no one around the house. "So we told 'it' to come in and knock on the table," McInnis recounts, "and at once the sound ceased outside and resumed knocking on the table." Further questions, answered by knocks convince the McInnis' they are indeed dealing with a ghost. They ask it to go away. It does.

On 21 August the 53-ton schooner *Margaret Ann*, laden with coal, comes to grief on Governor's Island Reef in Hillsborough Bay.

Mount Mellick native James Jeffrey Roche is named American Consul in Switzerland. One of Boston's leading men of letters, he has carved out an enviable reputation as poet, editor and author.

Grade 5 Class, Prince Street School, 1927

It was no part of any master's business to teach; his business was to "hear the lessons," in proof that they had been learned. If they were not learned, the boy was whipped. If he had to be whipped repeatedly, that was proof he could not learn, and had better devote himself to some more useful occupation.

— Andrew Macphail, *The Master's Wife*

Luckily for these children, educational theory had changed since the 1860s, which Macphail was recalling, and the time this photo was taken.

1905

The cornerstone is laid for Souris' stone Post Office/Customs House.

On 20 December, Kensington's beautiful new "boulder" railway station is officially opened with speeches and a dance. Total cost $5,000.

Kensington Station, c1910

The Province is granted armorial bearings — the basis for a coat of arms. It features "a lion passant" surmounting the familiar oak tree and saplings. In full, technical terms, the bearings are: "Agent on an Island Vert, to the sinister an Oak Tree fructed, to the dexter thereof three Oak saplings sprouting all proper, on a Chief Gules a Lion passant guardant Or."

One of the fixtures around "Olde" Charlottetown, the little harbour ferry *Southport* goes to the wrecker's yard.

On 26 October, the first train travels over the new Murray Harbour Branch line, the largest extension of the P.E.I. Railroad since the main line was built.

"We must have it" is the rallying cry as the campaign for a Northumberland Strait tunnel reaches fever pitch. The *Guardian* announces that demand has far out-stripped its supply of "Tunnel Stamps." (Several thousand more are on order.) Hot on the heels of a huge pro-tunnel meeting in Charlottetown, a delegation headed by Father A. E. Burke of Alberton meets with Prime Minister Wilfrid Laurier. (The meeting takes place on April Fool's Day.) In June, the Charlottetown Board of Trade notes that until a tunnel is built, the Island could make do with an ice-breaking car ferry for its main link to the mainland. July the fifth sees the largest-yet "Tunnel Tea" at Cape Traverse. Organizers promise addresses from "Canada's best orators" and "princely entertainments." Ottawa remains strangely quiet on the issue.

"We Must Have It"
Northumberland Strait Tunnel
Stamp, c1905

In November the *Guardian* introduces a *Saturday Magazine*, designed to replace the now-defunct *Prince Edward Island Magazine*. In addition to arts, history and literature, the *Saturday Magazine* also delivers the Island's first "comic page" – in full colour! The first issue features "Willie Westinghouse" and "Pretending Percy."

On 24 July, Charlottetown celebrates its first Old Home Week. It is a reminder of how many expatriate Islanders there are to come home.

After The Fire, Summerside, 1906

A newspaper editorial notes that Charlottetown has almost completely converted to coal for cooking and heating. Wood is cleaner and "more cheerful," but almost impossible to obtain. However, a recent trip to Murray Harbour on the new rail line revealed "some fine tracts of hardwood along the route. A little hard work and enterprise..."

Classes begin at Macdonald Consolidated at Mount Herbert. Funded by tobacco magnate William C. Macdonald, the experiment in school consolidation and manual training takes place in a state-of-the-art school building costing the huge sum of $20,000. Several years later, when Macdonald offers to give the programme and building to the Province, the government pleads poverty and closes the facility down.

"There can be no doubt," predicts the *Guardian*, "that the gasoline engine is destined to revolutionize to a certain degree at least," the province's agriculture and fishery. Engine builders, like Charlottetown's soon-to-be-famous Stewart Foundry, are counting on it.

"The crops of 1904 will long be remembered for their deficiencies," reports the *Guardian*, "and the winter of 1905 for its severity." December, January, and February have been the snowiest in living memory. On 25 February, the *Examiner* reports that John P. Morris of Donaldston was forced to dig a tunnel 70 feet long to reach the livestock trapped in his barn. In mid-March, the *Guardian* reports that near East Point, John Bruce's sawmill is still covered with snow to a depth of two feet over the ridgepole. It takes a two-engined train 40 days to get from West Prince County to Charlottetown. Heavy ice in the strait prevents imported hay from reaching the Island. With barns bare after last summer's poor harvest, livestock begin to starve. "I used to love winter as I loved all the seasons." writes L.M. Montgomery in her journal in March. "Will I ever love it again I wonder?"

One of the snowiest winters on record is followed by one of the driest springs. By the first of June, farmers are fearing they may be in for an extended drought.

Thanks to the need for fishing schooners, the Island shipbuilding industry stages a brief recovery. Between 1901 and 1905, Island shipyards launch 26 vessels.

1906

Prince County joins Queens and Kings in opting to replace the Canada Temperance (or Scott) Act with the much tougher Provincial Prohibition legislation.

Charlottetown receives a heavy dose of culture on 5 June as renowned opera diva

Shoe Department, Holman's of Summerside, 1911

Robert Tinson Holman opened a small shop on Summerside's Water Street in 1857. By the early 1900s "Holman's" was one of the largest retail firms in the Maritimes, with a thriving mail order business and a huge, three-storey department store.

Madame Albani performs at the Market House. Albani, "a Canadian . . . universally regarded as the 'Prima Donna' of the British Empire," gets rave reviews.

The *Examiner* for 13 June reports: "At the Opera House last night, Pauline, the Hypnotist and Mind Reader, entertained a large audience. A very difficult feat of mind-reading was performed under the critical eye of a committee of citizens."

On 22 August, the centenary of Rev. Peter Gordon's arrival as the first Presbyterian minister on the Island is celebrated at West Covehead Church. Over 2,000 people sit down to a full-course meal.

Over a million people in Northern Japan are suffering from famine, reports the *Guardian*. An appeal is made to Islanders' sense of charity. Within a month a cheque for $577.11 is in the mail.

Chief John Sark is proving very popular during a tour of Eastern Canada. After appearing at an automobile show in Montreal, he is introduced to Prime Minister Laurier. On his way home, he takes Moncton by storm. "Chief Sark attracted great attention in the streets yesterday in his picturesque attire," reports a Moncton newspaper. "The Chief is a very striking figure."

The *Guardian* calls on the English-speaking world to adopt the metric system, but concedes "we must undo the old, which is as hard as to learn the new."

The *Guardian* announces the results of its "Twenty Most Eminent Islanders" survey. The top three? Louis Henry Davies, George Coles and Edward Whelan (all Liberal politicians, curiously). The balloting is sparse.

Louis Henry Davies

First elected in 1882, Charlottetown lawyer Louis Henry Davies won four consecutive elections and served in Wilfrid Laurier's cabinet until 1902, when he was appointed to the Supreme Court of Canada. He went on to become Chief Justice.

On 29 August the schooner *William Dunbar*, loaded with railway sleepers, is dismasted in a storm, then towed to Charlottetown by S.S. *City of Ghent*. She makes it — barely; she arrives with decks awash.

Charlottetown Railway Station, c1910

On 2 September, the *Ella M. Rose* wrecks spectacularly at Souris. While trying to run for the harbour, she crashes into the breakwater. Captain and crew have to jump onto the semi-submerged roadway and dance through the waves to shore.

On 6 September a dismasted vessel is reported labouring off Point Prim, but when the tug *Brant* goes out, she finds nothing. It was the schooner *Alma*, driven aground at Pinette. When her crew jumped on shore, waves carried the boat back to sea.

On 10 October, the Great Fire of Summerside consumes 155 buildings, devastating the County capital.

On 2 November, a wild November storm drives the steamer *Turret Bell* onto a shoal at Cable Head. All hands are saved from the wreck, which is within an arm's throw of the shore. After herculean labours, the vessel is refloated in 1909.

On 3 November the Newfoundland schooner *Orpheus*, en route to Quebec with a load of dried fish, runs aground at Priest Pond on the Island's North Side. The crew are saved.

On 5 November, the Norwegian barque *Olga* drives ground at Black Bush on the North Side during a wild storm on her way to pick up a cargo of lumber in New Brunswick for the Australian Market. Captain and crew are rescued by local residents.

On 6 November, ten crewmen are lost when the Norwegian barque *Sovinto* wrecks on Carew's Reef, near Priest Pond.

On 16 November the schooner *A. J. MacKean*, en route from Tignish to Alberton, wrecks on the Alberton bar.

Shareholders agree to sell the Merchants' Bank of P.E.I. to

Mussel Mud Diggers, O'Leary, 1908

the Canadian Imperial Bank of Commerce. When the agreement goes into effect on 1 June, the Island loses its last indigenous bank.

On 11 December the province's leading businessman, Robert Tinson Holman dies in Summerside, aged 73. After a rocky beginning, the New Brunswick-born Holman fashioned a mercantile empire that made "Holman's" a household word in his adopted province.

1907

When it was built in the early 1880s for tobacco magnate Sir William C. Macdonald, the barn at his family's estate near Tracadie was reputed to be the largest and most modern in the British Empire. On 4 December it burns to the ground in a spectacular blaze.

The second Charlottetown railway station opens on Weymouth St. It is 118 by 43 feet, built of Island and Wallace sandstone.

On 1 March the *Stanley* gets pinched by heavy ice off Pictou Island. Driven by a strong tide, the ice smashes railings, deck fixtures and cabins and threatens to roll the vessel onto her beam ends. A worried captain sends his 40 passengers ashore by iceboat as the

crew frantically works to clear the ice away. When the tide slackens the boat rights itself and is able to limp into Georgetown. The next day the *Minto* gets caught in the same ice and takes two weeks to struggle free. Meanwhile, the *Guardian* notes that prices for the iceboat service have gone up. Full fare is now $5.00. "Strap" passengers – those willing to get out and help pull the boat – pay $2.50.

On 1 April, frustrated with the state of winter communications and the dwindling provincial treasury, MP Alexander Martin warns "unless the Dominion shows more desire to conciliate the people, Prince Edward Island may yet ask to revert to the position of crown colony.

On 8 April, L.C. Page & Co. of Boston writes to an little-known Island author to tell her that her much-reworked children's novel has been accepted for publication. *Anne of Green Gables* is launched in June 1908; by May 1914, it has gone through 38 editions and Lucy Maud Montgomery is famous.

On 6 July, the Charlottetown *Patriot* sponsors the first road race ever staged in the province, a six-mile run. The winner is Colin McNevin, who in 1908 will set a course record for a ten-mile race with a 67.07 2/5 time.

Operating out of Market Hall, "The Wonderland" begins showing motion pictures on a weekly basis. It's only a nickel to get in, compared to 15¢ to 80¢ for a ticket to live theatre or vaudeville at the Opera House.

Kimble Webster and Oswald Dingwell strike gold – in the form of mussel mud – in St. Peter's Bay. They estimate the deposit covers about eight acres and at is least 30 feet deep. "One of the most valuable discoveries of mussel mud in the history of this county," estimates the *Guardian's* King's County correspondent. With mud selling for a dollar per sleigh load, the deposit is worth about $400,000.

Sir Andrew Macphail
Oil portrait by Alphonse Jongers, 1924
Physician, professor, historian and political commentator, Orwell's Andrew Macphail was one of Canada's most respected authors. *The Master's Wife*, his memoir of growing up in the 1860s, is a priceless source for Island historians.

On 7 March the Board of Health imposes quarantine on several Charlottetown houses and orders public places be closed. Smallpox is already present in Auburn and Dromore, where close to 20 houses have already been "flagged." The epidemic passes with no fatalities.

In 1895 W.M. Myers of Hampton left for the gold fields of South Africa. In 1898 he decided to try the gold fields of Alaska. In 1901 he found a gold field at Candle Creek. Interviewed after his first visit home since leaving, Myers concedes his mine is worth over $700,000.

Michael A. McInnis was born in Seven Mile Bay, but as a young man emigrated to California. There he did well, founding a publishing company in 1895. This year he creates the *Maple Leaf* — a monthly magazine dedicated to keeping expatriate Maritimers in touch with each other and "the old home."

Orwell native Andrew Macphail is named McGill University's first Professor in the History of Medicine. Already an eminent Professor of Pathology, Macphail will also be known as one of Canada's leading essayists and social critics.

On 19 July, William Johnstone's little schooner *Silver Spray* is launched at Montague. It's the 50th vessel built at Montague, but the first in four years. There will be no more.

1908

Pressured by angry farmers who regard the automobile as a horse-scaring nuisance, the Island Legislature bans cars from all public streets and highways.

On 29 January Arthur Peters, one-half of the only pair of brothers ever to hold the Island premiership, dies in office. He had emerged from the shadow of his older brother Frederick to become Liberal premier in 1901. By year's end his replacement, F.L. Haszard, leads the party to re-election, winning a close, 17 seat to 13 victory. Resignations and by-election losses soon reduce this margin to nothing.

Basil King was born in poverty in Charlottetown in 1859. Trained as an Anglican priest, he also writes fiction. His novel *The Inner Shrine* is an immediate bestseller.

Georgina Fane Pope
A daughter of William Henry Pope, Cecily Jane Georgina Fane Pope chose a career in nursing at a time when the profession was regarded as barely respectable.

Georgina Fane Pope is named head of the recently created Nursing Service of the Canadian Army Medical Corps. While commanding Canada's small nurse's contingent in the South African War, Pope was the first Canadian ever awarded the Royal Red Cross Medal.

Operating against his better instincts, but at a distraught mother's insistence, Dr. A.A. "Gus" MacDonald re-attaches the almost-severed feet of a young boy run over by a hay mower. To Dr. MacDonald's astonishment, the operation is a success and soon the boy is able to walk without difficulty.

Summerside's waterworks and sewage system becomes operational.

1909

The new ice-breaking winter steamer, *Earl Grey* commences service on the winter run between Charlottetown and Pictou. Two-hundred-and-fifty feet long, driven by 6,500 horsepower, she's certainly the most powerful and possibly the most handsome boat yet to take on the Northumberland Strait. But like her predecessors, she is not impervious to the winter ice.

The government's financial report indicates that over a third of the province's $369,000 revenue goes towards education. Though there are concerns about the red ink, the $12,000 deficit is the smallest since 1882.

The Anti-Tuberculosis Society is formed to fight the deadly scourge that stalks many Island families. In 1937, the organization's name will be changed to the Free Dispensary.

For the first time since 1797, Island shipyards are entirely idle. Not a single vessel is registered this year. Over the 15 years between 1906 and 1920, only 28 vessels are launched from Prince Edward Island.

***Going Out To Stud,* c1910**

Herb Jelley poses with his prize cart horse in front of his O'Leary blacksmith shop. With the Island's horse population approaching 35,000 by the turn of the 20th century, the blacksmith shop was central to every community.

Simon Jordan and his Foxes

McAlpine's Prince Edward Island Directory for 1914-15 includes Simon Jordan of Beach Point among its listings for fox ranchers.

1910

The seaport town of Souris – third-largest in the province – is incorporated.

Imperial Oil erects the first bulk oil storage tank in Charlottetown. Until now the Island's gasoline supply has been stored as it has been shipped — in wooden barrels.

A private cable is laid between Pictou, N.S. and P.E.I., making possible telephone communication with Halifax.

Charlottetown merchant Benjamin Rogers is commissioned Lt. Governor. The Alberton merchant was President of the Legislative Council before its merger with the House of Assembly in 1893.

Lennox Island's Michael Thomas, running for the Abegweit Amateur Athletic Association, comes from nowhere to win the *Halifax Herald's* 10-mile road race on 31 October. The next year he is the favourite. He wins again. In 1912, he makes it three victories in a row before 35,000 spectators.

Three years after Robert Baden-Powell has founded the Boy Scout movement, YMCA officials request permission to introduce it to Prince Edward Island.

Pioneer fox farmers Charles Dalton and Robert Oulton market 25 silver fox pelts, their season's harvest, with C. M. Lampson & Co. of London. The sale nets $34,649 — $1,385.96 per pelt. The entire silver fox industry is controlled by the "Big Six Combine" — Oulton, Dalton and a select group of friends. The monopoly is broken later in the year when one of the "Big Six," Frank Tuplin, sells a breeding pair for $20,000. In 1910, the average yearly wage for a farm labourer is $225; for a professor at a large university: $1,200.

Islanders love their horses. According to federal statistics, the Island's equine population is 34,121. Valued at $3.6 million, they're worth more than the province's 113,000 cows.

 Farmers crowd the stableyard at the Revere Hotel on 13 December to ogle 30 Scottish fillies — Clydesdales, that is — imported for sale by auction by William Maharey. Marie Clerc fetches the highest bid — $400. By 1950, a good workhorse will bring only half that sum.

 Island field crops are worth an estimated $9,988,000. The most valuable crop is hay and clover, valued at $4.1 million. Potatoes are a distant third at $1.6. A good farm in the Garden Province costs $5,000.

The province is slipping backwards. According to one *Guardian* correspondent, teachers' salaries in 1910 were lower than in 1880.

With only 95 days between the last and first frosts, it's the shortest growing season ever on the Island. The average growing season is 151 days.

Charlottetown native Robert Falconer is named President of the University of Toronto. By the time he retires in 1932, the U of T will be the largest university in the British Empire.

1911

The cornerstone is laid for Zion Presbyterian Church on

Threshing Grain, c1910

the corner of Grafton and Prince Streets.

On 5 September, a fire in the switchboard office puts 560 Charlottetown telephones out of service.

After decades of protests over discontinuous communication between the Island and the rest of Canada, Prime Minister Robert Borden promises establishment of a modern ferry service. A powerful icebreaking vessel is ordered as engineers scout out suitable sites for the port facilities.

After 20 years in office, Liberal fortunes are sinking. Perhaps that's why Premier F. L. Haszard wants a provincial judgeship so badly. He gets it by snatching the appointment away from colleague James B. Palmer. As a

consolation prize, Palmer becomes premier!

On 10 December, the provincial Tories regain office the same way they lost it. A pair of by-election victories propel them into power for the first time since 1891. The new Premier, J.A. Matheson, quickly calls an election.

The country's population has grown to 7.2 million. The Island's has shrunk to 94,000.

The first meeting of the Prince Edward Island Women's Institute takes place in York.

One of James Rayner's foxes dies at his ranch at Kildare. Although its pelt is not even prime, he decides to sell it. At the March sale in London, it will fetch the formidable price of £410 — over

McCormack Reaper, c1890

$2,000. In the year since the Big Six Combine's monopoly was broken, 277 fox ranches have appeared in the province. The industry is valued at $15 million.

A large crowd gathers at a Charlottetown store to see a woman model the scandalous "harem skirt." When the heavily veiled woman appears, two policemen are needed to maintain order.

Islanders' conservation instincts are still rather underdeveloped. Willard Leard of Cape Traverse shoots a large eagle that was flying over his house. He sends it to Charlottetown to be mounted.

On 5 July Maud Montgomery, the creator of *Anne of Green Gables*, marries Rev. Ewan MacDonald of Valleyfield and goes to live in Ontario, far from her beloved Island.

The *Guardian* for 13 April announces the arrival on leave of two Island members of the fledgling Canadian Navy. The two sailors are crewmen aboard the cruiser HMCS *Niobe* — which comprises exactly one-half of the Canadian battle fleet.

1912

On 24 April, the old City Jail on Charlottetown's Pownal Square is demolished. Its replacement, the aptly named "1911 Jail," is still a Charlottetown landmark.

King's County capital Georgetown will become a town in law as well as name on 1 January. It selects its first slate of officers by acclamation. Longtime local official G. Albert Aitken is named first mayor.

On 12 March, Professor Kirkpatrick of Queen's University is hired to survey and select the best sites for terminals for the planned Northumberland car ferry service. A stretch of shore, soon to be named "Borden," lies waiting to be discovered.

On 11 April, on visiting a house in the small farm community of St. Mary's Road, the doctor finds five of the six children belonging to the McGee family either dead or dying. They appear to have been poisoned, but the doctor is unsure how. On 20 April, after the last surviving child dies of poisoning, suspicions of murder fall on his mother Minnie. "She is regarded as somewhat peculiar, and it is thought she may not be right in the head," reports the *Patriot*. Convicted of murder, she spends the rest of her life in the Hospital for the Insane.

Premier J.A. Matheson leads the provincial Conservatives to a smashing electoral victory, taking 28 of 30 seats. In some ridings, the Liberals don't even field a candidate.

On 21 March Senator Andrew Archibald Macdonald, last of the Island Fathers of Confederation, dies in Ottawa. Among the Canadian Fathers, only Charles Tupper outlives him.

Competing in the Stockholm Olympics, pole-vaulter Bill Halpenny is awarded a special bronze medal by the International Olympic Committee. It is their way of apologizing for the inadequate landing pit that injured him after a record jump, forcing him out of contention for a gold medal.

Tom Longboat the celebrated distance runner dazzles a large crowd at Charlottetown's Abegweit Grounds on 29 July. He laps local champ Fred Cameron of Amherst twice in winning a 10-mile match race. His time of 53:10 knocks 2:54 off Cameron's track record.

Lennox Island's Michael Thomas wins the *Halifax Herald* Marathon for the third straight year. Declaring it "the finest race of my career," the 29-year-old Thomas decides to retire from competitive running.

As the fox boom reaches its peak, Frank Tuplin sells 22 breeding pairs for $250,000. The provincial budget for 1912 is less than $400,000.

In a world gone mad for fur, the Island's first skunk ranches are established. Looking for a boom similar to the silver fox, hopeful entrepreneurs import captive stocks of the aromatic furbearer. When it becomes evident that skunk fur is not going to take off in the market place, captive stocks are released to fend for themselves. Until this point, the skunk was not found in the wild here.

Hundreds turn out for Dr. J. D. McCue's lecture on tuberculosis — "The White Plague." Alcohol, privation and intemperate habits, the doctor warns "will engender a condition which cannot

***Parker Foundry, Georgetown,* c1907**
From the turn of the century until after the Second World War, the Parker iron foundry was a mainstay of the Georgetown area economy.

resist the germ." The disease is especially common on P.E.I.

On 26 March, a Rogers Hardware Co. shipping clerk named Ernest Teed has the misfortune of falling down what is probably the Island's only elevator shaft. He dies, and most of the Queen Street business district closes for a half day to attend his funeral.

No one knows exactly when (or how) they arrived, but wild lupins have begun to spread throughout the province.

On 5 May, Kingsboro resident (but former Cape Bretoner) Jim Robertson leaves Souris with a dory load of fishing supplies. The 60-year-old Robertson is headed for home, just seven miles up the coast. He never makes it. Several weeks later the dory containing his dead body washes up on shore in Cape Breton — just a few miles, according to community legend, from the house he was born in.

"The people came out to see the airplane today." On 25 September Cecil Peoli, the 18 year-old "Bird Boy" of New York, makes the first flight on Prince Edward Island, a 15 minute jaunt above Charlottetown's exhibition grounds. The flight, in a biplane designed by Capt. James Baldwin, is part of a tour of eastern Canada.

On 14 April, the "unsinkable" *Titanic* hits an iceberg several hundred miles off the coast of Newfoundland and sinks. The first place in Canada to pick up her distress signal is the Marconi wireless station at Cape Bear, Prince Edward Island.

1913

The former settlement of "Stumptown" is incorporated as the Town of Alberton.

On 13 May, Charlottetown's Zion Presbyterian Church is dedicated. It was designed by prominent local architect C. B. Chappell.

Bishop's Palace and St. Dunstan's Cathedral, c1910
There have been three cathedrals on this site. The first St. Dunstan's was built in 1843. The second, pictured here, was completed in 1907 but burned down in 1913. St. Dunstan's Basilica, an almost exact replica, was built to replace it.

Of the 292 charges laid by Charlottetown's police force this year, 211 are for drunkenness. Only 28 charges have been laid for breach of the Prohibition Act.

The federal government awards contracts for construction of car-ferry service between Cape Tormentine and present-day Borden.

Despite widespread opposition in rural areas, the Legislature votes to allow Island motorists on the road on Mondays, Wednesdays and Thursdays. Horace Wright of Bedeque speaks for many Islanders: "We're going to keep them cars out if we have to take a pitchfork and drive it through them!" There are over 50,000 motor vehicles in Canada and the number is growing yearly.

The Legislature passes an act providing secret balloting for provincial elections. A similar act had been passed in 1877, but open voting returned two years later when it was decided secret balloting was too expensive.

On 1 April, the Island's first branch of the Women's Institute opens in Marshfield.

The Island's first Egg Circle is organized in Brooklyn, 61, to co-operate in the production and marketing of eggs and poultry. Eleven more will organize before the P.E.I. Co-operative Egg and Poultry Association is incorporated in 1914. The "egg wagon" soon becomes a common sight in many communities.

The Sir Charles Dalton Sanatorium for the treatment of tuberculosis patients is incorporated. It opens in North Wiltshire in March 1915. In 1922, after its federal operating grant runs out, the hospital is given back to Dalton by a penurious Province.

On 4 October, a band of "Hungarian gypsies" departs Summerside on the *Empress* after a month wandering around the Island.

On 7 March St. Dunstan's Cathedral, only six years old, is destroyed in a spectacular fire. The stone cathedral was 11 years in the building. By the light of the flames, a Protestant friend writes a cheque for $5,000 to kick off a new building fund.

Electricity, formerly an urban luxury, begins to make

inroads in the country. North Tryon miller Charles Ives hooks a generator up to his water wheel and is soon supplying power to his neighbours. Up east, the Souris Electric Co, the first outside Charlottetown or Summerside, is incorporated.

President Woodrow Wilson appoints Charlottetown native Franklin Knight Lane as his Secretary of the Interior. In 1920, Lane will be touted as a candidate for the Democratic Presidential nomination — apparently by people who don't know he is Canadian-born and thus not eligible for the office.

1914

The Legislature passes an act incorporating the Town of Kensington.

On 5 October, the launching of the *Prince Edward Island* gives the province its first truly effective ice-breaker. Unlike previous boats, which called at a variety of ports, the *Prince Edward Island* will shuttle between two ports only, ferrying railcars (and later automobiles) between New Brunswick and Prince Edward Island.

Fox king Charles Dalton donates $50,000 to St. Dunstan's College. Not surprisingly, the college names the resulting building "Dalton Hall."

The *Guardian* doesn't mean to sound crass, but it can't help speculating on how good the new war in Europe might be for the Island's farm economy. There should be extra demand for foodstuffs and, with Russia's sable trappers off fighting Germany, the main competition for silver fox fur will be at a disadvantage!

A motor vehicle tax was introduced in 1913. In its first year of operation it raises $480.

1915

Summerside's Town Council moves into its new brick Town Hall.

MacLean and MacKinnon Law Office, 1908
Views from the inside of office and commercial buildings are very rare. The older gentleman in this photo is the firm's senior partner, Angus MacLean. Beside him is Donald MacKinnon. An unidentified articling student is seated in the foreground. The firm's secretary, Marion McKinnon, works at a typewriting machine.

Premier Matheson leads his Conservative government to re-election with a close, 17 seat to 13 victory. His opponent, Benjamin Rogers, made constitutional history when he assumed the Liberal party leadership *after* serving a term as Lt. Governor.

Augustine Colin Macdonald, a Montague merchant, be-

2nd Canadian Siege Artillery, Flanders, 1917
Around dugout most of day. Did not sleep very much. Fairly quiet. Got the latest papers. Good news on the western front. Not so good out east. But soon will be OK. Received parcel from Josie. The top of the jam bottle was moved off about half an inch and the socks were soaked with it. I've a notion to eat them. Having a gum chewing frolic. About 10.30 PM Fritz started shelling our position, the first landing near our dugout. He continued during the night. One shell landed between two of the dugouts, demolishing them entirely and killing Corp. AB Needham in one and Gunner Fred Crawford in the other. In this one Sgt. DL MacPherson was slightly wounded but received a terrific shock and will likely go to England. Crawford had not received a scratch, death being caused by concussion.
— Diary of Percy MacNevin, 2nd Canadian Siege Battery, Oct 27th,1917

comes Lt. Governor, 31 years after his older brother Andrew Archibald was named to the post.

L'Impartial, the Island's first French-language newspaper, publishes its last issue. For 22 years it has largely been the Buote family's labour of love.

Island military officials are authorized to raise an artillery unit, later designated the 2nd Canadian Siege Battery. On 28 November, the 218 officers and men sail for England.

On 8 April, a serious fire rips through downtown Tignish, destroying the Tignish Trading Co. store, the Tignish Drug Store, and J.H. Myrick & Co.'s furniture and tailor shops.

Victoria's Alfred Arthur Sinnott is named Archbishop of Winnipeg.

On 15 December, after a stormy winter crossing of the North Atlantic, the former winter steamer *Minto*, Captain John Read commanding, reaches her new owner, Imperial Russia. The crew expects to go home; instead, they spend the winter breaking ice for the beleaguered Russians.

1916

Robert Harris' masterwork, "The Fathers of Confederation" is destroyed when the centre block of the Parliament Buildings goes up in flames. Harris is asked to paint a replacement but, pleading ill health, declines the honour.

On 8 July, despite a broken hand, Wild Bert Kenny of St. Teresa's gives future heavy-weight champ Jack Dempsey all he can handle in a bloody 10-round draw. Kenny goes down in the second, but floors Dempsey twice in the third. Dempsey later calls it, "one of the most brutal fights of my life."

When James E. Murphy of Augustine Cove registers the first native barley variety, it trades in its original name, "Old Island Two-Rowed," for the more prosaic "Charlottetown No. 80." Soon it is the most popular variety of barley in the Maritimes.

The Island's dozens of cheese factories adjust to new technologies as pasteurization is introduced.

On 12 August, Captain Anthony McInnis of St. Peter's Bay leaves Naufrage in the 18-foot skiff *Lilly May*, powered by a four horsepower, Island-made, Bruce Stewart Imperial engine. His destination is Boston. One month and 1,000 miles later, he putt-putts triumphantly into Boston Harbour.

On 4 October the *Santa Maria* discovers Prince Edwrd Island. Actually, she is a replica of Columbus' flagship, built by Spain in 1892 to mark the 400th anniversary of his voyage. Leased as a floating attraction, she is on her way home to Chicago, but is impounded here for debt.

The Great War's first Island infantry unit is officially designated the 105th Battalion (P.E.I. Highlanders). Thirty-seven officers and 1,107 other ranks sail for England, but the battalion receives no baptism of fire. On arrival it is broken up to provide reinforcements for units battered by the Somme offensive.

On 16 June, the 2nd Canadian Siege Battery goes into action for the first time. In action during the entire Somme offensive, the gunners will not get a rest until December.

Less than a year after the 2nd Canadian Siege Battery was recruited, authorization is granted for another Island artillery unit. Eventually, it will be designated the 8th Canadian Siege Battery with an authorized strength of 7 officers and 152 ranks.

The first Island-based community of nuns, the Congregation of the Sisters of St. Martha, is founded. Their mother house, Mount St. Mary's, is not acquired until 1920; until then, headquarters is St. Dunstan's University.

Kensington "gets the lights" as the first electric plant there goes into operation.

March comes in like a lion and roars all month. Prince Edward Island gets 66 inches of snow.

1917

Montague "the Beautiful" is incorporated as a town. Already, it has begun to eclipse the county capital, Georgetown, in size and importance and soon will pass

North Lake, c1960

89

Souris as the biggest town in the county.

On 28 April, with absolutely no fanfare, 142 years after the service began — 40 years after the arrival of the first "winter steamer" — the last ice-boat crossing is made across the frozen Northumberland Strait. The advent of a truly effective ice-breaking ferry, the *Prince Edward Island*, puts the ice boats on shore for good.

In the bitterly contested "Khaki Election," P.E.I. and Quebec return a majority of anti-conscription "Laurierites" – those Liberals who remained loyal to party leader Wilfrid Laurier. Tory and pro-conscription newspapers across the country are appalled. Three months later the province's honour is somewhat redeemed when the "soldiers' vote" is added to the totals. Naturally, those in uniform vote overwhelmingly for conscription. Their ballots are enough to overturn two of the previous majorities.

When Premier Matheson resigns to take an appointment to the bench, the Conservative caucus selects Aubin-Edmond Arsenault to complete his term. Son of Senator J.O. Arsenault, Aubin-Edmond is the Island's Island's first Acadian premier.

Aubin-Edmond Arsenault

The Island's first Rotary Club is organized in Charlottetown.

On 24 October, work begins on transforming Government House into a Convalescent Home for wounded Island servicemen. The renovation has a budget of $60,000.

On 13 February Lizzie Palmer, formerly of Nova Scotia but a long-time Island resident, dies at the age of 115.

Rochford Square School is born when the local School Board rents St. Joseph's Convent as a public school.

St. Dunstan's College receives a university charter. The Roman Catholic school waits another 24 years before using it.

Daylight Saving Time is adopted for the duration of war.

Captain D.J. MacDonald of Cardigan, skipper of the three-masted schooner *John G. Walker*, is just off the port of Le Havre when a German u-boat appears out of a fogbank and opens fire with its deck gun. MacDonald and his crew abandon their sinking schooner and are taken captive. While being interrogated by the u-boat captain about his cargo and destination, MacDonald catches a glimpse of a British destroyer through the fog. He lays his captor out with a punch to the head, leaps overboard and makes his escape when the u-boat has to flee.

On 15 April, the 8th Canadian Siege Battery goes into action for the first time.

On 12 December, Alberton's Wendell Rogers becomes the first Allied fighter pilot to shoot down one of Germany's giant Gotha bombers. He is awarded the Military Cross for the feat.

On 7 June Ronald Neil Stewart, descendant of an old Island family, wins the Victoria Cross for an action at sea aboard the HMS *Pargust*. The *Pargust* is a Brit-

ish "Q" ship, a war vessel disguised as a merchantman to prey on unsuspecting German u-boats.

On 7 September the Charlottetown block bordered by Great George, Kent, Prince and Grafton is "scooped" by fire. Several warehouses, livery stables, an ice house and the Union Hotel are gutted. The Strathcona Hotel, and Zion and St. Paul's Churches narrowly escape damage.

On 20 January St. Columba's Church, built in 1846, is completely destroyed by fire. For the next two years, services will be held at the East Point Cheese Factory.

On 13 February, tragedy touches the last year of ice-boat service, when 24-year-old crewman Lem Dawson is torn away from his companions' desperate grasp in a huge ice field and drowns. Amazingly, Dawson is the only crew fatality in the history of the service.

"Houses rocked, doors slammed, pictures swung from their places and people were dreadfully alarmed." So reads the front page of the *Guardian* on 7 December. At the *Guardian* building, the heavy linotype machines almost fall over and people are thrown from their chairs. It is thought at first that the munitions factory in New Glasgow (N.S.) had blown up. When word comes in that a ship in Halifax harbour has exploded, the immediate assumption is that a German submarine or spy is responsible.

On 7 December the *George N. Orr*, bound for New York from Montreal, runs aground in six feet of water at Savage Harbour after losing her steering gear. The captain and 32 crew are saved. The wreck is still there.

On 23 October, Georgetown "gets the lights." "Only a few of the lights are yet in operation," observes the *Examiner*, "but in a short time the darkness which has covered the town will be dispelled."

The View From the Top of Rogers' Store, Alberton, 1903

"I'll huff. And I'll puff..." On 30 October a Clifton farmer encounters, not the big bad wolf, but a severe wind storm. Hearing the door of an outbuilding slamming in the wind, he ventures out to fasten it. As he finishes the job, the entire building comes down on him, breaking his leg. "It was almost a miracle he was not killed, " the *Examiner* ventures. "Indeed he might have been, had not a terrific gust came immediately and carried off the debris."

A port is born. The lake at North Lake was freshwater until a 7 December storm broke through the dunes shielding it from the Gulf of St. Lawrence. Now it's a salt water inlet, and local inhabitants think it has the makings of a fine harbour.

Not knowing how long the war will drag on, and not sure if the British Empire's steel production can keep up with Germany's unrestricted submarine offensive, an Imperial Commission recommends £10,000,000 be invested in reviving the wooden shipbuilding industry. On Prince Edward Island, where the industry has been all-but-dead since 1880, more than a few interested eyebrows are raised.

1918

On 23 July, Chautauqua comes to Charlottetown with its unique blend of education, inspiration, entertainment and culture, all packed into a four-day package.

Beginning in early October, the deadly Spanish Influenza epidemic sweeping the world comes to Prince Edward Island. Paranoia is one side effect. One correspondent to the *Patriot* is convinced that the flu probably came in the clothes of German prisoners working at Borden: "We cannot be too careful of these Germans. . . . All along since the war has started they have been as deceitful as the Lord is true." Of the 900 cases reported in Charlottetown, 100 die. Across the province, an estimated 400 die before the epidemic runs its course in early 1919.

On 27 June, Nursing Sister Rena Maude McLean of Souris is drowned when a German submarine torpedoes the hospital ship *Llandovery Castle*. There are only 24 survivors.

On the 11th hour of the 11th day of the 11th month, an armistice ends the Great War. Of the approximately 4,000 Islanders who served, approximately 400 have been killed in action.

On 2 March, a major fire leaves Alberton's business district in ashes. Most of what escapes this fire will burn in 1927.

The *Victory Chimes*, built by John A. Macdonald at Cardigan, is the first large vessel to be launched from an Island shipyard in many years.

1919

Beaconsfield, in its day the most luxurious private residence in Charlottetown, has been refitted as a boarding house. When its owner, Henry Cundall, died in 1916, he willed it to charity to become a "home for friendless young women." On 22 May a large crowd, including the Mayor and Lt. Governor, attends its formal dedication as a YWCA.

Attended by a host of church dignitaries, Apostolic Delegate Pietro di Maria dedicates the new St. Dunstan's Cathedral. Designed by James Hunter, it is built on the ruins of the stone cathedral destroyed by fire six years earlier.

A federal act creates Canadian National Railways out of the bankrupt Canadian Northern and existing government lines, including the P.E.I. Railway.

"Progress" defeats parochialism. Banned from Island roads in 1908, motorists can henceforth drive where they wish — provided there isn't too much snow or mud or dust or . . . .

On 18 September, the first standard-gauge train travels from Borden to Charlottetown. Over the next decade, the Island's entire railroad system is converted to standard gauge.

On 24 September a war surplus Curtiss "Jenny" makes the first air-mail flight in the Maritimes from Truro to Charlottetown.

The new federal leader, Mackenzie King, is elected

by acclamation to represent Prince County in the House of Commons. His tenure in Ottawa is record-breaking; his incumbency in Prince County is brief.

Murdock MacKinnon becomes the first farmer to be named Lt. Governor.

J.H. Bell leads the Liberals back to power, taking 25 seats to the Conservatives' four. Former Conservative MLA John A. Dewar wins 3rd Kings as an Independent Farmers' candidate, becoming the only independent to date elected to an Island Legislature.

William Lyon MacKenzie King
The longest-serving Prime Minister in Canadian history sat as the MP for Prince County from 1919 to 1921.

Green Gables comes to the silver screen when Hollywood makes a movie from L.M. Montgomery's *Anne of Green Gables*. The film is, by all accounts, a *very* loose adaptation of Montgomery's novel.

The Société Saint-Thomas d'Aquin is founded in Bloomfield during the annual convention of the P.E.I. Acadian Teachers' Association.

Automobiles are driving horses from Island roads — and now the fields as well. The *Island Farmer* carries ads for International Harvester's "Good

***Royal Visit,* 1919**
The future Edward VIII was only the second Prince of Wales to make an official visit to the Island. His grandfather, Edward VII, made the first ever Royal Visit in 1860.

Kerosene Tractor," which is "fast replacing horses for all kinds of heavy farm work."

Opened as The Great War drew to a close, the Convalescent Hospital at Government House is officially named after Island nurse Rena McLean, killed in the torpedoing of a hospital ship by a German u-boat.

On 7 August, the Island suffers its first automobile fatality. Six year old George Ward and a friend had just finished getting some ice from an ice wagon on Elm Avenue. George stepped from behind the wagon into the path of an on-coming automobile. Although the auto was going slow, young Ward dies from internal injuries several hours later.

On 19 August The Prince of Wales (later Edward VIII) arrives on the Island as part of his Royal Visit to Canada. The young prince can be very charming — and Islanders are very charmed by him.

On 29 December W. S. Louson, a leading figure in the Charlottetown's YMCA, hosts a

***Launch of the* Barbara Macdonald, 1919**
Built as one of a trio of vessels by Cardigan merchant John A. Macdonald, the *Barbara Macdonald* was launched with the hope that another golden age of shipbuilding was in the offing.

banquet (followed by a free movie) for local newsboys. The salesman's philanthropy is praised, but his greatest legacy will be a treasury of turn-of-the-century photographs.

Cardigan merchant John A. Macdonald's attempt to resurrect the long-dead Island shipbuilding industry attracts a lot of attention. On 25 October a large crowd watches the launch of the three-masted schooner *Barbara Macdonald*, his second vessel in as many years. She costs $30,000. On 14 December, her maiden voyage ends in tragedy. Battered by storms, her captain drowned, she crashes ashore at Cape Pine, Nfld. Somehow, owner and crew scale a 350-foot cliff, in a storm, in the dark, to reach safety.

1920

Disgruntled farmers meet at Peakes Station to organize a branch of the United Farmers. While the U.F. score stunning upsets in provincial elections in Ontario, Manitoba and Alberta, the party never gets off the ground on P.E.I.

The P.E.I. Potato Growers Association is established to bring order, quality and better prices to the growing and marketing of Island potatoes.

The Prohibition Commission announces that between 15 July 1919 and 1 March 1920, 34,200 certificates were issued by Island

Bandstand and Public Gardens, Queen's Square, **c1910**

druggists and physicians to purchase alcohol for "medicinal purposes." The effects of the treatments are not documented.

Smallpox is no longer a great killer, but it still inspires fear. At Morell, an outbreak leads to quarantine for the afflicted and vaccination for the endangered. All of the patients recover.

The Prince Edward Island Agricultural and Technical School opens at Government House.

Schurman Bros. of New Annan advertise their Schurman Potato Grader (patent pending). Developed after "years of study and experiment," it costs the princely sum of $21.

1921

The Island's population has slipped to 89,000 — about the same level it was at in the late 1860s.

After 31 years, the Charlottetown *Watchman* calls it quits. The outspoken, staunchly Roman Catholic weekly has undergone several political conversions since its founding in 1890. In all this time, it has known only one editor, Peter McCourt.

The MacLean Method of Writing, devised by Mount Mellick native Henry Bovyer MacLean, is introduced in the British Columbia school system. By 1930, MacLean's *Method* is being

Dalton Sanatorium

"The White Plague" or tuberculosis was a particular scourge on Prince Edward Island until the second half of the 20th century. After watching helplessly while the disease ravaged his family, millionaire fox-breeder Charles Dalton financed this magnificent sanatorium in North Wiltshire and gave it to the province. When the province gave it back Dalton had it dismantled, donating many of the materials and furnishings to the new Charlottetown Hospital.

used across Canada and in parts of Australia and New Zealand.

"The Biggest Victory Since The War," reads the *Guardian*'s triumphant headline. The Island's 2nd Siege Battery wins the General Efficiency trophy at the Dominion Artillery competition. Another group of Islanders, the 8th Siege Battery, places third.

1922

On 19 July, the Scottish Catholic Memorial is unveiled at Scotchfort. The celtic cross has been fashioned in Aberdeen of Scottish granite to a design supplied by Island architect J.M. Hunter.

Prince Edward Island becomes the second-last province in Canada to give women the right to vote and run for public office.

On 24 March, the Abegweit Amateur Athletic Association's hockey team beats Windsor 5-3 to win the Island's first Maritime hockey title.

Despite the fact the Island has one of the highest tuberculosis rates in the country, the Government pleads poverty and closes the Dalton Sanitorium.

When internationally renowned inventor Alexander Graham Bell dies at his home in Baddeck, N.S., his estate contacts the Montague Furnishing Company — internationally renowned undertakers — to direct his funeral.

The former winter steamer *Minto*, now a Russian vessel named *Ivan Susanin,* runs aground and sinks in the Arctic Sea.

On 29 December, a howling nor-easter cancels all train traffic and confines the ferry to port.

1923

The Protestant Orphanage, a handsome brick structure designed by local architect "Bones" Blanchard, officially opens in Mount Herbert.

Parishioners in Tignish unveil a 10-foot-high Celtic Cross as a memorial to their late pastor, Father A. J. MacDougall.

On 20 February, two weeks after setting out, the train from Summerside reaches Charlottetown. Winter storms are playing havoc with the Island's rail lines.

The ruling Liberals are unseated by J.D. Stewart's Conservatives, who win 25 of the Legislature's 30 seats in a general election.

The Island is dry and getting drier. In a provincial plebiscite, Islanders vote overwhelmingly in favour of banning the importation of liquor into the province. Of the larger towns, only Souris votes "No."

A.B. Warburton's *History of Prince Edward Island* is billed as a great Christmas gift. It's the first book-length history of P.E.I. since professional historian Duncan Campbell dashed off his version in 1875.

On 26 March the legendary "Dumbells" comedy troupe, formed during the Great War, perform their new revue "Rapid Fire" in Charlottetown's Prince Edward

Theatre. The cast features expatriate Islander Jimm Good.

On 15 September, Barney Francis of the Abegweit Amateur Athletic Association stuns the crowd at the Canadian Track and Field Championships in Halifax. Using a powerful finishing kick, he wins the mile in a record time of 4:32 1/5.

On 28 April, fire destroys the *Guardian*'s offices at the corner of Kent and Great George Streets. But it takes more than fire to stop the presses; the *Guardian* doesn't miss an issue. A year later the paper is ensconced in new quarters in the former School of Music building.

On 8 February, while shovelling snow in a deep cutting on the P.E.I. Railway, W. B. Stewart is struck and killed by an oncoming train. The towering cutting muffled the sound of the approaching train and then left Stewart no place to go.

In early March, a two-day blizzard buries Island railways — and even some trains. It takes 12 days of back-breaking labour just to clear the main line from Borden to Charlottetown. Other lines take much longer during the

Summer Outing, 1913

When we took her driving, we strove to excel by never going faster than a walk. At length she would say "You might trot a little here; it is on the level." If she ever urged a horse to trot, she would explain it to him that it was downhill. She approved of the parish priest, afterwards Bishop, who always employed towards his horse the formula: "Get up, please."

– Andrew Macphail, *The Master's Wife*

Fishing boat race, c1920

Lobster boats claimed their place on the fishing grounds on opening day by "running the lines." Traps were tied to "back lines" — stout ropes one to two miles long. The success of the whole lobster season could hinge on where a boats' lines were run. With so much at stake, speed was essential to a lobster boat.

"Great Snow Blockade." On 14 March, just when exhausted workers — as many as 3,000 men and boys — succeed in opening the main line from Borden to Charlottetown, another nor-easter strikes and buries the railroad again.

On 1 October a terrific northerly gale, the worst storm in years, devastates the Maritimes. On the Island, high winds and huge tides destroy some 60 bridges.

1924

To help pay for a binge of road building that raised the provincial deficit from $100,000 to $750,000, the government establishes a new gasoline tax. In its first year it raises a mere $14,235.

The *Guardian* notes that A. C. Horne & Co. of Charlottetown are making a big splash with their new lineup of Chevrolets and Studebakers. Chev sports five new models, all "closed." The Studebakers sport the latest innovation, the one-piece windshield.

Islanders get on the right side — of the road. An amendment to the motor vehicle regulations follows American practice by ordering traffic to keep to the right. The change ends a century of left-side driving.

Fox breeders are nervous after daring thieves raid two ranches on Mt. Edward Road, near Charlottetown, making off with fox pups valued at $6,000.

Out-going Lt. Governor Murdock MacKinnon causes a sensation by vetoing the Church Union Bill, meant to pave the way for a union of Island Methodists and Presbyterians. Unionists are indignant; anti-Unionists rejoice. Constitutionalists worry over the first use of a vice-regal veto in decades.

Charlottetown banker and merchant Frank R. Heartz is named Lt. Governor.

On 27 March, the Abegweit Amateur Athletic Association Abbies beat Windsor 4-3 to claim their second straight Maritime Senior Hockey title.

Fishermen in Tignish form the first Fisherman's Union in Canada.

There's a move afoot to merge Canada's Protestant and Methodist Churches into a single, "United" Church. As in other parts of the country, the issue is very contentious on Prince Edward Island. Most of the province's Methodist congregations are committed to union, but Presbyterians are split.

The year is the Island's driest to date. Only 470 mm of precipitation, less than half the yearly average has fallen. But Islanders need not worry; a bad winter is on the way.

On 12 March, a late winter storm batters the Island. "On the western [rail] lines," the *Guardian* reports, "between five and six feet of heavy snow has fallen."

Vernon River's Francis Clement Kelley is named Bishop of the Roman Catholic diocese of Oklahoma City.

An Island Road, c1925

Only twice did she enter a motorcar. She thought it an unsafe and licentious way of traveling.

– Andrew Macphail,
The Master's Wife

Co-op Cannery, Abram's Village, 1941

In the 1930s, suspicious that established packers were conspiring to keep prices low, lobster fishers in many ports pooled their resources to build canneries of their own. This Co-operative movement was particularly strong in the western end of the Island.

1925

On 16 July the Great War Soldiers' Memorial, a bronze statue by sculptor George Hill, is officially unveiled on Queen's Square. "The Soldiers" is easily the most recognizable monument in the province.

On 10 August CFCY Charlottetown, one of the Mariimes' pioneer radio stations, is licensed. The brainchild of local businessman Keith S. Rogers, it becomes a fixture for generations of radio listeners.

On 15 July, fox-breeders Morrison & Milligan host a day-long gala opening for their new barn, "the biggest in the Maritimes," at Northam. The main wing is 100' by 40', with a 40' by 40' wing, and a cattle stable 40' by 80'. The program includes a cattle show, track and field meet, baseball game and a dance.

Lt. Governor Heartz assents to the second Church Union Bill (his predecessor withheld assent from the first) authorizing the Island's Methodists and Presbyterians to establish the United Church. The result is an ugly split among Island Presbyterians. In many districts bitter divorces are the order of the day as congregations argue over how to divide up property, buildings and other assets.

1926

The Pure Milk Co. opens Garden City Dairy in a building on the corner of University and Fitzroy. In later years, the second floor becomes a dance hall nicknamed "The Bucket of Blood."

On 18 February, police in New York City confiscate 138 cases of champagne hidden beneath a shipment of P.E.I. potatoes. The bubbly certainly couldn't have come from here — the Island's been dry for 20 years!

Archivist and historian D.C. Harvey publishes *The French Regime on Prince Edward Island*. The book is still regarded as a landmark in Island history.

On 30 March, Neil Cheverie of Elmira "plays classy" at Charlottetown's Strand Theatre to win a mammoth Island-wide fiddling contest. Cheverie will go on to place 2nd at the World Championships held in Boston.

The Royal Canadian Legion is established on Prince Edward Island. The first branch is in Charlottetown.

On 25 November, a "million dollar fox train" leaves Summerside with 855 breeding foxes in three railway cars destined

The Early Birds

"The Friendly Voice of the Maritimes," CFCY was the first commercial radio station in Eastern Canada. "The Early Birds" was one of its morning shows, created by Bill Brown and Syd Kennedy — or "Willie" and "Joe Stitch" as they are identified in this photograph.

Theatrical Group, Souris, c1929

for American customers. The owners, J. Edgar Milligan and George Morrison, own a network of 52 fox ranches anchored by their ranch at Northam.

The enterprising citizens of Kinkora incorporate their own electric company. They've got everything they need — except electricity. So they buy power from the Dunk River (later Scales) Hydro Electric Co. In 1929, Scales buys the Kinkora Company.

1927

Regular airmail flights between Moncton and Charlottetown begin. It's fitting that one of the first places to demonstrate the possibilities of airmail should get one of the country's first airmail routes.

Running on an "end Prohibition" platform, J. D. Stewart's Tories are routed 24 seats to six by A. C. Saunders' Grits, strongly supported by an angry Temperance Alliance. The flow of legal liquor in the province slows to a trickle.

Oil surveyors drill a 6,000 foot test hole on Governor's Island. They find no oil in that thar hill.

On 7 February, teenagers Bernard & George Leslie shoot the last known Island black bear near the Souris Line Road. Says Bernard, "[The bullet] got him through the left hip. And that ball came up through his hip and cut the jugular vein going out the side of his neck. That's what fixed the bear."

"Patronize home industry and save money for yourself by buying a HALL," urge ads for the Summerside firm's "Famous Hall Undershot Thresher." Half a century after is founding, Thomas Hall's company is still going.

Dr. John Duncan MacLean, C.B.E., formerly of Culloden, King's County, is elected Premier of British Columbia. He will serve until 1928.

1928

The *Guardian* reports that rum vessels have been "operating unchecked" for the last several days from a base at East Point.

The Harris family donates $20,000 in cash and $60,000 worth of Robert Harris paintings to help establish a memorial art gallery and public library on Queen's Square.

"At last" — an ad in the *Island Farmer* announces the publication of *Cummins' Atlas of Prince Edward Island and the World.* Three years in the making, the Island's first cadastral atlas since 1880 is expensive: $12.

All previous attendance records at the annual Provincial Exhibition are shattered as "a host of over 10,000" people jam the fairgrounds in Charlottetown.

On 9 May, famous Canadian naturalist Jack Miner arrives

Harvesting Potatoes, c1900

The beater digger in the foreground flailed the potatoes out of their drills. The harvesters would fill their baskets and dump them into the cart in the background. The potato harvest was so important that schools shut down every fall so students could lend a hand.

"An Island Home," c1920

James Mavor, that famous geographer and economist, during a visit made the discovery that PEI was more than an island, more than a continent even; it was a world in miniature. In a morning drive he traversed lowlands, crossed rivers, passed over watersheds, ascended into highlands, where he viewed bays, harbours and the ocean itself. On a longer excursion he reached the main summit of the Island, and upon the plateau beheld deserts, lakes and tundras.... He declared his opinion that a man who travelled from Antwerp to Bagdad would not see more.

– Andrew Macphail, *The Master's Wife*

Poole and Thompson, c1900

The Montague firm of Poole and Thompson was one of the biggest in King's County.

in Charlottetown to lecture on his favourite subject — birds. His talk, assisted by moving pictures, is highly praised.

Alberton's Maud Dyer becomes the Island's first registered woman pharmacist.

Blaming "the recklessness of the few," the *Guardian* fumes about Islanders' lousy reputation as drivers. "Experienced drivers have told us more than once that they feel safer on the streets of Boston or New York than . . . Charlottetown."

Newspapers call it the "Death Pier." On the night of 25 June the Walsh Family of Elliotvale mistake the old Southport Wharf for a roadway and drive at full speed into the Harbour. Two sisters and a brother drown.

It's a sign of the times; Jenkins & Sons Groceteria in Charlottetown shuts its doors. The building will now house a national chain, T. Eaton Co.

Gasoline is selling for 9¢ per gallon.

Scales Hydro-Electric Co. succeeds the bankrupt Dunk River Hydro. Though financially troubled, it is the biggest hydro-electric plant in the province.

The *Guardian* profiles 79-year-old inventor James F. Buckley, formerly of New Haven but now living in Bradford, Massachusetts. Buckley claims to have perfected a submarine that can make it from New York to Paris in 18 hours. Spiral fins mounted on a rotating outer hull drive the "Ocean Greyhound" through the water like a jackscrew — or will if someone would fund its construction.

On 30 August, the heaviest rain storm in years drenches the Island. On Charlottetown streets, the water is from six inches to a foot deep in places.

1929

On 26 June, three bishops and an archbishop attend the solemn dedication ceremony as St. Dunstan's Cathedral is raised to the status of a basilica. Rome has accorded this distinction to honour the centennial of the creation of the Diocese of Charlottetown.

Voting in a provincial prohibition plebiscite, Islanders retain the status quo; 11,471 voters favour strict prohibition; 8,080 would prefer sale of liquor under a government-control act.

An article in *The American Magazine* is lavish in its praise for the Island. Its correspondent found no divorce, no unemployment, very little crime. "The stores are prosperous, houses are painted, lawns are cropped and streets are clean."

On 11 July, some 500 guests honour Charlie Dalton, co-founder of the silver fox industry at a "Sir Charles" banquet. The event is sponsored by the Canadian National Silver Fox Breeders' Association.

On 18 September an earth tremor rattles the Island — and Islanders.

At the 75th anniversary celebrations for St. Dunstan's College, keynote speaker Francis C. Kelley, Bishop of Oklahoma, launches a $100,000 fund-raising campaign for his alma mater. Thirty thousand dollars is subscribed on the spot by enthusiastic alumni. Two months later, the stock market crashes — and the fund-raising campaign with it.

Car ferry Charlottetown, c1935

Designed to carry both railcars and motor vehicles, the powerful, icebreaking ferry *Charlottetown* was the Island's main link to the mainland from her launch in 1930 until her untimely (and controversial) sinking in 1941.

Motorists, c1930

Pull into the local Texaco for some gas and maybe a coffee, then finish your cigarette before hitting the road again. Except for the fact the gentleman is wearing an old-fashioned pocket watch instead of a newer wristwatch, this Island couple could not have been more thoroughly modern.

On 12 January, Charlottetown's finest hotel, the Victoria, is destroyed by fire.

On 10 March St. Mary's Roman Catholic Church in Souris is gutted by fire. The stone shell is re-built with some modifications.

29 October is Black Thursday on the New York Stock Exchange as a catastrophic market crash ushers in the Great Depression. It is another year before the Island, chronically depressed anyway, begins to feel the pinch.

1930

What's 1.8 miles long, 16 feet wide and three inches thick? The "McIntyre Highway": a stretch of the Malpeque Road near St. Dunstan's University. The first rural pavement on Prince Edward island is named for the flamboyant Public Works Minister, "Big Jim Bill" McIntyre.

Sir Charles Dalton, fox breeder and philanthropist, is commissioned as Lt. Governor.

Premier Saunders steps down from office, turning the Liberal leadership over to Walter Lea. Lea becomes the "Million Acre Farm's" first farmer premier.

The new Summerside Raceway opens.

Charlottetown Forum opens on Fitzroy Street. It is one of only three artificial rinks in the Maritimes. Seating capacity is 2,000, more or less.

On 22 November, Lot 16 residents witness the Island's first airplane crash. Junior Jones, the pilot, and passenger Charles Yeo walk away from the wreckage. Jones

"Gathering Shells," c1900

will go on to become Chief Pilot for Maritime Central Airways.

💲 The *Guardian* announces that Summers Fertilizer of Baltimore, A. Horne & Co. of Charlottetown, Poole & Thompson of Montague and Austin Scales of Freetown are joining forces to erect the Island's first fertilizer plant on the Bruce Stewart & Co. wharf in Charlottetown.

1931

🍁 Canadian National Railways opens a $750,000 hotel on Kent Street, giving the Island capital first-class accommodation at last.

🍁 Financial difficulties force the McDonald family to sell Dalvay-by-the-Sea, which re-opens as a first-class summer hotel. The new resort may have special perks for guests in this teetotalling province. It is soon owned and operated by the notorious rum-rummer, Captain Edward Dicks. When Dicks goes bankrupt in 1936, the estate is taken over by one of his creditors, Lt. Governor George DeBlois. A year later DeBlois sells it to the new National Park, which has been operating it as a resort hotel ever since.

🧭 On 20 May S.S. *Charlottetown*, the Island's elegant new ferry, is launched. At 2,795 tons

Upton Field, 1932

and 8,000 hp, she is considered the most powerful ice-breaking ferry in the world. In response to increasing automobile traffic, the vessel features a drive-on motor vehicle deck.

🧭 Upton Field, the Island's first real airport opens with speeches and festivities at Dr. J. S. Jenkins' farm in West Royalty. The Lt. Governor and the Mayor of Charlottetown each give an address, but the thousands of spectators are more interested in the performance staged by the Trans Canadian Air Pageant.

🏛 Chastened by four years of opposition, J.D. Stewart's provincial Conservatives sweep back into power with a 18 seat to 12 victory. Conservatives and Liberals have been trading the government back and forth since 1915. Conservatives learn to savour this victory; they will lose the next six general elections.

👥 After bottoming out at 86,000 in the mid-1920s, the Island's population rebounds to 88,000.

🌀 "Yo-Yo Craze Hits the Island Province," proclaims the *Patriot*. "Fascinating Philippine pastime has the city and country by the ears." The paper sponsors an Island-wide yo-yo tournament, with a cash prize of $20.

⚕ The Government closed down the Dalton Sanitorium in 1922, claiming it could not afford it. But it realizes in the fight against TB it cannot afford to do without a Provincial Sanitorium, and so opens one on McGill Avenue in Charlottetown.

🔥 On 14 December, Falconwood Insane Asylum is destroyed by fire. Its replacement, constructed on the same site, will be called the Hillsborough Hospital.

💲 Though the Great Depression shows no sign of ending, three Island businessmen take a chance and form the Health Pasteurized Milk Co.

☀ February features 134 cm of snow.

🌟 The growing season is remarkably long, with no frost for 199 days, 48 days over the yearly average.

Prince of Wales College, Charlottetown, P. E. I.

Prince of Wales College, 1912

"This is where I am spending my time now," wrote Miss Eliza MacWilliams of Eldon on the front of this postcard.

Golf Links, Charlottetown, c1905
Now known as the Belvedere Golf Club, this was the first golf course on Prince Edward Island.

1932

Lt. Governor Dalton moves into a newly-refurbished Government House. The last Governor to live at Fanningbank was A.C. MacDonald, who turned the building over for use as a military convalescent home in 1917.

On 25 January, Louise Jenkins becomes the first woman to pilot an airplane non-stop from Montreal to Prince Edward Island. The flight time: 4 hours 8 minutes.

Just a few months after its creation, the P.E.I. Provincial Police is replaced by the R.C.M.P. In addition to beautiful uniforms and an international reputation, the "Mounties" come with a Federal subsidy to help pay for them — an irresistible attraction to the cash-strapped province.

Benjamin Bremner publishes *An Island Scrapbook* — one in a series of popular anecdotal histories.

On 6 February, fire destroys Prince of Wales College. The cost of rebuilding the College and last year's casualty, Falconwood during the depths of the Great Depression will help defeat the Conservative government come election time.

On 10 February fire strikes another Island landmark as the Rustico Convent is destroyed.

On 21 February, four people are killed when a passenger train slams into a freight train stuck in snow at Handrahan's Cutting, near Tignish. Dead are an engineer and three snowshovellers trying to get the freight train free. Fortunately, there were no passengers on board. Two women had boarded at Summerside, but soon got off and proceeded to Alberton by horse and sleigh.

The *Guardian* dubs a 23 March effort the worst storm in a decade.

On 17 September, a tropical storm descends on the Maritimes devastating the Island lobster fleet.

1933

On 26 July, Victoria residents awake to the sound of enormous airplane engines. One of 24 huge flying boats in the Italian Air Armada, on its way back to Italy after an appearance at the Chicago Exposition, suffers a mechanical malfunction and lands in Victoria Harbour to make repairs.

On hearing that Charles Lindbergh will be landing in Halifax while scouting a possible flying boat route from New York to Greenland, the Island government extends an invitation to try its fine harbours. The Lone Eagle declines.

On 10 October, two years into his second term as Island Premier and after a lengthy ill-ness, J. D. Stewart dies in office. He is only 59. The premiership and the Conservative leadership fall to his colleague W. J. P. MacMillan.

On 9 December Lt. Governor Sir Charles Dalton, who parleyed his fox-breeding expertise into a fortune, dies in office, aged 83. Charlottetown businessman George D. DeBlois is commissioned as the new Lt. Governor.

On 1 September, fox magnates J. Edgar Milligan and George L. Morrison are killed in a car accident near Buffalo, New York. Partners since 1914, Milligan and Morrison "franchised" the fox fur industry, building up a chain of some 84 farms throughout North America — anchored by their main operation at Northam.

The third P.E.I. Hospital, a 100-bed facility, opens on six acres of Government House farmland bordering the Brighton Road.

The Carnegie Corporation of New York announces a grant of $60,000 for the establishment of a provincial library system on Prince Edward Island. The first branch opens in Montague.

On 25 January, Montague Hydro's dam on the south branch of the Montague River breaks. The wreckage helps an icy flood-tide sweep away a series of bridges in its path as it rushes towards the sea.

On 3 July, Herbert Mann of Margate is stunting over Summerside in his homemade airplane when a wing tears loose at 1,500 feet. Mann dies in the Island's first fatal air crash.

1934

The Dominion Minister of Railways agrees to drop the ferry rates for automobiles. The new rate will be $2.00 per auto ($3.00 round trip), down from $5.00 and $7.00.

Fishing on the Dunk River, c1890

The Island abounds in trout, and, I will venture to say, not easily to be excelled. If not as fine, they are very little inferior to salmon. They afford equal gratification to the sportsman and the epicure.

— John Lawson, *Letters on Prince Edward Island*, 1852

Sometime during the night of 25 March, thieves crack the safe at Charlottetown's toney Prince Edward Theatre. The substantial sum of $50-60 is missing.

L.M. Montgomery is among the select few invited to the first screening of the newest "Anne of Green Gables" movie. Her review? Two thumbs up! Much better than the silent version made in 1919. Her main criticism? "That the scene of the story is based in California... which does not have the same austere beauty of Prince Edward Island." "What then," asks the *Guardian* "became of the scenes taken here with so much publicity for supposed use in the picture?"

On 31 January, an all-French-language concert is held at Holy Redeemer Hall in Charlottetown. According to the Charlottetown *Guardian* it's a first for the anglophone city.

Earl G. Jenkins establishes a wildlife sanctuary at Southport.

"Your island lacks publicity," is the judgement of R.H. Davies. The noted American travel writer has been touring the Island, and feels free to dispense some advice. "Centralize on something, the number and kind of fish caught, a hunting and fishing synopsis, play up your golf."

On 21 March, sparks from a flue set fire to the roof of Government House. Fortunately, the fire is extinguished before any serious damage is done to the historic building.

To mark the 400th anniversary of Jacques Cartier's "discovery" of Prince Edward Island, a memorial cairn is unveiled by Lt. Governor George DeBlois in front of a slate of federal and provincial VIPs, as well as a delegation from France.

On 26 October, after four days adrift with a full cargo and a broken engine, the rum-runner *Tena II* is rescued by SS *Sanfonia*. To the immense relief of the *Tena II*'s owner-captain, the skipper of the *Sanfonia* agrees to tow them close to shore at Naufrage, where they can offload, instead of taking them to Souris, where the Mounties and Customs officials might take an interest.

On 30 January, Cardigan's only hotel — and restaurant — is destroyed by fire.

On 7 July, a disastrous fire sweeps through the West Prince community of Richmond. Among the 26 buildings destroyed are the Arsenault & Gaudet store, the post office, railway station, freight shed, a sawmill, a warehouse, a dance hall, three houses and numerous outbuildings.

Agnew-Surpass, the national shoe-store chain, opens a branch in Charlottetown.

On 7 February, the ice racing card on Summerside Harbour has to be postponed because of the extreme cold.

John Andrew McLeod of Park Corner is named President of the Bank of Nova Scotia. He's the second individual from his community to do well at the bank. From 1897 to 1907 the bank's General Manager was Henry Collingwood McLeod, also from Park Corner.

The *Daily People's Press* of Ouatenna, Minnesota, honours its proprietor, Benjamin Darby, at 86 said to be the oldest active publisher in the U.S. Mr. Darby is a na-

Prince of Wales College, c1950
Built in 1931 after the original College burned down, the expense of this building helped bring down the Conservative government of Dr. W.J.P. MacMillan.

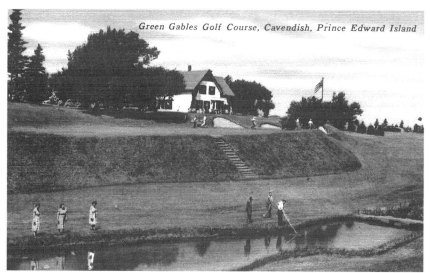

Green Gables Golf Course, Cavendish, Prince Edward Island

Green Gables Golf Course, c1940
Officially opened in 1939, the golf course at Green Gables was considered vital to the success of the Prince Edward Island National Park that was created in 1936.

tive of St. Eleanor's, Prince Edward Island.

The *Guardian* reports that Charlottetown native William T. McQuaid is the youngest member of the U.S. federal prosecuting staff.

1935

Any government in power during the Great Depression is likely to be unpopular, but today's provincial election produces a Commonwealth first. Dr. W.J.P. MacMillan's ruling Conservatives are shut out 30-0 by Walter Lea's Liberals.

On Christmas Day, Lt. Governor DeBlois hosts a party at Fanningbank for over 700 poor children. "Ice cream, oranges and candy were liberally distributed to each of the children, the boys receiving in addition a hockey stick and puck, the girls a doll and a box of chocolates...." To top off the day, each child is given a quarter before leaving. DeBlois' Christmas Day event will be repeated every year during his tenure in office.

The *Patriot* introduces a new feature — daily radio listings. On 14 November it publishes schedules for WZJ and WEAF from New York City and the new Cana-

dian Radio Broadcasting Corporation. The American stations offer "The Hit Parade," "Walter Winchell," "Jack Benny," and "Popeye the Sailor." The CRBC features "The Vesper Hour," "Garden of Music, musical tone pictures under the direction of W. Knight Wilson," and "The Viking Sword," a dramatization based on the exhibits at the Royal Ontario Museum.

A tornado touches down on the property of Father W.E. Monaghan in Albany. Dozens of trees are uprooted, several buildings are flattened and a heavy workhorse is blown 200 yards through the air. "I could see pieces of timber 60 feet

long hurled through the air like pieces of wheat straws," says a shaken Charles McCaughey, who himself was temporarily airborne.

The *Boston Herald* tells how, in 1917, former New Londoner George Clark converted Britain's top secret tracer bullet formula for use in American ordnance; "giving the US Army a machine gun tracer bullet that was better than any used by the Allies or their foes when all others had failed."

On 17 August, Charlottetown swelters in 36.7 C° temperatures, a record high for the province.

Hunter River's James Charles McGuigan is appointed Archbishop for the Roman Catholic Diocese of Toronto.

Murray River's John Sutherland Bonnell is named Minister to the Fifth Avenue Presbyterian Church in New York — one of the largest and most influential congregations in the United States. By expanding his ministry to the new medium of radio, Bonnell soon becomes one of the continent's most recognized and respected clerics and social commentators.

Marie-Anne Évangéline Gallant of Abram's Village is appointed Superior General of the Congregation of the Grey Nuns in Montreal. After her death, the city names a street in her honour.

Souris Beach, c1920
After World War I standards of beach attire grew scandalously loose. Before the War one would never have seen bare, adult elbows and knees on a public beach.

Cannery Crew, Graham's Creek, c1905

The operation of packing instead of being carried on in a capacious and well-conducted establishment at some central point is carried on in all kinds of out-of-the-way localities, in small establishments and under daily conditions which cannot be controlled, and which are detrimental to the best quality of packed goods.

— Shellfish Commission Report, 1913

1936

The Prince Edward Island National Park is established along the Island's north shore. Its centrepiece is Cavendish, "home" of the storybook heroine *Anne of Green Gables*. Miles of farmland along the North Shore is expropriated to create the Park. Sidney Ranicar of Stanhope is given special consideration for the "ginseng industry" on his 40 acres.

On 21 May, trustees of the Cundall estate decide to offer Beaconsfield house free of charge to the Prince Edward Island Hospital for use as a student nurses' residence.

Receiving his license from the P.E.I. Aero Club, Joe Anderson of Sackville N.B. is the first commercial pilot trained on P.E.I. Anderson will become a good friend of another Island-trained pilot, Carl Burke. On 6 December, 1941 he will be killed in a plane crash while returning to Canada after his final mission as a pilot for Ferry Command. He was coming home to become a partner in Burke's new airline, M.C.A.

On 10 January Walter Lea of Victoria, the Island's first farmer premier, dies after a lengthy illness less than a year after his Liberals made the first electoral sweep in Commonwealth history.

Walter Jones of Bunbury, author of the definitive work on fox breeding and world famous cattle breeder, is awarded the King's Silver Jubilee Medal for his "outstanding contributions to agriculture." The maverick Liberal will end up as premier.

Holman's offers the "Holman-Alsco Oil Burner," designed to convert any wood or coal-burning kitchen range into an oil range – only $52.50 or a dollar down and a dollar a week for a year. Homeowners with electricity – and lots of money – can also buy a Frigidare electric refrigerator. Ten dollars down and $10 per month for 18 months.

1937

Ottawa sets aside $200,000 to begin work on the new ferry harbour at Wood Islands.

A Royal Commission into illegal lobster fishing and canning begins inquiries in March. When A.B. Fisher, vice-president of Windsor-Fisher Ltd. is asked how long he thinks illegal fishing and packing has been going on in the province, he replies: "I can't say. I'm only 50 years old."

On 30 August, a major brush fire in the French Village area finally burns itself out after defying fire-fighters' efforts for nearly a month.

John T. McNally of Hope River is named Archbishop of Halifax.

Weighing the Catch, Fortune, 1940

It was good money. It got to be good money. It was very poor at first. In 1960 I had over 7,000 dollars coming to me for two months. When I started, I took 39 dollars for a month.

— Stewart Ross, *Belfast People*

Georgetown's Kathleen Fairchild becomes the first Canadian woman admitted to the Massachusetts bar.

1938

On 7 August, customs officials seize the rum-runner *Nellie J. Banks* off the North Shore. The most famous of the Island rum-runners will end her days as a hulk on a Murray Harbour beach.

On 26 January a Dodge half ton loaded with wood plunges through the ice about a kilometre from the ferry wharf in Georgetown. Although the driver and his companion get away safely, the ice surrounding the mishap is too thin to salvage the truck. So the next day about 15 local men devise a way to haul it 200 metres *under* the ice to a spot where they can winch it to the surface. The dripping Dodge is pulled triumphantly through the downtown before going to a local garage to be dried out.

On 30 March, while the Strait is still clogged with ice, residents of Canoe Cove wonder what a vessel "illuminated from stem to stern, both above and below decks," was doing off shore. It was apparently a steamer, but no sound of engines can be heard. Appearing at dusk, it sat in view until about 10:00, when it "slowly settled, without a sound, into the depths." Many are convinced it is the phantom ship – albeit in a modern guise.

On 26 November, in a blinding snow storm, the steamer *Nandi* runs ashore two miles north of the West Point Light.

O'Leary "gets the lights," courtesy of local entrepreneur Frederick H. Champion. For a town of its size, O'Leary is surprisingly late in its electrification. Its plant disabled by fire, Champion Electric is bought out by Maritime Electric in 1953.

On 28 April, a combination sleet storm and blizzard lashes the Island. Five deaths are

***The "Boston Boat,"* c1910**
Operated by a number of different companies over the years, the Boston Boat was a weekly visitor to Charlottetown in the early 20th century.

blamed on the vicious storm, which disrupts electric and telephone service for days.

Two Island youths, Lloyd Arsenault and Harry Perry, appear in a Montreal court on a charge of illegally riding a freight train. When Arsenault's charge is read to him in French, he replies that he can't understand and asks to hear it in English. When Perry's is read to him in English, he replies in rapid French that, though his name sounds English, he can speak only French. Both are found guilty and get a month in jail.

1939

On 14 June, George VI and Queen Elizabeth begin the first-ever visit to Prince Edward Island of a reigning monarch.

Automobile traffic has increased to the point to make another ferry service to the Island feasible. The new service, privately owned but government subsidized, will operate out of ports at Wood Islands and Caribou, Nova Scotia. The company calls itself Northumberland Ferries Limited. Canadian National charges automobiles $7.50 and trucks as much as $50 for a

***Loading Potatoes, Summerside,* c1935**
In the 1950s potatoes began to edge out hay and oats as the Island's dominant export crop.

round trip between Cape Tormentine and Port Borden.

On 17 May, in a barn at Day's Corner, Prince County, the R.C.M.P. make one of the largest liquor seizures in the history of Prohibition on Prince Edward Island. It just happens to be the day before a provincial election.

The Liberals under Thane A. Campbell roll to another election victory over the Tories, who can take some solace in winning three of the 30 seats. At least now they will have members in the Legislature.

Bradford W. LePage is commissioned as Lt. Governor.

"We're goin' to the barn dance tonight." On 11 November, Don Messer and his Islanders go coast-to-coast for the first time on CFCY radio. Don, Marg, Charlie and the gang become an institution in Atlantic Canada.

On 19 July, as part of the 75th Anniversary of Confederation festivities, "Anne of Green Gables Golf Course" is formally opened by the Hon. C.A. Crerar.

In a province that once banned automobiles, the gasoline tax has become the single greatest generator of public revenue. The yield for 1939 is $384,440.

1940

With a total of 35,000 visitors, the National Park at Cavendish attracts more than all of the Maritimes' other National Parks combined.

A Prohibition plebiscite indicates that Islanders are warming to the idea of lifting restrictions, but not yet. The majority votes to keep the province dry.

A new airport for Charlottetown on Brackley Point Road opens. The replacement for Upton Field costs more than $100,000 to build. When the Commonwealth Air

Don Messer's Islanders

Training Plan is announced, work begins on new airfields at Mount Pleasant, St. Eleanor's and Wellington.

When its only ferry, the recently-built *Charles A. Dunning* is commandeered by the government for war duties, the new Northumberland Ferry service buys a used boat named the *Sankaty* for $3,600. While in Halifax being refitted as the *Prince Nova*, the *Sankaty* is also commandeered. It will take the intervention of powerful friends in Ottawa to secure a boat for the service.

The idea of a fixed link to the mainland surfaces again when a provincial brief to the Royal Commission on Dominion-Provincial Relations revives the Northumberland Strait Tunnel proposal.

One of the most powerful individuals in the Mackenzie King government, James Ralston, is elected in Prince County. Ralston is not from the Island, and only rarely gets to visit his riding, but Prince County sees the advantages of having the Minister of Finance (later Defense) as its Member of Parliament!

The British North America Act is amended to allow Ottawa to institute an Unemploy-

ment Insurance Program. It's not known when we start to call it "pogey."

The Provincial Exhibition Association decides to cancel this year's fair for the good of the war effort. Old Home Week moves back to 12 August to fill the gap.

The government decides to relieve the agriculture and fishing industries from a portion of the gasoline tax. To differentiate the fuel used by farmers and fishermen, it will be stained with a dye. "Marked" gas becomes a part of the Island vocabulary.

Federal statistics indicate that hay and clover are still the number one crops on Prince Edward Island. Grain crops are a close second — potatoes are a distant third.

Oil surveyors return to Hillsborough Bay. This time they plan to drill at least 12,000 feet in search of oil.

The Federal Department of Fisheries imposes a minimum size limit of 6.5 inches on lobsters. Canners are happy, because small lobsters are more expensive to process. Fishermen fear for their incomes. In some areas, "smalls" make up over a third of the catch.

Provincial Exhibition Building, c1895

The fortunes of war. When Germany invades Denmark, Great Britain loses its main bacon supplier. Island farmers are put on notice that they will have to help make up some of the 3.5 million pounds of pork per week that Britain consumes.

A scarlet fever epidemic sweeps through southern King's County. Schools and other public buildings are closed in Murray Harbour as a quarantine is imposed.

Captain Edward Dicks, former rum-runner and owner of Dalvay-by-the-Sea, loses his schooner while fishing off Newfoundland. He claims he was torpedoed. No one dies, but he and his crew spend 36 hours in an open boat before rescue. Some wonder why the Germans would waste a precious torpedo on a mere coastal schooner.

As a wartime measure, Charlottetown adopts Daylight Savings Time.

Despite the reputation of Island drivers, British Columbia is named the most dangerous place to drive in Canada. Ontario comes in a close second.

Charlottetown's Fire Chief warns citizens they will be charged if they don't stop impeding his engines on their way to calls. Fire engine chasers are bad enough, but many enterprising motorists are trying to beat the trucks to the scene, often blocking their path.

On 4 September a German u-boat sets the tone for the war at sea when it torpedoes and sinks a passenger liner, the S.S. *Athenia*, without warning. The first Islander to die in World War II is Muriel Fraser of Summerside, who was among the 112 dead. Eastern Steamship Lines, who run the "Boston boats," reassure their customers that their vessels are American owned and fly the American flag. (In case the u-boat looks before it fires.)

Ottawa announces daily rates of pay in the armed forces. Senior officers will get $10 per day; junior officers: $4.25 to $7.50. Non-commissioned officers will earn as much as $3.90. A private will get $1.30.

Fearing that German spies might use it for a code, Ottawa bans the use of Gaelic in telegraph and wireless communication. Cape Breton and Prince Edward Island's large population of native Gaelic-speakers point out that their language has been in use in Great Britain for much longer than English.

On 22 January, Pte. Urban Joseph MacDonald of Cardigan is killed while on sentry duty in Dartmouth when a comrade's rifle goes off. He's possibly the first Island soldier to die on duty in World War II.

HMCS *Malpeque*, a Bangor-class minesweeper named after the Island community (and oyster), is launched at Vancouver. It is 11 years before she ever sees Prince Edward Island.

On 12 November, fire destroys much of the business district in the village of Breadalbane. Two stores are completely lost while two houses, another store and a hotel annex are damaged.

October is the wettest month since December, 1902. The province absorbed 8.85 inches of rain and enjoyed only 93 hours of sunlight.

The worst electrical storm in decades strikes eastern Prince County. Dozens of barns and dwellings are hit in Bedeque and Freetown. In Central Bedeque, the spire in the Baptist Church has two large holes punched through it.

Tignish native C.L. Nelligan, Bishop of Pembroke, is named head of the Canadian Catholic Chaplain Service. In the last war, Nelligan had served as a firearms instructor.

1941

Ottawa finds a vessel, a Great Lakes ferry named the *Erie Isle*, to replace the boats it commandeered from Northumberland Ferries. Renamed *Prince Nova*, the boat can carry 20 cars and two trucks. On 28 June, at 11am, it launches the Island's second ferry service when it sets out from Caribou, Nova Scotia.

Canadian Airways Limited drops Charlottetown from its schedule. Ottawa pressures the "government" airline, Trans Canada Airlines, to maintain the service, but this is a temporary measure. Trans

Lobster Smack, Colville Bay, c1910

A report on the Island lobster fishery in the 1880s estimated that the simple shore boat could be had for as little as $8.00!

Canada would prefer another company assume the route. Luckily one Canadian Airways pilot, a native of Charlottetown, would prefer to keep flying out of home. So he puts together a company to take over from T.C.A. On 7 December, Carl Burke's Maritime Central Airways makes its first flight. Within five years, M.C.A. is the biggest airline in the Maritimes.

Premier Campbell, who also serves as the province's attorney general, instructs the R.C.M.P to strictly enforce the Island's speed limits. Islanders are supposed to drive no faster than 45 mph — 30 mph if meeting another vehicle after dark.

In January, Islanders are horrified by the brutal murder of Charlottetown grocer Peter Trainor. Two men, Fred Phillips and Earl Lund, are quickly arrested. They stand trial in June, are convicted and sentenced to death. Their hanging on 20 August is the last state execution on Prince Edward Island.

The Island's population has grown to 95,057 — back to the level it was at in 1871.

Island fishermen feel the full impact of recent legal size limits for lobsters. Even though the war is pushing up prices for everything else, the value of the fishery is down 25%.

The Prince Edward Island Federation of Agriculture

holds its organizational meeting in Charlottetown. Ten agricultural organizations unite to adopt a constitution. Their aim: to coordinate, promote, and educate agricultural interests.

On 8 February, Canadian Airways pilot Carl Burke flies from Charlottetown to Musgrave Harbour, Nfld, to rescue a survivor from the crash of a Hudson bomber. He also brings out the bodies of the dead, including Dr. Frederick Banting, co-discoverer of insulin.

The government imposes gas rationing. Most motorists are allowed three gallons per week. Special exemptions are made for physicians, journalists and others deemed especially important to the war effort.

Man and Lobster, c1910

By the turn of the 20th century the increasing scarcity of large "market" lobsters like the one this man is holding prompted fears that lobster stocks were approaching collapse.

Islanders still make the best gunners. Following a shooting competition in England, an Island battery is declared the best in the Royal Canadian Artillery.

On 18 June, while en route to routine refit in Saint John, the carferry *Charlottetown* is mortally wounded when it hits an underwater obstacle. In the subsequent enquiry, Captain Read maintains his vessel ran over a submerged wreck, possibly a German u-boat victim. The court refuses to accept his explanation fixes the blame on him, and the career of one of the Island's most respected mariners comes to a sad close.

Horrified bathers watch as a Harvard flight trainer out of Summerside crashes then explodes behind the Cavendish sand dunes. Both pilot and instructor die.

January features 66 inches (165 cm) of snow.

Red Point native Cyrus Ching, president of the U.S. Rubber Company (now known as Uniroyal), is appointed by President Roosevelt to the National Defense Mediation Board. Ching is considered one of the leading labour mediators in the United States.

1942

While returning from refit in Quebec City, the Island's only carferry, S.S. *Prince Edward Island* is almost hit by a torpedo. Sailing in the front rank of a convoy, the crew of the *Prince* watch as a Greek freighter beside them is sunk by a German u-boat, and then as two torpedoes pass under their own keel.

Three years after nuns are given permission to attend the Island's Roman Catholic university, St. Dunstan's, the school begins an experiment in co-education as five lay women register for classes. The experiment is a resounding success.

On 11 September the Flower-class corvette HMCS *Charlottetown*, one of four Royal Canadian Navy ships named after Island communities, is torpedoed by a German u-boat in the Gulf of St. Lawrence. There are 58 survivors, but the commander and eight crew are lost. The same day in Quebec, HMCS *Summerside* is commissioned for service.

On 8 November, Charlottetown-born Frederick Thornon Peters, a Captain in the Royal Naval Reserve, leads a daring but futile attack against the harbour defences of Oran, Morocco. The only survivor on his vessel's bridge, he is killed in a plane crash five days later on the way back to England. He is posthumously awarded the Victoria Cross and the American Distinguished Service Cross.

On 8 June, the Halifax bomber piloted by future M.P. and Premier Angus MacLean is shot down over Holland. The crew are captured, but with luck and the help of the Dutch Resistance MacLean manages to escape. He is smuggled through Belgium, France and Spain to safety at Gibraltar.

On 7 January, two planes from RAF Charlottetown collide in mid-air at an altitude of 2,000 feet and crash in a field in Southport. All seven crewmen are killed.

With farm help at a premium and new tractors in short supply, Hall Manufacturing of Summerside suggests converting old cars into "Autotrac Tractors." They're like something from a myth: head of a car, tail of a tractor.

On 22 September, 164 mm (6.5 inches) of rain — an Island record — pours down in one 24-hour stretch. This will be the wettest September on record, with 315 mm (12.6 inches) of precipitation.

1943

Maritime Central Airways is offering three flights daily to Moncton. A return ticket is $11.70 plus tax.

As the *Prince Edward Island* struggles to maintain winter contact with the mainland, calls for

***Horse Pull,* c1930**
Judging from the numbers marked on the stone weights, this team is pulling about one and a half tons.

an additional icebreaker grow more urgent.

Police in Summerside seize 16 gallons of cherry extract. Prized for their alcohol content, cherry and orange have been added to the already popular lemon and vanilla extracts as favoured illicit beverages. Thanks to Prohibition, the Island has probably the most fragrant inebriates in the country.

Premier Thane A. Campbell is appointed Chief Justice of the Provincial Supreme Court — a position he holds until 1970, long enough to swear in his son as premier.

The new "Farmer Premier," J. Walter Jones, leads the Provincial Grits to a 20 seat to 10

electoral victory. The election is actually closer than it looks. A mere 200 vote swing, spread over six key seats, would have given victory to the Tories.

Island Foods, the province's first dehydration plant, opens in Summerside.

On 28 January, flying a one-passenger Department of Transportation plane, Captain Carl Burke of Maritime Central Airways makes five perilous landings on an ice floe off the North Shore to rescue four RAF airman, stranded after the crash of their Anson bomber. Able only to take off one crewman at a time, Burke makes an extra trip to rescue the airplane's radio!

Spreading Irish Moss To Dry
Irish Moss *(Chondrus crispus)* is an unprepossessing red algae with remarkable qualities. Within its structure is a compound called carrageenin, which is prized as a natural gelling agent in a variety of commercial products.

109

Charles A Dunning, c1955

Originally named the *Sankaty*, the *Charles A. Dunning* was purchased in 1939 but immediately requisitioned for war duty. In 1946 she finally began service as the second ferry on the Wood Islands-Caribou run. With a capacity of 26 vehicles, the *Dunning* remained in service until 1964, when she was retired and sold for scrap.

The *Guardian* estimates that over 10,000 Islanders have enlisted for war service. The Shaw family in Bloomfield has 10 of its 11 sons in uniform — plus a son-in-law.

Charlottetown's quota in the fourth Victory Loan Drive is $850,000 — just enough, officials point out, to build another HMCS *Charlottetown*.

A Halifax newspaper notes that Charlottetown's Gloria (Sally) Large is Canada's only female bomber ferry pilot. Enlisted in Britain's Air Transport Auxiliary, Large flies bombers built in Canada across the Atlantic for service in Bomber Command.

The Catholic church in St. George's, built in the 1850s, burns down.

1944

Dominion Transport Minister D.W. McLachlan announces a survey of the Northumberland Strait to see if the strata are suitable for the building of a tunnel. He warns, though, that "construction of the proposed tunnel appears to be of doubtful possibility."

Premier Jones describes Prohibition as "a noble experiment with human nature made by those who did not understand human nature." There is mounting pressure in the province to repeal the act.

On 13 November Defense Minister (and Prince County M.P.) James Ralston resigns from Cabinet. He and Prime Minister Mackenzie King cannot agree on conscription policy. Ralston is convinced that only conscription can provide enough reinforcements for Canada's battle-depleted army. King, fearing what conscription might do to national unity, is determined that only troops who volunteer will be sent to fight. Ralston's resignation forces King's hand. Ten days later the Prime Minister invokes the National Resources Mobilization Act to send conscripts overseas.

On 27 April the second HMCS *Charlottetown*, this one a River-class frigate, is commissioned for service.

On 5 December, Island pilot Don MacLean and the crew of his Avro Lancaster bomber complete their 34th and last mission. In an unusual step, the entire crew is decorated for bravery. MacLean and his fellow Canadians get the Distinguished Flying Cross.

1945

Federal officials officially nix the proposed Northumberland Strait tunnel. They promise, of all things, a new ice-breaking car ferry instead.

On 19 April, nearing the end of his term, Lt. Governor Bradford LePage refuses assent to a law that would have introduced government control over liquor sales.

Wanted for a series of armed bank robberies in central Canada, Ulysse and Eileen Lauzon are arrested on 13 September at the Covehead races. En route to Charlottetown, they make a daring but unsuccessful attempt to escape R.C.M.P. custody.

Lt. Governor Joseph Alphonse Bernard

On 18 May, Joseph Bernard becomes the first Acadian to be named Lt. Governor.

As the war in Europe ends, four of the Island's five

military airfields are closed. The airbase at Summerside-St. Eleanor's remains open while Charlottetown airport reverts to purely civilian status.

HMCS *Summerside* is de-commissioned after leading a charmed life through four years of naval warfare. A year later the little corvette is sold for scrap.

HMCS *Assiniboine*, a recently de-commissioned destoyer being towed to a scrapyard in New York, parts with its towline and runs aground at South Lake. There's no great rush to salvage the vessel, which remains on a sandbar until 1952. Portions of the vessel can still be seen at low tide. In addition to an epic battle with a German u-boat, which she sank by ramming, *Assiniboine* was part of the battle group which sank the *Bismark*, and once had the privilege of transporting Winston Churchill to Iceland.

1946

The Island's first Rural Beautification Contest is held. Mr. Cyril Toombs of Rustico wins first prize.

Six years after being bought by Northumberland Ferries (then requisitioned for government service) the automobile ferry *Sankaty*, renamed *Charles S. Dunning* begins service on the Wood Islands run.

On 11 August 20,000 Islanders, almost 1/5 of the population tours the new queen of the Northumberland Strait ferry run, the M.V. *Abegweit* at an open house in Charlottetown. The *"Abby"* is said to be the biggest, most modern, most powerful railway ferry in the world.

The Federal Department of Fisheries ships a population of Island lobsters to British Columbia to see if they can adapt to life on the West Coast.

In Urbainville, the last of the Island's grain banks shuts down. The once-common grain banks were precursors of the

Train Bridge, Pisquid River, 1949
By the late 1940s the Hillsborough Bridge was deemed too unstable to handle heavy, steam locomotives, which were sent to southern King's County via Mount Stewart.

modern co-operative movement. Urbainville's operation dated back to the 1860s.

A 96-bed "Veteran's Wing" opens at the Prince Edward Island Hospital on Charlottetown's Brighton Road, doubling the facility's available accommodations. A third wing will be added in 1960 to house the growing number of patients now able to afford hospital care.

Latin is removed from the curriculum of the Island's 400-odd one room schools. Although it will still be offered in larger schools, most rural students wanting Latin will have to take correspondence courses.

On 10 October, a major fire on the Charlottetown waterfront destroys the Bruce Stewart & Co. plant and Island Fertilizer. With engines like the "Imperial," Stewart & Co. helped motorize the Island fishing fleet in the early 1900s. Island Fertilizer will find a new home in two surplus airplane hangars which are moved from the airport and reassembled beside the Charlottetown Driving Park

Government officials estimate 200,000 tourists visited the Island in the 1946 season.

The Dominion Bureau of Statistics reports that Island farm labourers are the lowest paid in the country. The average daily wage (with board) here is $2.62 –

compared to Manitoba's national high of $5.26.

March may be a lion, but its throat is parched. It has been the driest month ever on Prince Edward Island, with only 5 mm of precipitation.

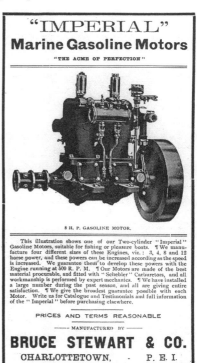

"Imperial" Marine Engine
In other places they were called "make and breaks," "one-lungers," "pickey-pucks" or "putt-putts." On the Island the simple, one-cylinder marine gas engines that revolutionized the fishery were usually called "Stewarts," after the Charlottetown foundry that made them.

Shore Cart, c1910

When boats were small and harbours scarce, the day's catch was simply taken to the water's edge and loaded onto shore carts.

Cardigan native Malcolm Dockerty is named head of the Pathology department at the Mayo Clinic. He is a pioneer in the specialty of surgical pathology.

1947

The Legislature selects the Lady Slipper as the Island's provincial flower. Unfortunately, they name the wrong species, then mis-spell its Latin name. A 1952 amendment further confuses the issue. Finally, in 1965 they get it right, and *Cypripedium acaule* goes into the books as our provincial flower.

A nurse's residence is completed alongside the Prince Edward Island Hospital. It will accommodate first and second-year students. The seniors stay at the nearby Cundall Home — a.k.a. Beaconsfield.

Canadian National decides that the Hillsborough Bridge is too fragile to safely support steam locomotives. So it despatches a lighter, diesel electric locomotive — the first in the province — to haul trains over the Murray Harbour line.

Led by J. Walter Jones, the Liberals trounce the Tories 24 seats to six for their fourth straight electoral victory. Although it receives a great deal of attention, the C.C.F. party gets few votes from Islanders. All 16 C.C.F. candidates lose their deposits.

On 11 September, Island meatpackers vote to strike. Farmers' concern over getting their meat to market starts a train of events that will end with government intervention and legislation to outlaw unions with out-of-province affiliations.

On 12 March, St. Dunstan's University Saints upset St. Francis Xavier 8-6 to win the Maritime Intercollegiate Hockey Title. Delirium reigns.

On 2 July, four Summerside residents see "a bright, luminous object travelling at great height in the air." The *Guardian* notes this "could have been one of the so-called 'flying saucers' reported having been seen in the western United States and Canada."

Local residents call for Green Gables House to be turned into a Provincial Museum. Premier Jones echoes their sentiments – in a pre-election speech.

Two years after the end of World War II, wartime rationing finally ends. The last two holdouts on the ration list, sugar and molasses, will no longer be rationed. Price controls will remain in force, however.

HMCS *Charlottetown* is paid off. Unlike her namesake a corvette sunk in 1942, her fate is less glorious. Sold for scrap, she becomes part of a breakwater in Oyster Bay, B.C.

Restless as cold weather delays the lobster season, four impatient fishermen from French River head out on 2 May into the teeth of a gale to set their traps. Their new boat is beaten to pieces on an off-shore shoal near New London light. All four are drowned.

On 17 August four young men drown at Cavendish beach — "all hauled under by a terrific undertow." The tragedy sparks calls for lifeguards, who appear the next year.

On 30 August, an Eastern Coastlines bus bound for Wood Islands is torn apart by a C.N.R. train at Wilmot crossing in southern King's County. Four people are killed and another 10 injured in the worst train-motor vehicle accident in Island history.

Christmas Day brings tragedy to Elmsdale, where a mother and two of her children are

Cape Turner, c1910

killed in a house fire that began when she mistakenly put gasoline into her stove.

It hasn't exactly been a drought, but the year sets a record for fewest days with precipitation: 141.

July is the hottest month on record, with an average temperature of 22 C°.

1948

On 9 June, after several months of discussion, Ottawa announces that the lower deck of the *Abegweit* will be planked to allow trucks as well as railcars to be carried. Not wanting to give its fastest-growing source of competition any assistance, C.N. had been resisting the move.

On 29 June, by a two to one margin, Islanders vote to replace prohibition with government controlled liquor sales. The vote is close in only two ridings: 2nd Prince, where prohibition loses by one vote and 4th King's, where prohibition is favoured 441 to 431. Turnout for the plebiscite is only 52%.

On 31 March, after 25 years on the air, R.T. Holman's Ltd radio station CHGS signs off for the last time. Summerside won't have to be without local radio for long, though. Plans are afoot to get a new station, CJRW on the air before the end of the summer.

On 17 July, without fanfare, the *Guardian* launches a new feature – the daily editorial cartoon. Cartoonist Vic Runtz is the first to feature Island stories and issues every day.

Out of a budget of approximately $7,000,000, the province is $350,000 to the good. Black ink is a rare sight in the government's ledger books. Since 1873 it has recorded 18 surpluses, compared to 56 deficits.

Hunter River's James Charles McGuigan, Archbishop of Toronto since 1935, is created a cardinal — the first English-speaking cardinal in Canada.

Cardinal McGuigan

1949

In 1948, Ottawa repealed the ban on margarine that had been in effect since 1886. Watching with horror the subsequent spread of the (cheap) edible oil product, the Island government bans its sale or manufacture here. Though the province's dairy industry applauds the move, the Federal Supreme Court rules the law unconstitutional.

On 2 February, two RCAF Lancasters fly diagonally across the continent from Sacramento, California to Summerside. Their flight — the first (and so far only) of its kind — covers 2,750 miles and takes 12 hours, 25 minutes.

Sixty-six years of catering to the concerns of Island farmers comes to an end when Summerside's *P.E.Island Agriculturalist* prints its last issue.

Work begins on the new Prince County hospital in Summerside.

Prince Edward Island wins the dubious honour of having the lowest-paid teachers in the country. The average teachers' salary in British Columbia is $2,042. In Ontario: $1,514. Here: $816. When the Island's Teachers' Federation brings these numbers to Premier Jones' attention, he replies: "Until farmers' incomes go up, yours won't."

Major General Ernest Weeks retires from active duty. Joining the army as a private in 1914, Weeks won two Military Medals and two Military Crosses — a rare accomplishment. During World War II he rose from the rank of Lt. Colonel

Lobster Factory, Fortune, **1940**
Two boys carry a load of live lobsters in for processing.

Hillsborough Bridge, c1910

Opened in 1905, the first bridge across the Hillsborough River was a second-hand railway bridge that originally spanned the Miramachi River. It was torn down after a replacement was completed in 1961.

to Brigadier General, and was the first Islander ever to reach the rank of Major General.

With spring ice keeping freighters far offshore, the tiny Newfoundland community of St. Mary's Bay runs out of food. On 8 April, the local Grenfell mission nurse radios that the population is starving. Bad weather keeps the RCAF on the ground, but a Newfoundland Airways DeHaviland Rapide, flown by Charlottetown-born Freeman Fleming is able to get through with 1,000 pounds of emergency supplies.

1950

Architects unveil plans for Charlottetown's new, $1 million Federal Building. The latest word in modern, concrete and glass design, the nine storey building will house the Post Office, Customs, Unemployment Insurance and Revenue departments.

Construction begins on the Island's portion of the Trans Canada Highway with a 16 km stretch of pavement between Bonshaw and North Tryon.

With the removal of the last steam locomotive, Prince Edward Island is the only Division in the C.N.R. to be completely "dieselized."

Beginning on 22 August, a ten-day national railway strike shuts down the Borden-Cape Tormentine ferries. The resulting, two-to-four-mile-long lineups at Wood Islands and Caribou testify to how reliant the Island has become on the automobile.

T.W.L. Prowse becomes Lt. Governor. The Charlottetown merchant will have the longest term of office — eight years — since George Dundas.

A near-record catch of 7.3 million pounds combines with strong prices to make the most lucrative lobster season yet. The $1.6 million helps make up for some of the disastrous seasons in the '40s.

"A new and important industry." Scallop beds are discovered in the Northumberland Strait south of Wood Islands and off Boughton Island.

While presenting a brief on education to the Massey Royal Commission into the Arts in Canada, Premier Jones can't resist a dig. "I don't think we should train a man too much," he ventures. "The first thing you know he's a professor and gone off to Upper Canada and we've had the expense of training him."

"A Morning Walk," Bonshaw, c1900

The vicinity of the town affords rides and walks such as the most enthusiastic admirer of nature in her softer beauties would choose to frequent; and presents at the same time, the evidences of increasing wealth, and a state of moral advancement, not exceeding in any country whatsoever.

— S.S. Hill, *A Short Account of Prince Edward Island*, 1839

On 1 August evangelist — later novelist and social commentator — Charles Templeton comes to Charlottetown. Over 6,000 cram into the Forum or listen to his sermon from loudspeakers on the street.

In the first full year after the repeal of prohibition, Island-

Sawmill, location unknown, c1890

114

Charlottetown Fire, 1951

On 18 August, 1951 fire ripped through the block bounded by Grafton, Kent, Prince and University Avenue. Among the buildings lost were Horne Motors, Whelan Memorial Hall, F.R. McLaine and Batt & MacRae.

 The Island's population increases to 98,429.

 John T. Croteau publishes *Cradled on the Waves*, a ground-breaking study on the co-operative movement on the Island.

The *Summerside Journal* and the *Pioneer* merge.

Farm income passes $25,000,000 for the first time in history. Thanks to post-war inflation, farm income figures are reaching all-time highs almost every year. Of course, so are costs.

Pulp is the new boom industry. This year, over $2,000,000 in pulpwood is exported from the province. The sudden, heavy cutting raises concerns over forestry conservation.

 On 9 November Princess Elizabeth and her consort, Prince Phillip, Duke of Edinburgh visit the Province. "Canada," she comments at the end of the national tour, "has become a second home in every sense."

Ottawa releases the first Canadian casualty list for the Korean War on 2 March. Among the 11 dead is Pte. Elliot MacKay of Charlottetown. MacKay had been serving with the Princess Patricia Canadian Light Infantry.

Fire destroys the 76-year-old Roman Catholic church in Wellington. It is estimated that over $50,000 will be needed to replace it.

1952

Hubert Rogers, born in Alberton but living in Vermont, has made an international reputation as a portrait painter. Now the National Gallery and Canadian Club of New York want him to try his hand at landscapes. They commission him to do two "typical scenes" of his home province — one to be part of the National Collection and one to hang at the Canadian Club's offices in the Waldorf Astoria.

ers spend $2,000,000 on alcohol.

Cardigan native John James Bowlen is named Lt. Governor of Alberta. In 1958, he becomes probably the only Islander ever to get a mountain named after him.

1951

On 11 March the C.N.R. orders an end to train traffic on the Hillsborough Bridge. Freight trains haven't been able to use the structure in several years, and now the railway is afraid that even lighter passenger trains are too much strain. The company agrees to keep the bridge open for motor vehicle traffic. Reluctantly. For now...

Premier Jones buys a bridge at bargain basement prices. The Dominion Bridge Company built the 12-span structure for Chaing Kai Shek for a little over $1 million. Now that the former dictator of mainland China has been deposed, the bridge has no place to go. Jones offers $470,000, and the bridge is soon on its way. The Premier is confident it will be big enough to span both the Hillsborough and North Rivers. It isn't.

"A problem with the widespread use of English cars here is the effect of various track widths in conditions of snow, ice or, off the paved roads, mud. Formerly when one car went through the road was broken. Now it depends upon who is ahead of you after a storm." Evidently Island motorists are not to expect that a snowplough will be ahead of them after a storm.

Winning 24 seats to six, J. Walter Jones leads the Liberals to their fifth consecutive term in office.

Provincial Exhibition Grounds, Charlottetown, 1955

This aerial photo shows all the elements of a classic "Old Home Week." To the right, the track and grandstand of the Charlottetown Driving Park; behind the park Kennedy Coliseum, where the livestock and other exhibits could be viewed and, in the foreground, the Midway.

Industry or scenery? The *Guardian* sums up the dilemma. "Islanders practically purr when visitors such as Montreal artist Campbell Tinning tell us that the Island is the most paintable part of Canada. On the other hand we would not seriously object to a few eyesores in the form of smoking factory chimneys."

Fisheries experts advise that improvements in technology will allow the region's fishery to expand at an unprecedented rate. "If the fishing experts are right," the *Guardian* reassures, "there is little danger that the world's oceans will become depleted for a long time to come."

The province opens a new tree nursery at Beach Grove, just outside Charlottetown. The first seedlings planted are Red Oak and four varieties of Larch.

The MacNeills of Cape Breton — 90% of the MacNeills in Nova Scotia — refuse to accept New York architect Robert MacNeill as their Clan Chieftain. Instead they swear allegiance to Colin MacNeill of Vernon River, a sectionman with the C.N.R. The split has been developing for 70 years. When the Gaelic College tries to mediate by inviting both to the annual Mod, the Cape Breton MacNeills refuse to attend.

On 25 February, M.V. *Abegweit* makes a small detour to pick up an exhausted deer seen swimming amongst the icepans. The animal is given a good meal and a cabin to dry out in and is released in New Brunswick on the return trip.

On 28 February the *Minnie Anne,* a trawler owned by S.H. Burhoe of Charlottetown, wrecks during a snowstorm off Yarmouth. The crew are saved by another trawler, the *Gladys Sweeney.*

The province's net debt passes the $20,000,000 mark.

Between 18 February and 2 March, three snowstorms drop 36 inches (90 cm) on the province. Firetrucks are kept from a blaze at a Southport store by 14-foot drifts. In Launching, Margaret McCormack loses her way while walking to a neighbour's house and dies of exposure.

From 1930 until his death in 1952, Charlottetown's Earl Young was editor of *Hansard* — the official record of Canada's Parliament. His replacement in the position? Thomas Hubbard, also of Charlottetown.

1953

The 24-member Liberal caucus elects Alex W. Matheson as Liberal leader. "Long Alex" (he stood 6'6" tall) is pledged to rural electrification and road improvement.

On 6 June, famed Island artist Mary Allison Doull dies, aged 87.

Five local dairies (Dunk River, Kensington, Tryon, Abram's Village, and Tyne Valley) merge to form Amalgamated Dairies Ltd. – ADL.

On 24 May, a massive storm batters the Island with 55 mph winds causing massive damage to lobster traps and fishing gear. Two veteran Tracadie fishermen, Charles and Gordon Watts risk their lives rescuing two boys trapped on a lobster boat.

Charlottetown-born "bungalow specialist" Albert Edward LePage expands his Toronto real estate company. Within a decade, "A.E. LePage" (now known as "Royal LePage") is one of the largest real estate networks in Canada.

1954

Premier Matheson announces that the Rural Electrification program, hitherto a pilot project, will be extended throughout the province.

In an effort to ease the growing tension between Town and Country over the issue of Daylight Saving Time, a Liberal cabinet minister suggests that it be made a local option, with each city, town and village deciding for itself whether to adopt the device.

The cornerstone is laid for Queen Charlotte High School on Charlottetown's North River Road.

The Pine Tree Line goes into operation. The string of radar

stations have been built in northern Quebec and the southern Northwest Territories as an early warning system against Soviet air attack. One of the main civilian contractors for the project was the Island's M.C.A., which gained priceless experience in operating in arctic conditions.

On 16 May, fire rages through Murray River. Nine buildings are lost: 2 businesses, 3 homes, a warehouse and several barns.

On 17 September, Hurricane Edna sideswipes the Island with winds of 65 mph and gusts of over 80. Trees, barns and telephone poles are the main casualties, though growers fear the entire apple crop will be lost.

1955

A plaque is officially unveiled at the powder magazine at Fort Edward in Charlottetown's Victoria Park. Now little more than picturesque scenery, the battery was once vital to the city's defences.

On 8 July, Islanders wake up to find that the C.N.R. has erected barricades at both ends of the Hillsborough Bridge. It says it is acting for the Dominion Department of Transport, and has closed the bridge because it isn't safe. Later that afternoon, Premier Matheson arrives,

armed with an injunction and a bulldozer, and traffic flows again. Having made their points, both sides in the dispute sit down to discuss a new bridge, which opens in 1961.

Elsie Inman

Two years to the day after he was sworn in as premier, Alex Matheson leads the provincial Liberals to their sixth straight electoral victory, 27 seats to three, over the Conservatives.

The Acadian Historical Society of Prince Edward Island is founded in Miscouche.

The United States and Canada begin planning one of the biggest defense projects ever undertaken in peacetime — a string of 50 early warning radar stations to be built near the Arctic Circle. Called the Distant Early Warning (or D.E.W.) Line, the project will cost $350,000,000. In on the very first planning discussions is Carl Burke. His Maritime Central Airways will be the main civilian air freight contractor for the project.

On 8 July, the 103-year-old St. Peter's Roman Catholic Church at Seven Mile Bay is completely destroyed by fire. Lightning is the culprit.

Eaton's opens a modern new department store on Charlottetown's Kent St.

1956

Charlottetown's long-awaited but much-delayed Federal building is complete and ready for occupancy.

Tests on the sandstone at Cape Tormentine indicate it would be suitable for building a causeway across the Northumberland Strait. Now all the project needs is about $50,000,000.

Premier Jones signs an agreement promising to pay for half of the Island's section of the proposed Trans Canada Highway. The provincial share is $5,000,000.

The new year begins with a new feature in the *Guardian* – the daily television schedule. Moncton's CKCW signs on at 2:00 in the afternoon. Before the day is done, viewers get to see American favourites like "Dragnet," "GM Theatre," "Howdy Doody," and "Jimmy Durante," as well as local programs like "Uncle Jack at the Piano" and "Citizens Forum." News, weather and sports at six and eleven. Televisions start at $185.95, but can be financed for up to 30 months at $1.85 per week.

***Main Street, Montague,* c1950**

After World War II the impact of the automobile on the Island way of life made itself increasingly felt.

Montague Harbour, c1900

 On 7 January an ice storm slams into the Maritimes. Worst hit on the Island is Summerside, which is declared a disaster area. An estimated 3,000 power and telephone poles are down – 2,000 between Charlottetown and Summerside alone. It is six months before power is restored to all areas. Luckily, electricity is still a novelty in most districts, so people are still quite accustomed to doing without.

Although winter came early to eastern King's, a long January thaw is makes things right. A field of turnips, covered for two months with snow, has recently been harvested in good condition. On 17 January the *Guardian* runs a photo showing a farmer finally finishing his fall furrows. But Islanders are soon up to their ears — and over — in snow. On 13 February meteorologists measure 156 cm of snow on the ground, the greatest depth on record in Charlottetown.

1957

 Jean (Reed) MacLean designs the Island tartan.

The Garden of the Gulf Museum is incorporated by an act of the provincial Legislature. Housed in Montague's former post office building, it is the province's first museum.

 On 29 August, the first load of fill for the approaches to the new Hillsborough Bridge is dumped.

Dr. W.J.P. MacMillan — OBE, papal knight, ex-pre-mier, long-time Tory leader, first Minister of Health and Education, victim of the 1935 electoral sweep — is named Lt. Governor. On 7 December, after only two weeks in office, he dies suddenly.

On 11 August, a DC-4 chartered from Maritime Central Airways in Charlottetown crashes in Quebec during a thunderstorm, killing all 79 passengers and crew — the worst disaster in Canadian aviation history to that date.

1958

Maritime Central Airways cancels its regular service between Moncton, Saint John, and Fredericton. Its reason? "Lack of patronage." Although M.C.A. is the nation's largest air freight carrier and its third largest passenger line, it's finding it difficult to maintain its position in the industry.

The crime wave has broken. Charlottetown Chief

MCA Aircrew, c1955
Senior Captain H.F. "Junior" Jones poses with his crew on the steps of a DC-3. Founded by Carl Burke in 1941 and based in Charlottetown, M.C.A. was the third-largest passenger carrier and the biggest air freight carrier in Canada by the late 1950s.

of Police C.W. MacArthur reports that an unusual number of break and enter offenses in November tapered off toward the end of December.

Insurance executive Walter Hyndman is named Lt. Governor.

J. Angus MacLean
With ten consecutive election victories between 1951 and 1977, it could be argued that J. Angus MacLean is the most successful Federal politician in Island history. He was one of only two Island MPs to run successfully in two different ridings (the other being James C. Pope) and was able to cap his federal career by becoming Premier in 1979.

In the middle of February, with a Federal election in full swing, Queen's M.P. Angus MacLean is running the country almost single-handed. In addition to his job as Fisheries Minister, he's Acting Minister of Defense, Agriculture and Secretary of State. When John Deifenbaker leaves for the campaign trail, MacLean is also named Acting Prime Minister. No other Islander has ever wielded such power in Ottawa!

High Tide at Noon, featuring Charlottetown's Errol MacKinnon in the role of Peter Grant, Shopkeeper, opens at the Capitol Theatre. Though all the Islanders are rooting for him, MacKinnon doesn't get any Oscar nominations.

Belle River, c1900

On 8 February, every Islander with a television is probably watching the first live hockey telecast in the Maritimes.

Summerside's Regent and Capitol theatres are finding television hard to compete with, so they decide to share the shrinking market. The Regent will close for six weeks while the Capitol stays open, then vice versa.

Oil prospectors drill test wells at Wellington, Port Hill and MacDougall

Dr. Lorne Bonnell, Minister of Health, announces that the new Salk Polio vaccine will be made available free to every Islander between 19 and 40.

Keir Clark, Minister of Education, officially opens Spring Park School.

On 30 April Charlottetown's beautiful stone Market House, designed by W.C. Harris and built in 1904, succumbs to fire. The gutted building is eventually razed to make way for the Confederation Centre.

1959

Although they take a bare 50.4% to the Liberals' 49.6% of votes cast, its enough to give the Conservatives a 22 seat to eight victory. Walter Shaw becomes the Island's first Tory premier in 24

Belle River, c1950

Fishing on the Fortune River, c1900

Persons fond of piscatorial pleasures can readily be accommodated and may be-take themselves to many a pleasant stream in the country where the finny tribes abound

– Pictou Eastern Chronicle, 1856

years. Liberal leader Alex Matheson quips that at least there now will be a decent Opposition.

Andrew Hill Clark publishes *Three Centuries and the Island; A Historical Geography of Settlement and Agriculture in Prince Edward Island*. Though the title is long and sounds dry, *Three Centuries* will become regarded as one of the most important books ever written on Island history.

The former *Earl Grey*, now a Soviet icebreaker named *Fedor Litke*, is retired from service. Her bridge is removed and put on display in a museum in Moscow.

On 30 July Her Majesty Queen Elizabeth II and her husband, Prince Philip, make their second visit to Prince Edward Island, but her first since becoming Queen of Canada. Fifteen hundred guests are invited to a lawn party at Government House.

On 19 June a sudden overnight storm, with winds peaking at 75 mph, lashes Atlantic Canada, smashing fishing boats to kindling and wrecking gear. In its wake, 35 men, including one Islander, are declared dead or missing.

The United States Navy appoints William Silliphant of Hunter River to the rank of Rear Admiral. A specialist in pathology, Silliphant has been in the USN Medical Corps since 1930.

1960

19 August Dee's Boy takes the inaugural Gold Cup and Saucer Race, finishing with a first and a third in the two-dash event. (The Gold Cup and Saucer Girls won't appear for another year.)

The farmers are furious, but Prince Edward Island officially adopts Daylight Saving Time for a three-month period every year.

The first meeting of the Evangeline School Board decides to build the intended regional high school at Abram's Village.

By 3 September, the worst forest fire season in two centuries reaches a peak. Drought-fuelled forest fires rage all over West Prince County. Hundreds of acres are blazing around Black Banks, Foxley River, Portage, Murray Road and Ellerslie. Part of Tyne Valley is evacuated before the fires are under control. At the same time, fire-fighters in northern King's County battle another blaze burning out of control near Dundee.

The tourist industry attracts 208,000 visitors.

Charlottetown-born Edgar W. McInnis is the first faculty member hired at the country's newest university — York. In 1944, while teaching at the University of Toronto, he won the Governor General's Award for his book *The War, Fourth Year*.

1961

 After three trouble-plagued years of construction, the new Hillsborough Bridge is officially opened by Islander Angus MacLean, federal Minister of Fisheries.

On 29 May, Margaret Macdonald becomes the first female M.P. the province sends to Ottawa when she wins a by-election for the Conservatives in the riding King's County. The by-election was made necessary by the death of the incumbent, Margaret's husband, John A. Macdonald. She wins the seat again in the following general election.

The Island's population climbs back to 104,000.

The Department of Agriculture declares that the province is virtually free of ragweed — at least in "the resort areas."

On 14 March a Summerside landmark, the Clifton Hotel, is razed by a deadly early morning fire. Of the 35 occupants, three are killed and 16 injured as they flee the burning building.

Nature's contribution to New Year's celebrations in Summerside is 53.6 cm of snow, a provincial one-day record.

The Island endures a particularly wild spring. March features no fewer than five major snow storms. A surprise storm on 21 March, with winds gusting to 75 mph, strands many children in their schools — some for four days. Another storm on 25 March forces the Government to declare a state of emergency. Helicopters make mercy flights as 30-foot drifts submerge power lines. On 1 April a record 3.5 inches of rain in 24 hours causes unprecedented flooding. Bridges are washed out all over the province — two at Ross's Corner alone, and the dam bursts in Tyne Valley. Mid-April sees two more snowstorms; the ploughs are helpless in the hard-packed snow.

1962

Prime Minister John Diefenbaker announces plans to construct a causeway between Prince Edward Island and the Mainland at an estimated cost of $105 million. Then, a remarkable coincidence, he calls a federal election.

C.N. Marine introduces the M.V. *Confederation* to the Borden-Tormentine ferry run. She's the Island's first "ro-ro" vessel. Traffic can "roll on, roll off" without having to turn on the deck, or the boat having to turn at the dock.

Maritime Central Airways cancels plans to expand its fleet with three additional Dart Heralds. Although the turboprops are the hottest passenger planes around, M.C.A. feels the business outlook is too bleak.

Victory is sweet for Walter Shaw's provincial Conservatives. A snap election call has resulted in a comfortable, 19 seat to 11 majority for the 75-year-old premier. He's the first Conservative since J.A. Matheson to win back-to-back elections.

Oil prospectors are back, drilling test wells at Wellington, French River, Alexandria and Earnscliffe.

Tryon's St. Anne's Catholic church, built in 1897, is destroyed by fire.

Islanders never had it so . . . wet. In 1962 the province re-ceives a record 1,465 mm of precipitation (300 mm over the yearly average). A single, three-inch (75mm) downpour in April washed out bridges in Bedeque, St. Peters, Bridgetown and Montague.

1963

On 2 February, the first sod is turned in construction of the Fathers of Confederation Memorial Building. Premier Robert Stanfield of Nova Scotia does the honours. In a rare show of harmony, the provinces and the federal Government have agreed to split the bill.

The cornerstone is laid for Charlottetown's new West Kent School, not on the west end of Kent Street, where government offices will soon replace the original brick building, but in the new residential district of Brighton.

Prince of Wales professor W. Joseph "Billie Archie" Mac-Donald is named Lt. Governor

Barra-born Jim MacNeill launches the *Eastern Graphic* in Montague. The feisty weekly newspaper dubs itself "the lively one."

On 9 January M.V. *Abegweit* is called out of her overnight berth at Borden to rescue 16-year-old Kenneth Blacquiere, adrift on the Strait after his smelt shack broke free of the ice pack in Summerside harbour and carried him out to sea.

On 2 May the Coast Guard vessel *Wolfe* battles through high winds, a rain storm and heavy ice to rescue three lobster boats trapped in the ice off Basin Head. The three were on their way to North Lake to await the start of the season. Instead, the *Wolfe* breaks a path back to Souris for them.

A severe wind storm with winds of up to 130 kph blasts the Maritimes on 19 December, causing extensive property damage. At Covehead Harbour, it demolishes the six-year-old bridge linking Stanhope and Brackley.

1964

The Legislature creates a provincial flag. The design is taken from the armorial bearings granted in 1905 — "a lion passant" surmounting the familiar oak tree and sapling device — but with a narrow border of red and white rectangles on three sides.

At a meeting in the Miscouche Convent, Acadian leaders vote to establish an Acadian museum. Dr. J. Aubin Doiron is elected president of the organization.

Dr. F.W.P. Bolger publishes *Prince Edward Island and Confederation*. Bolger's is the first history of the Island's side of the Confederation years.

Confederation Centre, c1970

On 24 April Adele Townshend's one-act play, *For the Love of A Horse*, debuts at the Provincial Drama Festival in Summerside. The re-telling the story of land agent Edward Abell's murder by Lot 56 tenant Patrick Pearce reflects the provinces increasing interest in its history.

On 18 May, the Dominion Drama Festival kicks off the first-ever presentation in the still-unfinished Confederation Centre of the Arts. British Columbia does the honours, staging Arnold Wesker's *Chips with Everything*.

The Public Archives Act provides for the establishment of a provincial archives.

In an era of school consolidation, Charlottetown - applauds the opening of Birchwood High School on Longworth Avenue.

On 20 February, Roman Catholic worshippers attending Mass at St. Dunstan's Basilica feel the impact of Vatican II's liturgical reforms as the priest reads the epistle and gospel in English instead of Latin.

On 2 December a memorable gale pounds the Maritimes with winds reaching gusts of 160 kph. Twenty-three lives are lost at sea.

1965

On 15 February, the Red Ensign comes down for the last time as Canada's new and controversial Maple Leaf flag is raised over the Charlottetown Armouries.

Prime Minister Lester B. Pearson announces a call for tenders for a $148 million causeway across the Northumberland Strait. An election is obviously near.

Alex Campbell, a 32-year-old lawyer, defeats Dr. Lorne Bonnell for the Liberal leadership in a convention held at the newly opened Confederation Centre. It's the first time that an Island political party selects a leader by the American "convention" format. Prior to this the selection was made by the party caucus.

On 27 July, *Anne of Green Gables*, the much-loved musical by Don Harron and Norman Campbell, makes its premiere at the Charlottetown Summer Festival. The debut performance earns a standing ovation.

Alex Colville's painting "To P.E.I." takes first prize in its category at the Atlantic Winter Fair. It's also for sale: $6,000 plus commission.

1966

The final design for a fixed link to the mainland proposes a combination causeway/bridge/tunnel. Ottawa calls for tenders and discovers the price tag might be as high as $300 million. The project is put on hold.

On 30 May, the closest election in Island history ends in a 15 to 15 seat deadlock. A by-election in 1st King's — the voting was deferred when one of the candidates died in mid-campaign — will decide the fate of the government.

"Seafarers Haven," c1960

The small boat harbours that characterize the Island's coastline are mostly a creation of the 20th century. As fishing boats became bigger and more expensive, wharves and harbours became essential. Many boat harbours were created by cutting a channel or "run" through to a saltwater pond or inlet.

Victory Chimes, *Cardigan,* **1918**

Views of wooden sailing vessels under construction are rare and precious.

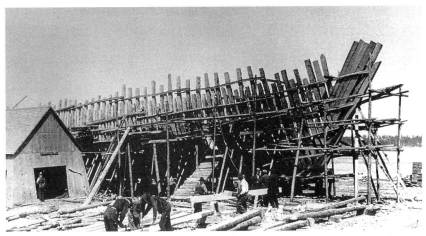

Victory Chimes, *Cardigan,* **1918**

The Tories make one of their candidates Minister of Public Works and Highways, and 1st King's gets a sudden bonanza of pavement. "Please don't pave it," pleads one farmer. "It's my only field!" On 11 July the Liberals win both seats, and the right to form a government.

Beach Scene, c1890

It wasn't until the 20th century that fine, sandy beaches became attractions. The 19th century ideal was more like this.

 Harness driver Joseph O'Brien of Alberton is named to the Canadian Sports Hall of Fame. In 1961 he was the top driver in the United States. In 1971, he will become only the third driver in history to win 3,000 races.

 On 14 October, the cornerstone is laid for a new senior high school on Charlottetown's

Spring Park Road. Col. J. H. Gray, an Island Father of Confederation born nearby, wins out as namesake for the new school. The also rans include Samuel Holland, Governor General Vanier and Lord Selkirk.

On 23 April, the Stanhope Resort Hotel — once known as the Seaside Inn — goes up in smoke. It has been accommodating visitors since 1889 under the successive ownership of the Mutch, MacMillan, and Warren families.

1967

The Acadian Pioneer Village in Mont Carmel officially opens.

Basil Hill and Ann Giffard publish *Westcountrymen on*

Prince Edward's Isle: A Fragment of the Great Migration. Ninety years after the industry's collapse, it is the first academic exploration of shipbuilding on Prince Edward Island.

Government grows. Queen Elizabeth II officially opens the new Provincial Government Buildings on Rochford St. There is irony in the choice of site; in the 19th century, the area was a swampy slum known as "the Bog."

On 8 August, 104 years after the last visit, an Earl of Selkirk returns to Prince Edward Island. There are no permanent immigrants in Sir Nigel Douglas-Hamilton's party.

On 25 February, caught in blinding snow, mountainous seas, and hurricane force winds, the 91-foot trawler *Iceland II* of Souris runs for shelter from a killer storm in the Gulf of St. Lawrence. She wrecks on a shoal near Forchu, Cape Breton. All hands are lost.

On 10 October a cloudburst of Biblical proportions dumps a record 32 mm (1.3 inches) of rain on Charlottetown in just one hour.

1968

At 16,000 horsepower, the new *John Hamilton Grey* — "Big John" — is the most powerful

Brae Harbour, 1949

Though most of the Island's fishing fleet was motorized by the 1940s, the owner of this fishing smack has kept open the option of sail power.

Cottage Life, 1894

This photo was taken at Holland Cove, just across the harbour from Charlottetown. This area was particularly attractive to Charlottetonians looking for a summer retreat. It was deep in the country, yet only minutes away from town by ferry.

icebreaker ever to tackle the Borden-Tormentine run.

On 17 February, the Canadian National hockey team settles for a bronze medal at the Winter Olympics in Grenoble, France, after losing 5-0 to the Soviets. He'd prefer gold, but team member Bill MacMillan becomes the first Islander ever to win an Olympic medal.

Bill 72 provides for the establishment of the University of Prince Edward Island, engendering bitter controversy among many supporters of the two existing universities, St. Dunstan's and Prince of Wales.

On 21 October, Hurricane Gladys slashes across Prince Edward Island with sustained winds of 80 to 100 kph. One man loses his life when a 130 kph gust fells a tree on top of his truck.

1969

The federal Government shelves the causeway project in favour of a "comprehensive development plan." The studies at the heart of the plan were commissioned in the early 1960s. It is designed to reshape the province's economy and — as a by-product — its society.

The end of an era occurs on 25 October when Canadian National Railway makes its last passenger run on Prince Edward Island.

Farmer and politician J. George MacKay is named Lt. Governor.

The *College Times*, Prince of Wales University's 46-year-old student newspaper publishes its final edition. One of the last issues it covers is the demise of its own university. The St. Dunstan's newspaper, *Red and White*, has been in operation for 60 years. The newspaper for the new provincial university will be called the *Cadre*.

On 2 July, the University of Prince Edward Island takes over from Prince of Wales and St. Dunstan's to become the provincial university.

Beginning on 7 November, Islanders get 144 hours — six days and nights — of precipitation.

1970

On 6 June, amid rain, sleet, and hail, hardy descendants commemorate the 200th anniversary of the arrival of the Scottish settlers at Stanhope by unveiling an Island sandstone cairn.

Campaigning on the Comprehensive Development Plan's promised millions, Alex B. Campbell's Liberals turn a two-seat majority into a 27 seat to five

Queen and Grafton Street, Charlottetown, c1900

The cannon stuck in the sidewalk at the corner of Queen and Grafton was put there in 1860 to commemorate the visit of the Prince of Wales.

124

electoral rout of George Keys' Tories. Among the successful Liberal candidates is Jean Canfield of Crapaud. In her second bid for a seat, she becomes the first woman ever elected to the Island legislature.

 Angered that he has been passed over for the Governor General's Award for Poetry, Milton Acorn's fellow poets meet in a pub in Toronto to proclaim him "The People's Poet." Although the Island native will later win the Governor General's Award, he prefers the former title.

On 19 December, three weeks later than intended because of a series of snowstorms, winter harness racing debuts at the Summerside Raceway.

The Prince Edward Island Heritage Foundation is incorporated.

Charlottetown's School Trustees vote to revise a provision of their General Policies. Henceforth, female students attending junior or senior high schools will be permitted to wear slacks. Presumably, pants are preferable to mini skirts.

On 7 September, the oil barge *Irving Whale* goes down

"Sunnyside," Charlottetown, c1870

in the Gulf of St. Lawrence 30 miles northeast of North Cape, taking 4,200 tons of bunker "C" oil with it to the bottom. It becomes an ecological time bomb, defused only 25 years later when it is salvaged and re-floated.

1971

To kill a planned rock concert, the Legislature hurriedly passes an act empowering the Attorney General to prohibit any public gathering that may "contribute to the disruption of public order." *Time* magazine dubs us "the uptight little Island."

On 8 September, two employees of the Canadian Bank of Commerce branch in Summerside head for the mainland with $414,647, the biggest bank robbery in Island history. The two men later turn themselves in.

At 112,000, Prince Edward Island's population reaches an all-time high. The previous peak, recorded in 1891, was 109,000.

1972

Armed with monies provided through the federal government's Prince Edward Island Centennial Fund, Catherine Hennessey, Fred Hyndman, and Wanda Wyatt purchase the Cundall Home — Beaconsfield — from the Cundall Trust. It will become home to the Heritage Foundation.

Two high-speed, high-capacity carferries are added to the Borden-Tormentine crossing. M.V. *Holiday Island* and *Vacationland* might not look like much, but they can move a lot of cars in a short amount of time.

Prodded by concerns over the rate at which non-residents are buying up land, Premier Alex Campbell appoints a Royal Commission to investigate land use and ownership. The Land Question has been re-born.

"Sunnyside," Charlottetown, c1900

Looking east from the intersection of Queen and Grafton Streets, this section of Grafton Street, shopfronts facing south, was nicknamed "Sunnyside."

125

Old soldiers do die. On 19 February Daniel P. MacRae, identified as the last surviving Island veteran of the Boer War, dies in Waterside, aged 90.

On 10 July thousands of Islanders and visitors, including scientists from Harvard, the Smithsonian, and the Hale Observatory, witness a total eclipse of the sun. The Island is on the centre line of the astronomical event for the first time since 1780.

On 10 May, the ferry *John Hamilton Gray* makes a slight detour 45 miles northwest of Cape Tormentine to free the Liberian freighter *Lambda* from an obstinate ice-field that refuses to acknowledge spring.

In one of its snowiest winters on record, the province receives 539 cm — 18 feet — of snow.

On 13 October, the earliest snowfall in recorded history dumps about two inches of snow, causing several car accidents and minor power outages.

1973

On 3 July, Her Majesty Queen Elizabeth II officially opens Beaconsfield, the newly renovated home of the Prince Edward Island Heritage Foundation.

On 11 July, Basin Head Fisheries Museum officially opens.

On 16 July, Orwell Corner Historic Village opens.

On 17 August, Green Park Shipbuilding Museum is formally opened by Governor General Roland Michener.

Smack-dab in the middle of the Island's centennial, a railway strike brings ferry traffic at Borden grinding to a halt for 10 long, frustrating days.

On 6 September, Islanders are puzzled by a mysterious earth tremor. Tremors are re-

ported in Summerside, Charlottetown, and Borden. Yet nothing is registered at the Dalhousie University seismograph in Halifax and no planes are in the area to cause a sonic boom.

 Landmarks and Symbols

 Transportation and Communications

 Law and Order

 Politics

 Population

 Arts and Letters

 Sports and Leisure

 Land and Sea

 Health and Medicine

 Everyday and Extraordinary

 Education

 Military Events

 Religion

 Natural and Other Disasters

 Commerce

 Science and Technology

 Weather

 Away

 Shipbuilding

Index of Surnames and Placenames

A

B

Miner, Jack, 97
Miquelon (Fra.), 71
Miramachi (N.B.), 18, 24, 32, 44
Miscouche, 14, 49, 63, 117, 121
Monaghan, Ambrose, 76
Monaghan, Father W.E., 103
Monaghan (Ire.), 20, 24
Moncton (N.B.), 81, 97, 117
Mont Carmel, 78, 123
Montague, 54, 77, 83, 89, 90, 101, 117, 121
Montgomery, James, 5
Montgomery, L.M., 68, 80, 82, 86, 92, 102
Monticello, 46
Montreal (P.Q.), 36, 39, 71, 81, 90, 103, 105, 116
Moore, David, 14
Morell, 49, 92
Morris, Charles, 5
Morris, John, 27
Morris, John P., 80
Morrison, George, 96, 97, 101
Morrison, Albert E., 78
Mount Herbert, 72, 80, 94
Mount Mellick, 79, 93
Mount Pleasant, 106
Mount Stewart, 39, 57, 71
Mukely, Elizabeth, 7
Munn, Thomas H., 60
Munro, A., 32
Murphy, James E., 89
Murray Harbour, 20, 35, 79, 80, 107, 112
Murray, Hugh, 24
Murray River, 103, 117
Murray Road, 120
Musgrave Harbour (Nfld.), 108
Myers, W.M., 83

N

Naufrage, 21, 89, 102
Nelligan, C.L., 107
New Annan, 93
New Chepstow, 19
New Glasgow, 62
New Glasgow Bridge, 48
New Glasgow (NS), 90
New London, 6, 8, 12, 15, 24, 39, 53, 55, 60, 103, 112
New Perth, 70
New Zealand (N.Z.), 36, 40
New York (N.Y.), 41, 64, 73, 87, 90, 96, 101, 103, 111, 116
Newcastle (N.B.), 67
Nicholson, John, 14
Nicholson, Samuel, 14
Nine Mile Creek, 29
North Cape, 24, 42
North Lake, 76, 91, 121
North River, 3, 26, 58, 115

North Rustico, 68
North Tryon, 87, 114
North Wiltshire, 87
Northam, 96, 97, 101
Northeast River (see Hillsborough River)
Nowlan, Edward, 36

O

O'Brien, Cornelius, 62
O'Brien, Joseph, 123
O'Leary, 71, 105
O'Leary Road, 46
Oban (Sco.), 12
Oran (Morocco), 109
Orlebar, John, 35
Orwell, 17, 126
Ottawa (Ont.), 50, 54, 64, 66, 73, 74, 77, 80, 86, 104, 106, 107, 108, 113, 120
Ouatenna (Minn.), 102
Oulton, Robert, 71, 84
Oxley, Henry Havelock, 64
Oyster Bay (B.C.), 112

P

Palmer, Edward, 31, 36, 40
Palmer, Lizzie, 90
Palmer, James B., 85
Palmer Road, 70
Panmure Island, 31
Park Corner, 15, 102
Parry, Mary, 22
Patterson, Walter, 4, 6, 7, 8
Paul, Capt. R., 78
Paul, Percy C. S., 78
Peake, James, 25, 37
Peake, James (Jr.), 53, 72
Peakes Station, 93
Pearce, Patrick, 16, 122
Pearson, Lester B., 122
Pempraise, James, 59
Pensens, Jacques De, 2
Peoli, Cecil, 87
Perrey, Rev. S. E., 19, 49
Perry, Harry, 105
Perry, Stanislaus, 73
Peters, Arthur, 75, 78, 83
Peters, Frederick, 69, 70, 73, 75
Peters, Frederick Thornton, 109
Peters, James Horsfield, 29, 69
Peters, John B., 8
Phillips, Fred, 108
Pichon, Thomas, 4
Pictou (N.S.), 13, 21, 25, 27, 44, 59, 65, 76, 82, 84
Pidgeon, John, 53
Pillman, Thomas, 50